Contesting Community

The Limits and Potential of Local Organizing

James DeFilippis

Robert Fisher

Eric Shragge

Rutgers University Press

New Brunswick, New Jersey, and London

Library of Congress Cataloging-in-Publication Data

DeFilippis, James.
    Contesting community : the limits and potential of local organizing /
James DeFilippis, Robert Fisher, Eric Shragge.
        p.   cm.
    Includes bibliographical references and index.
    ISBN 978–0–8135–4755–8 (hardcover : alk. paper)
    ISBN 978–0–8135–4756–5 (pbk. : alk. paper)
    1. Community organization.   2. Community development.   3. Political
participation.   4. Social change.   I. Fisher, Robert.   II. Shragge, Eric,
1948–   III. Title.
    HM766.D44 2010
    307.1′4—dc22   2009038464

    A British Cataloging-in-Publication record for this book is available
from the British Library.

Parts of Chapter 2 build on earlier versions of material that first appeared in
Robert Fisher, *Let the People Decide*, and Michael Fabricant and Robert Fisher,
Settlement Houses under Siege.

Chapter 5 was developed from a shorter article entitled "What's Left in the
Community," *Community Development Journal* 44(1) (January 2009): 38–52.

Text ornament by John Barnett / 4 Eyes Design

Copyright © 2010 by James DeFilippis, Robert Fisher, and Eric Shragge

All rights reserved

No part of this book may be reproduced or utilized in any form or by any means,
electronic or mechanical, or by any information storage and retrieval system,
without written permission from the publisher. Please contact Rutgers University
Press, 100 Joyce Kilmer Avenue, Piscataway, NJ 08854–8099. The only exception
to this prohibition is "fair use" as defined by U.S. copyright law.

Visit our Web site: http://rutgerspress.rutgers.edu

Manufactured in the United States of America

CONTENTS

Acknowledgments

THIS BOOK HAS GONE through a long process of writing and revision. Accordingly, we have compiled a set of debts to friends and colleagues who have commented on earlier forms of it and its arguments. The arguments we are making were first aired at the annual conference of the Urban Affairs Association in Montreal in 2006. We learned a lot from the discussion that ensued. We then tried out many of these arguments with the "Right to the City" group convened by Susan Fainstein, David Harvey, Peter Marcuse, and Neil Smith (among others) and hosted (most of the time) at the CUNY Graduate Center. We made it through that presentation humbler about our project, but with a better project for that humility. We then road-tested the ideas of this book at an all-day workshop with practitioners in Montreal at the Institute for Community Development Summer Program, Concordia University, and their comments and thoughts contributed to how we think about and communicate the issues discussed here. Finally, as the project was nearing its completion, we had the members of the Place and Politics Collective at Rutgers University read the first half of the book. Their comments about our blind spots, omissions, and lack of clarity have certainly made this a better book than it would have been otherwise. Marlie Wasserman, Alison Hack, and the people of Rutgers University Press have been very supportive of this book, and have contributed useful and productively critical comments as well. A special nod of appreciation to Alden Ace Clarke-Fisher for his inspirational ideas on the book cover. Along with the group's acknowledgments, we each have people we would like to acknowledge.

James DeFilippis: Nobody ever writes anything on their own, and everything anyone writes has an accumulation of debts attached to it. For my part, this project is in many ways the culmination of a set of writing I have been doing for more than a decade on community, community development, and the politics of community—work that I could not or would not have done without learning immensely from others. In particular, people such as Susan Fainstein, David Imbroscio, Bob Lake, Kathe Newman, Pete North, Susan Saegert, and Randy Stoecker are friends and colleagues who have greatly shaped how I think about all of these issues. My co-authors, Eric and Bob, are two people I started reading and learning from when I was graduate student. Having the chance to write with, and learn much more from, them has been amazing. My life has seen some big changes in the four years since this book was first conceived. There has been a move (back) to Rutgers University, and I am grateful for the support and encouragement of my colleagues here. But the most important has been the birth of my second daughter, Marley Elizabeth DeFilippis. She possesses an almost other-worldly optimism and joy in life, and she never fails to lift the spirits of everyone around her with her incredible smile. My portion of this project is dedicated to her.

Robert Fisher: I would like to thank my co-authors for this rich intellectual and political experience. At times I thought we were drawing it out just to keep up the wonderful dialogue. I would also like to thank the University of Connecticut for a grant to research community organizing, which enabled me to hire Sally Tamarkin, graduate assistant extraordinaire. Our work together continues to serve as the basis of my understanding of New Right and Christian Right organizing. Danielle Corciullo, another graduate student at the University of Connecticut with whom I have had the privilege to work, was a careful and tenacious editor in the final stages of the manuscript. Most important, I would also like to dedicate my contribution to the book to my sister, Marcy Fisher-Reiners, who is not a community organizer but who has always remained steadfast in her abhorrence of social injustice and her support for the less fortunate. She is a model for us all.

Eric Shragge: Working with a great group of activists and organizers in and around the Immigrant Workers Centre keeps my politics sharp and contributed to the desire to challenge how community practice has evolved. Urban Affairs Association nametags made this book possible.

After looking at his then new book, *Unmaking Goliath*, at the conference, I was in the hotel shop and so was James, thus beginning a friendship and collaboration. My friendship with Bob goes back further to the late 1990s, when a former student of mine who was working in his department suggested we meet. It is rare that working together can be fun. This project was.

Contesting Community

Introduction

THIS BOOK GREW OUT of our shared concerns about what has happened to community, community organizations, and the politics and policies that shape them. Although we all teach in universities, we have long personal engagements in community and social justice work, and are active in, or allies with, a number of community organizations whose work informs our understanding of contemporary practice. Our interest in local community is tied to a broad social and economic critique of neoliberal forms of capitalism. We believe that the struggle for social change, shaped by the goals of social and economic justice and equality, is still critical. And this is especially true now, when these ideals are often dismissed by the mainstream and when economic injustice is so apparent. Further, we believe that the local community is an important, but not an exclusive, place to work for these goals. As co-authors, we began our discussions and made the decision to write this book because, in our own positions as academics and activists, we had witnessed the marginalization of the longer-term goals of economic and social justice as part of the agenda of community organizing. In its place, we see a narrower focus on much more limited practice. This limited practice is justified because it meets specific needs with a deliberate pragmatism. Further, it is often shaped by the needs of the neoliberal context, and the related priorities of government and of the large private foundations that fund these organizations. In discussing this observation, we thought that a book that broadly examines the direction of community practice would answer the questions of why this has happened and what other possibilities exist. We believe that being situated both in and outside of community organizations, with a critical orientation, gives a perspective that can bring theory and critique to a discussion of the practices in which we have engaged or observed in the day-to-day of community life.

While we are frustrated by the shortcomings and failures of most contemporary community efforts, and the theories that inform them, we nevertheless disagree with those who dismiss the community and its local organizations as potential and actual actors in the struggle for progressive social change. After all, community-based efforts have a long history of successful work at the local level. Even contemporary resistance, whether grassroots territorial organizations in Latin America or radical community efforts in the northern hemisphere, is grounded in local work. Almost all transformative social change and social justice work historically—the struggles of workers, racial minorities, women, and so forth—is the product of organizing and mobilization of local communities. Instead of dismissing, in the first instance, community-based efforts and community organizations, this book views community-based efforts through the lens of such vital questions as: Who are the appropriate agents of change in the centers of world power? Where are the sites of mobilization of resistance and opposition? What are the elements needed to contend for power and challenge neoliberal hegemony? For all these questions we argue that part of the answer rests in community-based activism and organizing.

We do so, however, with no small degree of ambivalence. This is because we maintain a critical understanding of the contested debates and practices that embody community initiatives under contemporary neoliberalism, and capitalism more broadly. On the one hand, we are advocates for, and participants in, community-based organizing and development efforts. We understand their power and their potential. We have seen them work in the past and present. On the other hand, we are critical theorists keenly aware of both the political limits to organizing in communities in the contemporary political economy, and the problems of power relations and oppression *within* communities. For us, community-based efforts are simultaneously vital and marginal, filled with democratic potential but laden with inherent limits, necessary but not sufficient. Not sufficient, that is, if the goal is to contest for power and change society in ways that create more equitable and just cities and communities.

This book contextualizes local work. It grew out of how community is understood and used in the contemporary era. As community work has become increasingly conservative since the 1980s, it has been embraced by policy makers and the state, analysts, academics, advocates, and the growing not-for-profit sector. This is true in much of the world, but is probably most pronounced in the United States, United Kingdom and Canada. In these countries, which are the focus of this book, community-based efforts are being promoted as *the* solution to a whole host of social, political, economic, and cultural issues and problems. But this embrace has been of community initiatives that, in both theory and practice, are politically constrained and limited in their goals and aspirations. It is based on an understanding of community that is largely divorced from the goals of social, economic, and political justice. Instead, community and community-based initiatives have increasingly become part of the regulation and management of social problems such as poverty, and have often emphasized some of the most conservative understandings of community. Community, in short, is being embraced by the state and capital precisely because it is being used in ways that are not only uncritical of the larger political economy but actually largely in line with the needs and interests of that political economy—and those who benefit most from it.

While we see strong convergence of community-based policy and politics in the three nations under neoliberalism, we also see differences. We do not argue that each nation, with a different history and political culture, responds in the same manner to each challenge. Nevertheless, we intentionally travel between the three nations, emphasizing ones when they are the center of activity—such as the United States around the history of community organizing or the United Kingdom around contemporary "third way" politics—or when we want to emphasize the breadth of the phenomenon across national contexts. We do not treat each subject equally for each nation, and this is not meant to be a definitive study of community efforts in the Anglo-American world. We use a cross-national approach because the shift in context and community-based efforts is so obvious across the three nations and because the cross-national approach broadens the discussion beyond any national parochialism.

Finally, a brief note about terminology. Because we study the subject in three nations there are often different terms used to describe what, in reality, are quite similar processes and programmatic activities. But rather than imposing a standard label, we simply use the specific phrases and terms that are used in the different countries. This has the benefit of being precise, but the drawback of potentially being both a bit confusing and giving the impression that there is greater variety in practices than there actually is.

If contemporary community efforts are marked both by a loss of radical politics and an explicit commitment to social and economic justice, they also suffer from recurrent failures to critically analyze their contemporary political and economic context. Thus *Contesting Community* is also prompted by the need for community organizations to better understand contemporary processes of neoliberalism and capitalist globalization. We see the political economic context as vital in shaping the potential and actual impact that community efforts have—both in their magnitude and in their political meanings, goals, and implications. While the focus of the book is on community organizations and community-based efforts, our emphasis on the importance of context means that we devote a great deal of attention to understanding the political economic roles played by communities in contemporary forms of capitalism, as well as the ways in which community is understood theoretically—and therefore enacted and acted upon politically and practically.

The chapters in the book build an argument that is, on the one hand, critical of the way community practices and the policies that shape them have developed since the 1980s, and on the other, sympathetic to the practices of organizations that both challenge dominant practices and fight for economic and social justice. In chapter 1, we set out a basic framework for understanding community, why it is limited and why it is important, and what is its context. The second chapter examines the history of how community has been used as an idea and in practice. There are important lessons to be learned from the historical record, in terms of the shifting relationships between community and the state, and the different organizing strategies, tactics, and political goals of efforts over time. One of the central lessons is that community is a politically neutral term, that is, it can be used by practitioners and theorists whose politics span the spectrum from Left to Right. There are dominant ideas of community and community-based work in each historical period, and the progressive ones—from settlement houses and Saul Alinsky to more contemporary counterparts—form the "canon" of community organizing. It is what most people who study and/or work in the field think of when they hear the terms. But the past and present of ideas about community and community practices also includes conservative and right-wing efforts, and it is these efforts which form an "anti-canon," that is, ideas about community and practices in the community which stand in opposition to the values and goals of the efforts which form the canon. Because community is almost always contested, the existence and importance of this anti-canon, not to mention its tension with left and liberal ideas and efforts which form the canon, must be included in any critical analysis of community. Through this chapter, we begin to understand that community is historically complex, shaped by many forces and contested theoretical perspectives.

In the next two chapters we focus on the period after 1980 and the impact of neoliberal politics and policies on grassroots efforts. The shift to neoliberal policies profoundly influenced practice in the community and the ideas that shaped it. Chapters 3 and 4 present and critique these concepts and practices. In both these chapters, we cite examples of practices in the community sector that emerge within the frameworks and theories we evaluate. In 3, we examine two core changes brought in with neoliberal policies: (1) the expansion of the market into the social sphere, including its use in community development, and (2) the decentralization of the state, giving greater responsibility to the local. With these changes we observe a double movement. The community becomes more important, but its role becomes restricted and narrowed. In chapter 4, we look at some of the core ideas that have been used to support the conservative direction in community development and organizing. Under the general rubric of communitarianism, we explore and critique such concepts as social capital, asset-based community development, consensus organizing, and more progressive approaches we describe as "Left promoters." The implications of these ideas are explored, especially how they are taken up on the ground in practice. The chapter concludes with an analysis of an anti-canon group in the United States, the Christian Coalition, and its grassroots efforts, underscoring not only the contested nature of community but also that studying efforts on the right has value for those interested in advancing progressive social change.

We argue throughout the book that community has virtues and limits for those interested in fomenting social change. We certainly do not see it as a lost cause in this regard. On the contrary, we see it as integral to such efforts. Thus, in chapter 5 we present several examples of organizations that do not follow the dominant trends in ideas and practices since 1980. We see these organizational examples as representative of a wider trend that has the potential to expand. We discuss organizing efforts that are promising in terms of connecting community-based efforts to larger social change. These exemplary organizations go beyond the limits of community, either transcending the realm of community (and working on issues of labor, for instance), or transcending the geographic scale of the community (and working at the citywide, nationwide, or global levels). The lessons we draw from these "imperfect" examples are pulled through to the last chapter, in which we outline several propositions that can guide community efforts, as well as theory and writings about them, to become part of a larger movement for economic and social justice.

CHAPTER 1

Community and Its Discontents

IT TAKES MORE THAN a community to address a global economic crisis. Policies of unregulated capitalism have resulted in a global economic tsunami, for nation-states and for community activists and the organizations in which they work. This "state of emergency" is not uncommon; it is, as Walter Benjamin put it, "not the exception but the rule" (1969, 257). We should be used to the bust cycles of capitalism, since these cyclical downturns happen so frequently, but people somehow think they, or the new economic paradigm of the moment, are immune to a severe downturn. The role of community in and after this economic crisis remains uncertain, depending in part on the actual depth, reach, and overall response to it. The crisis clearly offers proponents of social change an extraordinary opportunity, as the neoliberal political economy of more than thirty years is both exposed and questioned. Still, it is not inappropriate to ask, in the face of this global economic crisis, what is the potential for social change in the current context, and what is the place of community efforts in any progressive advance.

Given that context always heavily shapes community activity, the answer depends in part on the extent and impact of the crisis. One forecast suggests that the impact will not be that great, that this crisis is no more than a "cyclical downturn" followed by a "panic." Nevertheless, in the short run the economic crisis seems likely to cause enough of a "punctuated equilibrium" in the neoliberal consensus, to which all major parties in the United States, Britain, and Canada subscribe, to force a modest change in the overall political economy. Even a punctuated equilibrium might undermine the thirty years of conservative, corporate-dominated flux, which has characterized politics and policies for the past generation. In many ways the newly elected U.S. government has set the tone in responding to the crisis. One can see such change already in the agenda and policies of the Obama regime, at this writing just one hundred days old, in the United States, challenging decades-long conceptions antagonistic to the role of big government on social issues such as health care, the environment, and housing.

Another forecast proposes that the impact of this economic crisis will be as dramatic as Lenin is said to have once remarked about the Russian Revolution: "Some decades nothing happens. Some weeks decades happen." There are clear indicators that contemporary capitalism and the neoliberal policies which have framed and sustained it have been shaken. In this scenario, not only is free market capitalism being questioned but socialism has reappeared as a possible alternative, after almost a generation in the United States where Liberal, the "big L word," was the furthest left anyone seemed to be able to imagine, let alone utter. The economic crisis may have undermined the neoliberal hegemony of the past thirty years with the election, in the United States at least, of a regime that says it is open to addressing the economic crisis and advancing a long-overdue progressive agenda. Putting the state back into regulating the economy and general welfare has returned as acceptable policy, especially in Western Europe, after decades of libertarian theory that identified big government as the problem and sought to limit it to police and imperial functions.

Critics who have been arguing for decades about the impending disaster that would result from an unregulated business and corporate sector are no longer seen as cranks. Within a few weeks, the capitalist economy seemed to border on collapse. Global financial corporations folded or were saved by government bailouts. With government bailouts, particularly in automobile manufacturing, restructuring involved wage and job concession by workers and their unions. Unemployment rose dramatically, much of that in manufacturing centers, and much of that unemployment effecting low-income workers whose jobs are more concentrated in boom-and-bust industries, such as automobile and oil production. As a result of the crisis, GDP in all capitalist economies contracted. The effects of the crisis are dwarfed by the 25 percent decline in GDP in the major world economies in the first three years of the Great Depression and the 25 percent unemployment rate. Still, in a very short period of time, billions of dollars have been lost in the stock market and (more important for working and middle-class people) retirement savings, both of which declined more than 50 percent. Those who have not lost their jobs face stagnating or declining wages, more demanding work due to hiring freezes, reduced work hours, furlough days, and temporary factory shutdowns (Samuelson 2009). At the same time, home foreclosures and evictions continue to expand, forcing out the victims of predatory practices as well as those who made bad decisions that coincided with the get-rich-quick mindset of the past generation. People most decimated by this economic crisis and the ones least responsible for it are being asked to shoulder a disproportionately large part of its burden.

Across Europe there have been massive protests targeting the way government has bailed out the rich without compensating those who will suffer from the global recession. In the United States, the initial response has been to organize in a fashion more common to the Great Depression of the 1930s than the past thirty years. For example, in Boston, led by the community group City Life/Vida Urbana, and in Florida, led by Right to the City, successful eviction blockages— complete with protests and arrests of occupants and allies—remind one of scenes of militant organizing from the 1930s. As early as January 2008, City Life/Vida Urbana was blocking evictions resulting from predatory lending practices on subprime mortgages. They not only engaged in eviction defenses, with attendant blockades, but their actions also resulted in owners buying back buildings at their real value after the eviction defenses. They have also sought to link to other anti-displacement organizations nationally, including Right to City efforts and, more recently, ACORN.

Comparing this radical work to similar efforts in the 1930s, Sandra Hinson (2008) remarks that while the community-organizing efforts and the economic crises are different, eviction blockages then and now share common elements, ones invaluable to any understanding of contemporary organizing. First, "the hardest hit are those who can least afford the blows: low- to moderate-income tenants and homeowners." Second, "in both cases, people need the government to intervene on their behalf." Third, "it takes good organizing and a broad alliance of community groups, workers, faith-based groups and social service advocates to force officials to act." Early events and responses to them seemed to have catapulted the United States out of its neoliberal delusion and into a more progressive context, one that is on a trajectory to be marked not only by such basic and long overdue reforms as universal health care and environmental policy, more befitting the twenty-first than the nineteenth century in the United States, but also by a rebirth of left activism. A global economic crisis poorly managed with bailouts for banks and the wealthy amid worsening under/unemployment, lack of health care, and environmental degradation could spark more radical responses and dramatic changes.

Commentator Peter Dreier and others see the confluence of economic crisis and political victory as a golden opportunity for those interested in progressive social change in general and community organizing in particular. In the United States, the economic crisis came on the heels of former community organizer Barack Obama's election as president and eight disastrous years under George W. Bush's right-wing regime. These elements created a broad interest in grassroots, local organizing, not least because Obama's experience as a community organizer in the 1980s was highly publicized through harsh attacks by his opponents during the election and by rejoinders from those sympathetic to the goals and values of progressive community efforts. As Dreier (2009) puts the current opportunity, "there is no doubt that Obama's campaign and victory lit a spark, accelerating student interest in politics in general and grassroots organizing in particular. Millions of young people, including college students and recent graduates, got involved in the Obama campaign. Thousands learned organizing skills at Camp Obama training sessions. The efforts of these young people—as well as the expanded youth vote—made a big difference in Obama's triumph last November. Many of the students who volunteered in the campaign got a taste of organizing and now want to pursue it as a career." We share Dreier's emphasis on the potential of community organizing and his hope that the current convergence of economic crisis and a progressive-oriented political regime provides an opportunity to transform the political-economic context and help create a new era that buries the ideological underpinnings and corporate-dominated practices and policies of the past generation, ushering in, at the least, dramatic, progressive reforms within nations and across the globe.

But the outcome of the economic crisis and the election of Obama as president remains uncertain, as does the contribution of community-based efforts. As Christopher Hayes put it at the end of April 2009, "Amid the euphoria of election night, it seemed the left side of the ledger was all that mattered. For the past three months it's been hard to ignore the right side. Now it all feels balanced on a knife's edge" (Hayes 2009). It is very possible that not much will actually change. If it can be said that the past thirty years were fundamentally about the dominant class figuring out new ways to expand its power, it is not certain that much has changed thus far in any of the three nations discussed in this book. David Harvey thinks a substantial part of the problem is this whole turn to community. He remarks that "the Left in the United States already suffers from an NGO culture." We think this "NGO culture" is a global phenomenon, certainly central to social change in the United States, but not limited to it. If this culture does not change, however, if the anti-statist politics of much of the Left persist, the questioning of and challenges to neoliberalism levied by political elites, even progressive regimes, will probably remain superficial. This has been all too evident in the continued support thus far for the financial industry rather than for the victims of unbridled capitalism who have lost their pensions, jobs, housing, and possibly decades of their lives.

It is clear there is opportunity for change everywhere. Such is the nature of crises. But the opportunities may exist as much for the Right, which in the United States, at least, has been counted out again and again, and its resurfacing each time proves these obituaries premature. We may see a continuing romance of community-based efforts, but grassroots organizing is no longer, and never has been, under the sole ownership and direction of the Left. The Right too has experimented with great success with grassroots organizing, sometimes simply tied to local insurgencies regarding property values, schools, and racist policies of exclusion, and sometimes tied to national parties or organizations.

Populist organizing and revolt are in the air and part of many people's experiences. In this regard, the Bush regime was a great help to grassroots groups, especially those on the Left. Clearly there is much enthusiasm in the United States for the promised Obama progressive agenda to succeed, and people are being organized at the local level to help support it, just as the Right organizes in opposition to it. To state the obvious, centralized, top-down forms of power politics that regulate unbridled capitalism and provide social and health benefits are still essential to any changes in the United States, Britain, Canada, or elsewhere. But there is also every reason to think their direction will be contested, by the Right opposing it and the Left expanding its boundaries. There is broad consensus on the Left that it will need to mobilize to both push Obama's agenda and go beyond it, and in so doing actually make it more acceptable as its moderate nature becomes apparent. Both sides, Left and Right, with all the variety included in that simple dualism, understand that much of this activism and dissent will mobilize at the grassroots. For more than a generation, community and community-based efforts have been the primary site and method for addressing social need and promoting social change. Accordingly, we think this book could not be more timely. No matter how this economic crisis unfolds or whether in the United States, United Kingdom, Canada, or elsewhere, local initiatives will play an important role in affecting the nature and direction of future politics and policies.

A central theme of *Contesting Community* is that community efforts can play a critical role in challenging contemporary neoliberalism, but it is essential not to romanticize the power and potential of local efforts. Community is a contradictory and contested concept, not simply an inherently good thing. That is what Raymond Williams warned as he ended his discussion of community in *Keywords*. He stated: "Community can be the warmly persuasive word to describe an existing set of relationships, or the warmly persuasive word to describe an alternative set of relationships. What is most important, perhaps, is that unlike all other terms of social organization (*state, nation, society,* etc.) it seems never to be used unfavourably" (Williams 1988, 76, emphasis in original).

Williams proposes two critical and separate issues vital to our understanding of community in social change. First, the political content of community is open and undetermined. It can reinforce the status quo, or it can embrace deliberate rejections of that status quo. This is vitally important because too many observers have saddled community-based organizing efforts with a priori political meanings, and reacted to those political meanings, rather than to the content of actually existing community-based efforts. Second, the term "community" is almost always presented and understood as a good thing. Perhaps this results from community's association with the organic and spontaneous, whereas the other forms of social organization have a more deliberate quality to them—which to some can be read as inauthentic. Or perhaps it is due to the nostalgic longing for a mythic, sanitized past, which community can often be connected to, and is always more appealing than the unambiguously flawed present. Whatever the basis, and regardless of the often impressive historical uses of community activism, this reason alone means that the Left should not give up on the concept of community. To do so would be to leave reactionary and conservative forces with a monopoly on the only conceptual description of social organization that is always understood as good. And that would be a horrible concession to make. Thus, Williams's observations, and their implications, are a challenge for those on the Left. How do we understand the importance of community in struggles for social and economic justice, without losing sight of the limitations inherent in community work? This book is about taking up that challenge.

The underlying preoccupation throughout this book, is how, if at all, local communities and their organizations can contribute to the process of social change. One of the problems with the term "social change" is that it can be taken from the point of view of either the Left or the Right. In fact, until very recently it is the Right that has been more effective in bringing about changes pushing toward the current neoliberal arrangements. In this book, we begin with the assumption that basic social change implies at least the redistribution of wealth and income, and that the process to achieve this, and as a goal in and of itself, is the redistribution of power toward the working class, poor, and groups that have faced forms of oppression in contemporary capitalism, such as racial minorities and women. This raises basic questions regarding the process of social change and the role of the state.

The process of social change is complex, and it is beyond the scope of this book to present all the programmatic, strategic, or tactical forces involved. Fundamentally, we do not believe that there is one blueprint or group, for example the working class, that acts as the primary agent of social change. A combination of working-class organizations, linked with broader social movements and community organizations, are the components that need to work in alliance to challenge the structure of power in contemporary capitalism. In contrast to many on the Left, who have dismissed the community as not useful to this process, we understand local work in the community as essential to social change. We elaborate the reasons throughout the book; briefly, in local communities, as in workplaces, because of shared space and often shared social position, people can be brought together to act. In addition, it is possible to build local organizations that can be sustained over time to contribute to a longer-term movement that opposes the status quo. Our concern and one of the motivations for writing this book is to critically analyze why community has moved in the direction of collaboration with and integration into the wider neoliberal agenda. But we also seek to challenge left theorists who see such regulation of community efforts as the only possibility. We see community and local work as vital to a wider oppositional movement of the Left.

This is not the place to write a theory of the state, but a couple of points are essential to set up later discussions. First, in the struggle for social and economic justice, the community has neither the resources nor the power to gain these resources. We would argue for some degree of decentralization as a way to enhance local democracy, but this does not in any way replace the role of the state as the locus in the society that has the power to redistribute wealth and income and limit the power of capital. We agree with Hardisty's analysis:

> Like many progressives I tend to see government as responsible for assuring a critical level of social justice. If I trusted government agencies and agents more, I would argue for a government program for every social ill. . . . Progressives need to maintain a careful balance in our attitude toward government. We must, of course, oppose uncompromisingly government that practices corruption and abuses power, and/or become[s] a vehicle for the interest of the rich or of authoritarian forces. But we should not confuse the need to scrutinize and control government with delegitimizing it altogether. Under the capitalist economic system that, for the near future, has a lock on the American economy, democratically conducted government is still the greatest hope for serving the needs of the vast majority of people, and, especially, for protecting the interests of the least powerful. (1999, 194–195)

However, even if left-wing progressive governments were elected to power, these changes would not happen without continual and ongoing demands from many places to push for basic change. Active community organizations can play an important role in local mobilizing, education, and leadership building in this kind of contestation. Historically, social democratic parties and progressives in elected positions, whether it be school boards or municipal or more central governments, require broad movements either to maintain their politics once in office or to defend changes that curtail the excesses of the rich and powerful. We find that the declaration of the Zapatista Front of National Liberation captures this orientation in its discussing the role of citizen organizing that can become a: "political force that does not aspire to take power . . . that can organize citizens' demands and proposals so that he who commands, commands in obedience to the popular will[,] . . . that does not struggle to take political power but for the democracy where those who command, command by obeying" (cited in Lynd and Grubacic 2008, 9). Even if there are alliances between community organizations and progressive and left parties, it is not enough to relinquish responsibility to those in elected positions; therefore, ongoing local work and alliance with other movements are key to pushing through a social change agenda.

At another level, the interaction between community and the state is one of the central problems explored in the chapters that follow. Local organizations find themselves both the recipients of recognition and support from government and, at the same time, they often mobilize and oppose direction of state policy or make demands to improve it. However, as we will argue, the former has had an impact on diminishing the latter. In other words, state support and recognition have shaped the ways in which community organizations intervene, and limit their activities that are oriented toward contestation of public policy and wider issues of social and economic justice. The chapters that follow build on this perspective, exploring those shifts under neoliberalism that have acted to draw community into roles of local service provision and development agents. At the same time, despite the wider pressures to move in these directions, there are many examples of organizations that contest neoliberal capitalism, organizing and mobilizing locally, and more broadly to challenge government and private capital. These tensions are at the core of the book along with an exploration of how local work can contribute toward the building of a wider opposition movement.

In this chapter, we set out the concepts related to how we understand community in its complexity. First, we discuss why community is important, and emphasize that community is fraught with tensions and contradictions. We then propose that contestation is central to understanding community and community-based organizing and organizations. Third, we argue that community is never independent of its wider context, but neither is it determined by it. Because of the structures of society and the place of community in them and the wider context, we turn to our fourth topic, the limits of community. Fifth, the chapter concludes with an analysis of the role and potential of community in social change. These five concepts frame our treatment of community and community organizing and organizations throughout the book.

WHY COMMUNITY IS
(AND HAS BEEN) IMPORTANT

Communities are important because they are the places of daily life in which people are housed, fed, care for each other, and raise children. They are the sites of daily convenience shopping, and the other activities that sustain us. However, these activities are not carried out by an abstract community but through a complex interaction of state services, community-based nonprofit organizations, private sector companies, and voluntary and informal processes. The forces that shape these activities often come from outside the community, either with state policies and related services or through the private market. The interaction of the external forces and the basic needs that are provided locally is the central tension that makes community a place in which interests and power are shaped, and in which important social, economic, and political conflicts occur. In a basic way, communities are the sites where people are prepared and supported to enter into the wider marketplace of capitalism in whatever class position they find themselves. Marxists refer to this as social reproduction, and communities are the sites of conflict around these issues and the tensions they create.

While capitalism, as a macrosocial system, needs functioning communities to produce and sustain healthy and skilled labor, the same is true at the micro level. Individuals and households need processes, organizations, and institutions such as schools, housing, recreation, and so forth, in communities to function in order to be able to achieve their personal and familial goals for their lives. Importantly for us here, having these organizations and institutions function properly is almost always beyond the capacities of individuals and households—especially in poor communities where people lack the material resources to purchase many commodities. But the need for communities to provide the means of reproduction as a social product is not limited to poor communities. Most people, for instance, attend public (state) schools rather than private ones, and no matter how large individual suburban backyards, most city people still rely on public parks for the kind of physical, social, and psychological restoration that parks can provide. Moreover, the quality and condition of people's housing is inevitably linked to that of the other people who live around them. Thus, people in communities—especially, but not exclusively, those without material wealth—need to act collectively to insure the organizations and institutions in communities function properly.

But the importance of community in the political economy is not solely as the site of social reproduction, and to assert as much would be both ahistorical and a misreading of the contemporary moment. Historically, factories, mines, and other components of the wage-labor productive economy were rooted in communities, and the divide between places of employment and places of residence was much narrower and less dichotomous. Similarly, in the contemporary economy increasing segments of reproductive labor have become wage labor (albeit often poorly paid and hyper-exploitative—see, for instance, Anderson 2000; Domestic Workers United 2006; McGrath and DeFilippis 2009). People, particularly in the middle and upper classes, increasingly "contract out" the work of daily life. Take-out and delivered food, child care, housekeeping, and landscaping are all examples of how much of what used to be unwaged work in the daily life of communities has become commodified into relations between consumers and producers, and employers and employees. Thus, as capitalist wage relations penetrate further into communities, the idea that the realms of home and paid work are somehow distinct from each other is increasingly untenable.

Being both the realm of reproduction and intimately connected to (and part of) the realm of employment means that community is connected to a variety of different institutions and kinds of social relations. First, social services are for the most part administered and experienced at the community level—and this was true even before the nonprofitization of social services that we have seen in the last thirty years. Second, the institutions involved in the provision of housing—public, private, and not-for-profit—while simultaneously working at various scales, impact people at the scale of the community (rather than the citywide or individual levels). Housing is the central realm in which social reproduction takes place, and this is particularly true in the Anglo-American world, which has, since the late eighteenth century, shrunk notions of the ideal family down toward the "nuclear family" (see Hayden 2002). But domestic property, for homeowners, is the largest source of wealth, and thus is particularly prone to inspire political action at the community scale. As Kling and Posner (1990, 36) put it: "Any activist knows that in the United States probably the easiest issue to mobilize people around is the protection of their property rights. Second easiest is the demand that 'the community' participate in decisions that effect the life situation (e.g., property value, child raising and education, shopping, traffic patterns)." This has certainly been true for the "suburban warriors" of the Right, starting with the tax revolts of the 1970s, who, according to Lassiter (2006, 7), "have significantly expanded the grassroots narrative" beyond left activism based in New York and Chicago to conservative efforts based in Sunbelt suburbs.

Third, communities are not only important in reproducing labor but also in the operations of labor markets. Perhaps most notably, social networks that are centered around the community play an important role in connecting potential workers with job openings, and employers with potential workers (see, for instance, Kasinitz and Rosenberg 1996). The old cliché that "it's not what you know, but who you know" has more than a grain of truth to it—and it is in communities that "who you know" often gets established. This is perhaps most true in immigrant communities, but it is true more generally as well—regardless of which labor market segments and what kind of communities are involved.

At the same time, the community is a place of face-to-face contact. This is particularly true for the geographically or territorially based communities in urban areas that are the concern of this project (although communities of culture or interest also can emphasize face-to-face contact). The potential for collective action is always present. For example, collective action around child care can range from informal practices such as shared child care responsibilities among a set of parents in an apartment building or community, to the more formalized self-help of cooperative daycare, to politicizing the issue by demanding state subsidies for child care. But the political implications of communities need not always be so intentional as this. The face-to-face interactions that are such an important part of urban communities act to influence—often without anybody noticing or recognizing it—how people understand the world around them. People see each other on the street, in the supermarket, at their kids' school, in church, mosque, and synagogue, in the public library, or at bookstores. Relationships develop and grow. Although this is not easily measured or even understood, one expression of the impact of communities on people's political understandings is what urban geographers have long called "neighborhood effects" in voting behavior (see Agnew 1987; Baybeck and McClurg 2005). That is, when you control for other variables that influence political understandings and behavior (race, income, gender, education, etc.) the place in which people live continues to act as an independent force in shaping people's political lives.

There is something inherently logical about political understandings being shaped by common territory. This is because people in urban communities have their daily lives mediated through shared institutions in the political economy. A community's sharing of, for instance, a common position in a metropolitan area's real estate market forces people to try to work together to face issues such as abandonment, foreclosures, or gentrification, because these processes, while rooted in larger political economic relations, play out at the community scale. Similarly, when a government disrupts a community by either establishing an unwanted land use or promoting a large development that will displace people, it is a threat to the lives and interests of many people in that community—and transcends any one person or household. People, in short, can and do form communities by virtue of facing common sets of issues in their daily lives. And, importantly for us here, this making of communities often takes an organizational form, and people formalize, to one degree or another, their commonalities through groups, associations, and organizations.

These territorially shaped common sets of forces themselves overlap with other commonalities of people in communities. In North America and Britain, when people are sorted into residential space in urban areas, it does not happen independently of their race, class, and ethnicity. The causal processes involved in that sorting are beyond the scope of this book, but the more pronounced the segregation (race, class, and/or ethnicity) that results from those processes, the more likely the shared concerns of common territory will be a basis for community politics. In his famous discussion of "Do Communities Act?" Tilly argues that the most important condition for communities to act is shaped by whether or not "communities are homogeneous with respect to the main divisions of power at the regional or national level" (Tilly 1974, 219).

Because of the importance of community, it is only logical that it has been used and invoked since at least the late nineteenth century as a base of countless efforts at democratic participation, mobilization, and opposition. While the significance and political content of the efforts have certainly varied, community organizations have a long and continuous history, especially in the United States but not exclusively there. Community efforts run the political gamut from radical efforts that challenge corporate exploitation and systems of racial apartheid, to more liberal/adaptive charity-like efforts that provide services such as health care and food to enable people to survive, to reactionary efforts that oppose racial integration or left social initiatives. The persistence and variety of community efforts underscore their integral nature historically in the United States, Canada and, more recently, the United Kingdom. Britain and Canada have deep traditions of charitable efforts at the local level to address basic needs. But with the expansion of the state in those two nations, community-based efforts played a much more minor role in social provision than in the United States—at least until the convergence around the United States's community-oriented model in those nations since 1980.

Finally, given the importance of community in shaping collective action, and given that community is the realm in which services are provided and experienced, it is unsurprising that the collective action within communities has been geared toward, and steered through, the largest institutional framework for collective action in any society—that is, the state. The state, encompassing all levels of government and its agencies, as well as nongovernment entities that perform the tasks and functions of government, is therefore central in any discussion of the organization of community. On one level, this is because the quality of life within communities is greatly shaped by the provision of services—schools, parks, hospitals, streets, buses, and so forth—by the state apparatus. And those services, and their quality (or lack thereof), are defining components in the commonalities of people in shared residential spaces. They therefore are often the launching point for nonstate-based collective action in neighborhoods. But on another level, because community-based collective action is often undertaken vis-à-vis the state, when communities take organizational forms they do so in a set of relations (either explicit or implicit) with the state structure. Accordingly, state policies toward communities and their organizations become critical in any discussion of the importance of community in the larger political economy. We examine this in more detail in chapter 3, but stated briefly, the changes in state policy in neoliberalism mobilize actors and organizations at the local level to play an active role on their own behalf. Some of these policies have benefited organizations by bringing them recognition and financial resources, but they do not come without a political and social cost. The relationship between community and the state does not disappear. Instead it becomes crucial, wherein many organizations choose pragmatic self-interest over raising demands and contesting the state.

We argue, in short, that the political importance of community contains five key components. First, community plays a central role in the capitalist political economy and its reproduction. This role complexly connects community to a set of other realms not normally thought of as community. Second, the community is where people have many of their interactions with the state and its social services. As such, political consciousness vis-à-vis the state is often formed in the community, and issues related to reproduction and services become points of contestation in which the relationship between the state and community members becomes concretely expressed. Third, and related to this, community is the site where political ideology and understandings of the world are very often formed—often organically, without purposeful or deliberate reflection or analysis. Fourth, community is where people learn to participate in politics and political life, and they often do so in local organizations in their neighborhoods. Historically, this has been perhaps more true in the American context than elsewhere (as de Tocqueville famously observed), but the convergence of political-economic forces in the last thirty years in North America and Britain has pulled the Canadian and British contexts toward the American model. Finally, social movements need communities. They need them because communities have historically been the staging grounds for social movements. And they need them because of the vital roles that communities play in the creation of the larger political economy—roles that enable changes at the community level to have implications well beyond what is considered community per se. But they also need communities because of how important communities are in the daily lives of people. One of the axioms of organizing is that you organize people where they are, and where people are, in much of their lives, is in their communities.

COMMUNITY IS (AND ALWAYS HAS BEEN) CONTESTED

Because of the significance of community, it has been, and continues to be, mobilized for a variety of political projects. Building upon the discussion in Fisher (1994), we identify five types of community mobilization:

1. *Reactionary*: which try to turn back the clock to a prior, real or imagined, time and state of affairs;
2. *Conservative*: which attempt to maintain a status quo that resists the advancement of social, economic, and political justice;
3. *Adaptive/Reformist*: which accept the basic premises of the status quo, but try to tweak it a bit around the edges. They try to reform gross inequities to improve and maintain society;
4. *Radical/Revolutionary*: which use the language and realm of community as a basis to try to fundamentally transform the social relations of their time;
5. *Opt-out*: which use the context of community to try to withdraw from the larger-scale social relations of their time.

Although this may seem fairly straightforward, we must stress that the mobilization of community is actually more complex than is often assumed. For instance, the nineteenth-century rural communes inspired by the British political economist and philosopher Robert Owen might appear to be radically critical of industrial capitalism. But they were, rightly in our view, disparaged by Marx as being reactionary for trying to turn back the clock to a world before industrial capitalism and the urbanization associated with it. Or, to use a more contemporary example, anti-gentrification organizing is often assumed to be politically radical—especially if the tactics involved are confrontational. But the rhetoric that is often used in such struggles is often a very conservative understanding of community. Gentrification is often opposed because outsiders are moving into and taking over "our" community—a "we were here first" language that echoes that of anti-immigrant organizing. Conversely, anti-gentrification organizing can be, and often is, underpinned by a critical or radical analysis of class in urban space. Therefore, the use of community must be understood and analyzed, in terms of its political content and implications, not just by *who* or *what* is being opposed or promoted, but *why* and because of what analysis and ideology. In short, the vision and ideology of the organized community is a decisive variable in the political content of community-based work.

All political projects encounter political opportunity structures that enable or constrain their efforts, and those opportunity structures vary according to both the political content of the projects and the political economic context in which the projects are located. Because of community's central role in social reproduction, community is most easily mobilized to simply reproduce the current set of social relations. The political content of this, however, is not completely or straightforwardly conservative. That is, maintaining the status quo and defending hard-won current gains can be radical—it depends on what is being defended and why, and who is attacking the status quo of the moment (Calhoun 1982). Nevertheless, some of the most politically successful projects invoking community have been ones that fall into the category of conservative projects. This is particularly true for communities that, because of the privileged class and race position of their residents, are products of the choices made and preferences expressed by those residents (choice itself being a privilege). Therefore those residents' inherent tendency will be to maintain a status quo that they have chosen to be part of and constitute. For reasons we will discuss below, the political opportunity structure is much more constraining if the goals of community efforts are radical or revolutionary—if they oppose or run counter to vested interests and the strictures of the dominant political economy.

Communities can not only function to reproduce a structurally unjust status quo but they also have connotations of homogeneity. People in communities are often assumed to be almost uniform in their interests, lifestyles, perspectives, and so forth. And in casual conversation (as well as more formalized academic writing) people often talk about communities as though they are such uniform entities that they become agents that act. Thus we hear phrases like, "the community is opposed to . . ." or "the community wants . . . ." But such an assumption of homogeneity often manifests itself in the oppression or exclusion of all those who are perceived as different, or in the erasure of class, race, gender, and other differences within communities. Combined with the conservative, status quo–reinforcing tendency of much of community politics (and the structural limits on efforts that are politically more radical), this tendency to parochial exclusion has led many on the Left to reject community as a framework through which transformative politics can find expression. We obviously do not agree with such a conclusion. We think that community-based efforts historically have, currently do, and potentially can, play vital roles in fighting for more equitable and just societies. Otherwise, we would not have written this book. On the other hand, we certainly realize the mistaken nature of efforts to promote a consensus at the community level based on an assumption of community that emphasizes its commonalities. As Michael Ball noted of consensus-oriented community regeneration efforts in London, "anyone who lives in Waterloo—with its battles between landowners, residents, service providers, and local and central government—will know this is a nonsense. There is no single truth. There is inherent conflict" (cited in Imrie and Raco 2003, 29).

COMMUNITY AND ITS CONTEXTS

Communities are, to no small degree, products of their larger social contexts. This has always been so, and what has varied has not been the extent to which the context shaped communities but how this has occurred, through what social forces and relationships, and whether such forces and relations enable or constrain actions within communities.

The extent to which community is shaped by its larger context led many social theorists in the second half of the nineteenth century and first half of the twentieth century to argue that community was being inevitably destroyed by capitalist urbanization. Theorists such as Tönnies, Simmel, Weber, Marx, Nisbet, Park, and Wirth all argued that capitalist urbanization would inevitably disrupt the smaller-scale, interdependent social relations that had long been fundamental units of people's lives. Some lamented the demise of communities (notably Tönnies with his framework of contrasting *Gemeinschaft und Gesellschaft*; Tönnies 1957 [1887]). Others celebrated the demise of community (notably Marx, who argued that capitalist urbanization had rescued "the population from the idiocy of rural life"; Marx and Engels 1967 [1848]). Still others simply wanted to understand how capitalist urbanism had created new forms of social interaction that undermined community (Wirth 1938). But all these theorists were in agreement that smaller-scale communities had ceased to be important in society. And as larger-scale forms of economic organization brought more and more people to cities, the density of people, the complexity of the division of labor in society, and the variety of social interactions would combine with the lack of economic necessity of smaller-scale units to inevitably undermine community as an important realm in people's lives and the larger world.

But, of course, communities have not ceased to exist as a result of capitalist urbanization, modernization, TV, or anything else. Instead, capitalism created new forms of communities—with new interdependencies and relations. For example, at the very moment Louis Wirth was famously writing in Chicago in 1938 that "community" had been replaced by "society," Saul Alinsky was organizing the Back of the Yards neighborhood of that same city, in what would become one of the dominant forms and expressions of urban politics in the twentieth century. And before Alinsky, communists had been engaged in massive community organizing efforts on Chicago's South Side to mobilize against evictions, racism, and the collapse of capitalism. The same critique can be applied to the ideas of contemporary theorists such as Robert Putnam, who write about the decline of community at the same time that there is a broad proliferation of community-based initiatives in the United States and throughout the globe. Thus, while the larger political economic context plays a central role in shaping how communities operate, and in the potential of political efforts based in communities, the often-heard argument that the larger context is destroying community has not been evident in the cities of Canada, the United Kingdom, or the United States. In fact, many elements of the contemporary context accentuate interest in community.

In the contemporary political economy, community is, quite frankly, "hot." And it is so largely, but not solely, because of the neoliberal turn of the last thirty years in the Anglo-American world and more broadly. Although this is not the place for a thorough discussion of neoliberalism, which has been done very ably by others (see, for instance, Brenner and Theodore 2002; Hackworth 2007; and Harvey 2005; among others), we think it is necessary to take a moment to briefly describe the processes of neoliberalism that are important to understand the contemporary "turn to community." Neoliberalism as a general orientation of governments has an impact on many dimensions in society. According to Brenner and Theodore, it can be understood as "a historically specific, ongoing and internally contradictory process of market-driven sociospatial transformation" (2002, 6). Several elements of this definition are important for the discussion that follows. The historical dimension means that the transformation to neoliberalism will vary from society to society, depending on national and local conditions and political traditions. There seems to be a convergence, however, in the three countries discussed in this book that differentiate them from, for instance, the social democratic countries of Scandinavia (Esping-Anderson 1990). The market-driven nature of neoliberalism also means a transition from what Bob Jessop describes as Keynesian welfare national states to Schumpeterian workfare postnational regimes. In distinguishing the latter from the former, Jessop argues that at the economic level, competitiveness and innovation become more important than full employment and planning. Social policy is subordinated to economic policy, with downward pressures on working conditions. One related goal is to get people to become "enterprising subjects" and become less dependent on state welfare programs. The market is clearly at the center of these changes. Neoliberal ideology implies that markets should be open and as far as possible "liberated from all forms of state interference," so that they "represent the optimal mechanism for economic development" (Brenner and Theodore 2002, 2). In short, the turn to neoliberalism has meant a fundamental transformation in the relations among the state, capital, and communities. This began with the "roll-back" neoliberalism of the Reagan-Thatcher-Mulroney period (see Peck and Tickell 2002), when the goal of the governments was to dismantle the welfare states that had been incrementally built up since the 1930s. The 1990s to the present, however, marks a shift in the practice of neoliberalism as communities, and community organizations, have been newly empowered to try to pick up the pieces left by the retreat of the state. The regimes of Clinton, Blair, and Chretien offered a more ameliorative brand of neoliberalism that differed from their immediate predecessors in some of their forms, but not, ultimately, in their core orientations or in the centrality of the market.

Within this context, there has been a major shift in the provision of social services and the meeting of basic human needs in Western political-cal economies. The public sector has, by and large, been in a protracted process of removing itself from the direct provision of basic services. It has also been decentralizing economic and social development to local communities and their governing regimes. This began in the late 1970s and early 1980s, and has continued largely uninterrupted in the period since then. Accordingly, a whole host of human needs are increasingly being met by public-private partnerships and the not-for-profit sector. This shift, which is one of the organizational expressions of neoliberal urban governance, has been called "neocommunitarianism" (Jessop 2002) or "neoliberal communitarianism" (DeFilippis 2004). The deliberate, visible withdrawal of the public sector from social services has occurred in the realms of housing, workforce development, health, and even income and in-kind assistance. Community is implicitly, and sometimes explicitly, expected to fill the gaps left as the state retreats. To be sure, the expanded interest in community-based organizing comes not only from the public retreat or restructuring since the late 1970s but also from 1960s activism, which emphasized the virtues of decentralized, anti-government, small-is-better, participatory forms of local democratic activism. Both of these trends have converged to spawn not only a vast proliferation of such efforts but also efforts with broadly varied forms and politics.

The neoliberal context has had contradictory and paradoxical impacts on community efforts. In some ways, the current moment is incredibly supportive of community-based efforts. The community is being promoted by influential theorists and policy makers in all three countries as being the definitive realm of society (see chapters 3 and 4). Accordingly, governments and foundations are putting greater resources into community organizations, through contracting out of public sector services, new public sector initiatives, and capacity-building funding of community-based, not-for-profit initiatives. But while the contemporary moment would appear a fortuitous one for community organizations, the reality is actually rather different. First, the ability of community organizations to use government money is highly constrained, and the theoretical frameworks that inform most community work are similarly truncated—thus leaving community groups unable to utilize the additional attention and support to achieve much beyond particular services and developments. Second, the larger political economic processes associated with neoliberalism—that is, globalization, capital mobility, and state retrenchment—have combined to geographically extend and even undermine the relationships that constitute communities by moving key economic decisions further away from the local and local state power. This distancing further removes people acting within communities from the forces that shape their lives and isolates people from each other in communities undermined by global capitalism. Third, the converse of this, not only does contemporary capitalism stretch out capitalist relations over greater distances but it also involves itself in more intimate relations in peoples lives. In so doing, it commodifies social relations by bringing the market into key aspects of what was previously provided by either the state or local nonprofits, or via unwaged (usually female) labor. We will elaborate in chapter 3 how the shifts to the market have reshaped community and changed the forms of local organization, shifting projects to a depoliticized form with high levels of professionalization, thus limiting local participation and mobilization.

Thus, paradoxically, at the very moment that communities are more burdened and constrained, they have also become increasingly more salient and popular sites for responding to and struggling with the world they have been handed (Fisher and Karger 1997; Pendras 2002). The turn to community may be a reaction to precisely the structures of the contemporary economy that marginalize large components of urban societies, creating poverty and exclusion from participation in the "fruits of capitalism." Manuel Castells has argued this point forcefully. Segregation and marginalization of communities lead to a "tendency to shrink the world" to the scale of that community (in Susser 2001, 311). This has led to a turn inward, toward efforts at the community level in arenas and practices as far ranging as public school reform, crime prevention, and social service delivery efforts, as well as efforts to democratize social, political, and cultural practices. Community is promoted as a site for greater democratic participation and an alternative to conservative state policies and bureaucratic programs. But these processes, as we argue in chapter 4 and elsewhere, are usually limited, not least by their lack of mobilization beyond the local. Nevertheless, community has also been an opportunity for political work. For example, activists who cut their teeth in the anti-globalization movement have turned to local work, which has created new, more politicized initiatives, particularly in solidarity with immigrant communities. Thus even in a neoliberal context, community plays roles that both reinforce and contest the dominant political and economic relationships.

In the world of community practices, heavily influenced by decades of neoliberal policy and politics, most community-based efforts have adapted to a conservative and constrained context for social change (Fisher and Shragge 2000). Practice has too often ignored or rejected prior social action and conflict models. Community development and community building efforts adapt to the shift right. An emphasis on "the bottom line," building "partnerships" with local businesses and corporations, developing "relationships," and focusing on "community assets" has narrowed conceptions of community activism, for example, squeezing out conflict models from the community organizer's arsenal of strategies and tactics. Moreover, most contemporary models of community building and development focus exclusively on the local internal community, not the economic, political, and social decisions that rest outside the community and create community needs and concerns. They thus turn away from the broader context at the very moment that the neoliberal context pushes people into communities and theorists into conceptions about community, neither of which can independently address the contextual challenges. It is that context which needs to be integrated into analyses by community organizations and theorists, not ignored or supported with adaptive theories about community intervention that implicitly adjust social change efforts to prevailing norms.

THE MARGINAL COMMUNITY

At the same time as community has become increasingly important in contemporary capitalist societies, it is also politically marginal. There are several reasons for this. First, the economic relations that produce communities within capitalism extend well beyond any given community. How a community is situated in the global economy, in turn, is largely dependent upon institutions and a set of relationships that exist outside of or beyond the community itself. Banks and their mortgage lending practices, industrial corporations and their decisions to locate a plant in (or, more commonly in North America and Britain, away from) a metropolitan area, and towns in other countries with soon-to-be emigrants to Canada, the United Kingdom, or the United States are all very real examples of how communities are shaped by a host of economic relations that extend well beyond any one community. Therefore, rightly understood, there is a difficult and ambiguous question of the extent to which problems in a community are actually community problems—given that so much of what produces communities are relations and decisions that exist well beyond any single community (a similar question was asked by Massey 1995, about regions).

Of course this was not always the case, or not to such a degree. During the period of dramatic industrialization in the United States, for example, from the mid-nineteenth to mid-twentieth centuries, capital was often community centered and even bound in local factories. Communities had direct access to and impact on these sites of capital. A labor strike, supported broadly by people in the community, including local police and politicians who were neighbors as well, could bring companies to a standstill. In response, companies dispersed and decentralized operations throughout the nation and the world, so that communities (and organized labor) would have less influence over corporate decisions. This comparative historical perspective underscores the point that contemporary communities do not have much control over the local economy, and that is the way capital prefers it.

There has certainly been a growth of community organizations and an increased inclusion of community in some decisions that affect local life. But fundamentally, many community organizations depend on relations that extend beyond community over which they have little control. Most important in this are governments and their policies that shape local activities and development. But the same can be said, albeit on a smaller scale, about the role of foundations in community work. In both sets of relations, the community organizations are structurally reliant on the outside institutions—and while this reliance does not mean that community organizations are powerless in their dealings with outside funders, it does render those relations structurally unequal.

There is also an element of political informality in community in which power and the capacity to influence decisions are uneven and depend on the capacity to mobilize and organize at the local level. At the same time, the implementation of community-based and controlled programs and services does give some power if there is a participatory democratic process. These processes are complex and are often linked to local traditions, as well as to how outside forces shape the local. Power is central. Although communities per se do not have formal power, they are the places of organizing for power. Through local organization, citizens can take some control over social political and economic processes that shape daily life. For this to happen, communities, through local organizations, need to see outside targets that should be challenged and not accept the inward-directed policies and practices that shape so much of contemporary local practice. We take this up in chapter 5, which presents examples of organizations that have continued to organize for power in order to make demands on the state and private sectors in their quest for economic and social justice.

To sum up the points emphasized thus far, community is both objectively and subjectively important. It is objectively important because of the vital roles it plays in the reproduction of capitalism. And it is subjectively important because of its significance in both people's experiences and memories and happiness, and also their interactions with the larger political economy and the understandings they have of that political economy. Often the wedding of the objective and subjective bases of communities leads to people organizing around their interests in communities. Thus community organizations—some durable, some transient—emerge. Community, in short, matters in ways both material and immaterial, and people act accordingly. And yet, despite the importance of community, community organizations are often politically marginal due to their fragmentation and relative dependence on outsiders.

COMMUNITY AND SOCIAL CHANGE

Given all of these constraints on community, the key question for this book is what role community organizations play in the process of social change in the contemporary political economy. We have written *Contesting Community* to explore this question. Our analyses of issues related to community, and the thematic examples throughout, are underpinned by this question. It is clear for us that the kind of social change we are discussing goes beyond local communities and cannot be achieved within them solely through the work of organizations tied to them. Despite their importance, communities and the organizations present within them are too limited and fragmented to achieve much on their own. But we still believe in community because of the importance of local work in reaching people who can organize themselves for power and critically understand the underlying causes of social and economic problems. And, as we elaborate in the last chapter, broader definitions of community, and the community action and community organizing we are discussing, can act as bases for longer-term social change.

The advantage and contribution of local work is the stability and place for participation in day-to-day activity that it offers to citizens. Local work can provide a base for long-term action and mobilization. Local communities are the places where people meet, discuss issues of common concern, and find strategies to respond to them. It is the great political potential of communities to take the objective qualities that come from shared territory (which include the aforementioned social service and education provision, labor market networks, and relations of domestic property) and combine them with the subjective processes of identity formation that happen through the everyday interactions of daily life in community.

However, without a conscious wider vision, community organizations will remain focused on the local. The challenge is to build an agenda that transcends local work and to find ways to connect with broader organizations, and build alliances to work for fundamental social change. Community organizing by itself cannot affect these changes.

For this to happen, broader-based initiatives that transcend local work are necessary. The community is simply too limited a scale. It is not easy to build the alliances that bring together social movements, which include labor and local organizing work. Further, compared to traditional labor or Marxist organizing, agency in community is far more multidimensional and crosses class with multiple issues such as race and gender. This is both a strength and a complexity of community. Community per se is not an agent, but the site for diverse actors and actions that have the potential to bring together alliances cutting across divisions at the local level and beyond.

Community organizations, through their leadership (staff, board, or members) must have strong, explicit commitments to the struggle for social and economic justice. This is a starting point. It may seem a bit obvious, but we say it because the explicit naming of such goals is increasingly uncommon in community-based efforts in the Anglo-American world. If it is not said out loud then how could it possibly be the focal point for organizations' work? Clearly, social and economic justice is not going to be realized at the scale of the community, but it must remain the goal. Related to this, there has to be a commitment to some form of procedural justice in how organizations operate. And if they are engaged in development or service provision, the ideal of justice must inform how such activities are structured and operate. Justice is not a vague goal "out there," but must be part of the defining characteristics of the internal relations of the organizations.

Community efforts must have an analysis of the processes and relations that cause injustice in their communities, and of the institutions that play vital roles in those processes. It is not enough to call for economic justice. In order to properly interpret issues and developments when they arise, and organize for the long term (beyond any one issue), there needs to be critical analyses of the causes of the problems in communities.

Because of their political goals and analyses, community efforts need to maintain conflict at the core of their activities. This centrality of conflict does not imply constant conflict, but rather a recognition of its potential, even if that potential is often (or usually) dormant. Nor does this imply that work in communities does not or should not contribute to community building and development, but that such processes are part of wider analyses of social and economic inequality, and such analyses necessarily include a role for conflict.

Finally, community-based efforts must transcend the places in which they are rooted. There is a substantial difference between working "within a place" and working "about a place." In order for community-based efforts to productively contribute to the goal of social justice, their understanding of community must be "within a place." In short, they must not be limited in their perspective to just the level of community. Focusing solely at the level of community not only allows for communities to become parochial and exclusionary but, even more important, it also reproduces and internalizes within community organizations the very marginality that makes community-based efforts so difficult, without realizing any of the benefits of the centrality of the community to the larger political economy. This book contributes to thinking and organizing both locally and beyond the local as a precondition for communities to be part of a needed broad-based movement for economic and social justice.

CHAPTER 2

History Matters

CANONS, ANTI-CANONS, AND
CRITICAL LESSONS FROM THE PAST

THE HISTORY OF COMMUNITY INITIATIVES reveals a complex past, one which if viewed with a wide-angle lens instantly expands understanding of the varied goals, politics, and shapes community efforts take. The complex history and diverse forms result from a number of factors, chief among them the historical context that shapes and helps produce a dominant form of community-based effort in each era. This dominant type not only mirrors broader contemporary phenomena but responds to and affects them as well. This history is a contested one, because community efforts are fundamentally political and, whether groups like it or not, implicitly or explicitly they are part of the social struggles of their historical context. Eras characterized by more liberal reform, ones that Piven and Cloward refer to as eras characterized by dissensus, foster and allow opportunities for the proliferation of more left-oriented community initiatives. These are the epochs which are usually seen as providing key lessons from the past for contemporary progressive efforts, and which serve as the "canon" of community organizing. More conservative or reactionary eras, which Piven and Cloward refer to as periods characterized by consensus, produce not so much a decline of community efforts, as the literature seems to suggest, but rather a decline of left-oriented community efforts and a rise of not only highly moderated but especially reactionary forms of local organizing, what we see as the "anti-canon." In discussing these developments, we will draw primarily from the history of the United States, with some reference to similar events in Canada and the United Kingdom. The material on the United States is especially rich because of the long tradition and variety of community organizing and development initiatives and their extensive documentation.

For a generation now we have found ourselves in a conservative/reactionary context, one characterized by a broad proliferation globally of community efforts as well as an equally widespread rise of reactionary and conservative uses of community. At the same time, there has been little understanding of the complex and contested nature of community action and the transformation that occurs in community practice in reactionary and conservative contexts. On the one hand, these reactionary and conservative pressures on the field of community organizing are being relatively ignored. Or they seem to be ignored but actually reflect organizational decisions that perceive the context as so constraining that the organizers have little choice but to pursue accommodating strategies which maintain the organization and financial bottom lines. On the other hand, we find a growing popularity, even romanticization, of the concept of community and community-based work. But the history of community organizing is filled with lessons for contemporary practice, chief among them that conservative and reactionary forms of community-based efforts flourish and proliferate in eras of consensus, just as more reformist liberal and radical forms do in eras of dissensus; they need to be included not only in the overall historical canon of community organizing but also in contemporary discourse and strategizing about the nature, potential, and limits of community action.

Such dualisms as eras of reaction and reform, conservative and liberal, consensus and dissensus are, of course, too simplistic to capture the depth of complexity revealed through the study of community efforts over time. And, of course, every historical era not only includes efforts that reflect the dominant form of the time and the politics of the moment but also includes oppositional forms that challenge contemporary community practice and the broader status quo. But for our purposes here, the dualisms actually reveal a great deal not only about the diverse motives and goals of initiatives in the past but also about contemporary community theory and practice in our current era of conservatism and reaction.

Conservative political economies and social contexts produce and support conservative initiatives. The relationship is commonly accepted throughout our society. Reactionary regimes since 1980 have had a profound direct effect, shifting policy and discourse to the right on issues ranging as widely as the environment, poverty, income inequality, crime, and war. For some reason, the obvious connection has escaped most community organizers and people who write about community efforts. In general, practitioners and scholars proceed almost as if the nature, form, and politics of community efforts are unaffected by the broader reactionary context. Nothing could be more wrongheaded. Most community efforts of a progressive nature have been heavily curtailed and constrained in the past three decades. Many of them have been incorporated by public and private funding, transforming the field to emphasize community building and consensus models rather than community organizing or conflict models. And, at the same time, right-wing and conservative efforts have proliferated.

Even in eras hostile to oppositional efforts or left activism, there is always a dialectical process in which community initiatives develop and respond to the tensions and contradictions of the time. For example, civil rights dissent developed at the community level in the South in the 1950s to address the obvious contradictions and tensions of apartheid racism (Morris 1986). Accordingly, even in our current context there are critical community initiatives doing essential work to challenge the neoliberal hegemony that dominates the era (and they are discussed in later chapters). These efforts, as with civil rights efforts in the 1950s, win victories, raise consciousness, engage people in struggle, plant seeds for social change, and provide models for future radical practice. They do so usually as oppositional efforts. The flip side is true for more progressive eras such as the 1960s, which, while often seen as glory days for left initiatives at both the local and national level, were also the seedbed of conservative and reactionary efforts that arose ten to twenty years later as a powerful right-wing movement.

Not only are minority forms of community organizing ignored, marginalized by a dominant form in each era but conservative and reactionary efforts are a clear and ongoing presence throughout the contested history of community organizing and community-based social change. While we argue here that the political-economic context of every era heavily influences the dominant tendencies of community organizing in that era, we emphasize with equal weight that there is a dialectical interaction, a contested—not reductionist—relationship, between the broader political economic context and grassroots efforts. Context is always relevant and critical to understanding local efforts, but it is never determinative.

One caveat. We should not give the impression that the dominant form of social change since the late nineteenth century has been local-based initiatives. The dominant pressure in industrial societies has been toward centralization. This is expressed both in the growth of capitalist enterprises and their concentration and in the centrality of the state in shaping areas of health, income, and labor. From the late nineteenth century onward in the United States (earlier in the United Kingdom), "bigger is better" was a truism for all sectors, including business, government, labor, and what has come to be known as civil society. No sphere of life was immune to the pressures for increasing size and power in order to compete more effectively under industrial capitalism. Nevertheless, despite this pressure to centralize and to expand size and scale in order to be large enough to compete at national levels, industrial society increasingly segregated and disaggregated residence and work by class, race, and ethnicity. The first neighborhoods under industrial capitalism served as geographic communities that not only pushed people into interdependent specializations but encouraged those who were largely left to their own devices to develop association and power at the community level. Accordingly, while the major story since the late nineteenth century has been one of centralization of power and organizational form, there has always been a significant parallel phenomenon emphasizing decentralized, community-based, local responses. Although activists and regular working people might have preferred a more centralized and powerful response, such as state provision of programs to address basic needs, they worked at the community level because that was the site where problems manifested, people experienced them, and organizers could mobilize a response. This is especially true in the United States, where weak political parties, a federated national government, and broad support for highly individualistic forms of capitalism provided vast space for voluntary activism.

CHARITABLE ROOTS, NATIONAL DIVERGENCE, AND CONTEMPORARY CONVERGENCE

Nowhere is the penchant for community and local activism better seen than in the voluntary and charitable associations that have been a mainstay of community life and social service distribution in the

United States, the United Kingdom, and Canada. Alexis de Tocqueville in the mid-nineteenth century understood the importance in a highly individualized society relatively free, certainly compared to Europe, of traditions and obligations of communal solidarity. In the United States, people built associations and community to meet their needs and advance their interests. The United Kingdom and Canadian experiences were in many ways similar. As in the United States, charitable, religious-based forms of addressing social problems dominated in these societies through the nineteenth century. But as social welfare became incorporated in expanded state functions and obligations, especially in Britain and Canada, in the twentieth century, religious-based charities and the civil society sector of voluntary associations receded in number, impact, and significance. Centralized state policy and programs replaced many decentralized charitable and voluntary efforts. In the United States, even with the professionalization and secularization of these efforts, decentralized charitable forms and missions of the past remain strong into the twenty-first century. Of course, as Wagner and others argue, late-nineteenth century charity usually had a negative side; it was never simply benevolent. "Charity's focus was hardly on social, economic, or political change, but on character reform. . . . Charitable institutions to assist the poor in America combined benevolence with repression" (Wagner 2000, 65). This different context in the United States continued dependence on voluntary associations to meet needs and problems, but also provided space for community efforts to emerge and develop. Settlement houses were a vast improvement over "scientific charity" of the late nineteenth century, as will be discussed below, but like all other forms of social welfare, it was not as pure as presented. These forms did reflect, however, the American love affair with decentralized charity and local voluntary associations, and the implicit and explicit hostility in American capitalism toward more centralized statist initiatives for addressing social needs and problems.

The historical experiences of the United States, United Kingdom, and Canada thus follow a pattern of convergence, divergence, and reconvergence. Prior to the late nineteenth century, before formalized social welfare state formation in Britain and Canada, all three pursued a social welfare model similar to community-based charitable approaches that reach back to the first millennium. Beginning from the late nineteenth century and following their own specific trajectories, the three nations diverged, with the United Kingdom and Canada developing a stronger social welfare state and state apparatus to address social welfare needs and the social byproducts of industrial capitalism. In the United States, the welfare state did not develop until the 1930s, and then only in a compromised, more modest form in response to a global crisis of capitalism. It was never intended to challenge capitalist businesses and private insurance or replace voluntary associations at the community level. It was meant to be supplementary. Community efforts continued to play a significant role in both policy and discourse about how to address social problems (see O'Connor 2008), and community efforts found opportunities and space to develop. This civil society alternative to the state and market continued to grow in the United States, sometimes with an expanding and complementary state, sometimes in response to or in tandem with a contracting one. With the democratic insurgency of the 1960s throughout the world, the Left, or in this case the New Left, continued the historic social change trends in the United States by using loosely organized social movements, local protest efforts, and community-based action to address contemporary challenges. Decentralized, anti-statist, community-based forms with a preference for local-based, democratic initiatives remained more a hallmark of organizing efforts in the United States. The Canadian experience was a mix between the United States and Britain, where there was a heavy emphasis on democratic participation in localist activities such as popular clinics; but overall the experience was closer to Britain, with its social democratic and socialist demands for state intervention. As the world began to shift right in the mid-1970s, partly in response to the democratic initiatives of the 1960s and partly in response to corporate strategies to maintain profits in an increasingly competitive global marketplace, the welfare state began to be disassembled and rebuilt, as did conceptions of community and local-based initiatives, even in more socialized systems in Western Europe, the United Kingdom, and Canada. And it is in this era since 1980 that we see a convergence in all three nations of proliferating community associations and initiatives, expanding importance and reliance on civil society, and the use by the state of community as a concept and site for addressing social needs. It is this current epoch, and the uses and potential of community-based efforts, on which this book focuses. But it is in the historical precedents, primarily but not exclusively in the United States, where most of the history of community action in the hundred years between the 1880s and 1980s takes place, which are the primary subjects of this chapter.

LESSONS FROM THE PAST

We start with selected key points from this history of community-based efforts in the United States. We emphasize that community organizing has a long history and that historical context is critical in understanding current community efforts. Then, in the selected history that follows, we embed essential lessons, especially the importance of conflict organizing and social movement building. We conclude by illustrating how community organizing cuts across the political spectrum; it's not inherently progressive; it includes efforts ranging all the way from Left to Right.

Community Organizing Has a Long, Rich History

The history of community action dates back at least to the late nineteenth century and extends throughout the twentieth century. The popular imagination might believe it began in the 1960s, as a product of the oppositional efforts of that generation, but intentional community organizing started with the decentralized, communitarian responses of the late nineteenth and early twentieth centuries, most notably the social settlement house movement. To be sure, there were earlier efforts. Prior to the Industrial Revolution, de Tocqueville noted the importance and proliferation of local voluntary associations—what is now called civil society. Around the same time, various romantic communitarian ideas took form in utopian "opt-out" efforts such as those set up by the Owenites, Shakers, Fourierites, and others. But it is in the twentieth century that community-based activity, in contrast to the more centralized thrust of the broader society, takes on a more intentional and significant role. As noted earlier, with industrialization, with the segmentation of urban life into neighborhoods and blocks, and with increasing density and population mass in large cities, especially New York and Chicago, urban residents formed community associations and voluntary activities for a wide variety of goals that they could not meet on their own and could not rely on private sector or the local, state, or national public sector to effectively address.

The more or less accepted canon of the field of community organizing, as edifying and limiting as any canonical device, emphasizes three major heydays in the history of community work in the United States: approximately 1900–1920, 1930–1946, and 1960–1975. It highlights, among other examples, the social settlement, community center, and other communitarian initiatives of the years 1900–1920; the more radical efforts of Saul Alinsky, Left political party work at the local level, and the community-labor work of the nascent CIO in the 1930s and 1940s; and the community-based initiatives of the civil rights, New Left, and nascent women's movement in the 1960s and early 1970s. This canon of noted community efforts is rich with lessons from the past for community action efforts in the present and future.

As with most canons these days, there is disagreement on which examples to include. The above list is selective, and there are a large number of efforts excluded, especially efforts led by women and people of color. Social work scholarship has possibly the richest and deepest canon, emphasizing its own roots in the settlement house movement and tracing its interest and role in local-based organizing through leading roles in New Deal programs in the 1930s, War on Poverty programs in the 1960s, and the women's movement. Those associated closely with the Alinsky tradition of community organizing ignore at best, often disdain, these social work examples. They instead might begin with Alinsky's efforts in the 1930s, implicitly anointing him as the father of community organizing in the United States, and emphasizing his work, that of the Industrial Areas Foundation in the 1960s, and similar efforts associated with the "backyard revolution" of the 1970s. Similarly, activists of color will include Alinsky but not exalt his contribution, arguing ironically that "Alinsky founded community organizing like Columbus discovered America." They focus their attention instead on the deep resistance of African Americans before the twentieth century, and include not only efforts of luminaries such as W.E.B. Du Bois but also community-building and service delivery work in the early twentieth century; the efforts of Marcus Garvey and Father Divine in the 1920s and 1930s; and especially black community, labor, and electoral efforts tied to civil rights and Black Power movements of the 1960s and 1970s.

The dominant examples and texts noted above compose our general understanding of the origins, history, and models of community-based social change. While the examples in this multiple-stranded canon of community organizing vary, they all share a common ingredient. During the twentieth century, they draw on the heritage of struggle and resistance in the three eras of left struggles and liberal politics: 1900–1920, 1930–1946, and 1960–1975. Of course there are exceptions. All historical eras have porous, not fixed, boundaries. Garvey did his work in the 1920s. The Montgomery Improvement Association staged its bus boycott in the mid-1950s. Still, despite minor discrepancies in the canons, there is agreement on the importance and richness of this history. There is also almost complete agreement on the types of historical context that help produce such efforts. The progressive canon emphasizes that community efforts have a long history throughout the century, but largely in specific eras and historical contexts—which they helped create—which provided more opportunities and supports for progressive social change.

The Importance of Historical Context

As we have already argued, the broader political-economic context is vitally important in shaping the nature, form, choices, and success of community-based efforts. Because organizing efforts and writings about organizing are always specific to a particular time and place, the history of community organizing must situate practice in the context of the varied sites that generated it, including both the national and local context.

From that perspective, each historical era has a dominant form of community initiative, one produced by the interaction between the broader political economy and the social struggles and oppositional efforts that respond to it. Although there is always a broad range of competing efforts at any time, a distinctive form tends to emerge in each era, reflecting as well as influencing the broader political economy of the specific era. This is not a one-way street where national political economy dictates the nature, form, and success of community initiatives. The process is always much more dialectical, a give-and-take between a dominant type of national political economy at any given historical period and the resistances and initiatives produced both by the local tensions and contradictions of this context; The process is also affected by the oppositional imagination and democratic passions of citizens mobilizing as public actors. Certainly issues of human agency—defining the very nature of a community organization, its goals, methods, daily choices—play a critical role in the life of any community organization effort. But the larger historical context heavily influences what conceptualizations and choices are available or encouraged, what goals are salient, and what strategies seem appropriate and likely to succeed. It helps shape a dominant model of community work (and almost everything else) in each historical context.

Progressive Era Organizing

The dominant example of community-based initiative in the last decade of the nineteenth century and especially the first decades of the twentieth century was the social settlement house. It was both a strong reflection of the political economy of the Progressive era—its virtues and limits—as well as catalyst for the critical progressive changes of that time. Settlement leader Vida Scudder saw the turn-of-the-century city as a "cleavage of classes, cleavage of races, cleavage of faiths: an inextricable confusion" (cited in Shapiro 1978, 215). Society seemed to be coming apart at its class and ethnic seams (Husock 1990; Kogut 1972). In response, reformers developed a counterideology and social movement which argued that society, not simply the individual, was responsible for social conditions, and that the environment, not simply one's personal characteristics, heavily shaped life experience (Quandt 1970). Many reformers in the national Progressive movement believed in bigness and centralized initiative, but another strand of progressivism was a variant of communitarian reform, best epitomized by the social settlement movement, which advocated for community-based initiatives and interventions.

Begun in England in the late nineteenth century and flourishing in the United States and Canada in the early twentieth century, settlements attracted social reformers to engage with the problems of the new urban-industrial order at the local level by living in settlement houses based in slum neighborhoods, especially those with a high percentage of recent immigrants. The settlements reflected well the social gospel missionary impulse as well as the middle-class Progressive era animus to reject the individualism, greed, and faith in laissez-faire capitalism of this earlier era. They responded collectively to the oppressive conditions of slum areas and the dire needs of people living in these deplorable conditions, and, given their concern for order, aimed to do so before social unrest between the classes tore the society apart. They also were responding to the obvious limits of charity associations that dominated the social welfare field in the United Kingdom and United States. To that end, settlers in the most Progressive houses in New York City and Chicago developed a community practice that included four essential elements, which reflected the thrust of the broader Progressive era context: (1) a rejection of the individual causes of poverty common to charitable work and an emphasis on the social and economic conditions that misused, constrained, and impoverished workers and immigrants; (2) an integrated approach that provided desperately needed services, engaged with residents at the individual and community level, and focused on developing cross-class solidarity between neighborhood residents and settlement workers; (3) a communitarian perspective on the essential importance of building community and community connection as a means of increasing participation of primarily poor recent immigrants and developing solidarity networks at the local level; and (4) a willingness to organize and advocate for social, political, and economic justice at the local, state, and even national level, including participation in the electoral process and policy advocacy (Fisher 2005).

Only a few settlement houses and leaders such as Jane Addams, Lillian Wald, and Florence Kelley actually challenged capitalism's role in creating class divisions and exploiting industrial workers, and actually supported efforts and protests to change the system. For most settlement leaders, the general thrust of the period, which the settlement houses both reflected and aided, was a renewed understanding of the social causes of problems and the need for nonviolent, reform-oriented collective responses and solutions to the challenges of the emerging urban-industrial order, especially the mass migration of millions of immigrants to major cities. As communitarians who understood the value of community building and community organizing, especially in densely settled neighborhoods in such cities as New York and Chicago, they worked to not only use the local as a site for democratic participation and service delivery but also as a staging ground for broader initiatives. They aimed to affect the overall political economic context and move policy and initiatives at the local, state, and national levels around specific issues such as housing reform and child welfare, which were part of a much broader concern about slum life and increasing inequality between rich and poor. Aware of the limits of individual settlements in particular and individual community work in general, they formed the National Federation of Settlements (NFS) in 1911 to coordinate the hundreds of settlements nationwide and advocate for broader initiatives that could not be addressed fully at the local level. But the NFS had limited power and effectiveness due to the voluntary nature of the national organization (Primary Source Media n.d.).

To be sure, the settlements achieved a great deal, even continuing into the twenty-first century to serve as a model for an integrated community practice. And yet the middle- and upper-class nature of most early twentieth-century reform efforts also heavily influenced settlement initiatives, providing a pragmatic and optimistic reform fervor and faith in public life and public service, while limiting efforts to nonradical and nonstatist initiatives and solutions. A more radical response and more effective initiative at the national level would not develop until a later historical context, the Great Depression, did tear society asunder and expose not only the limits of unregulated capitalist economies but also the limits of local-based initiatives to address them. Ultimately, of course, it was the activism and actions of people engaged in these struggles, including the emerging labor movement, that pushed the broader political economy to dramatically shift, and to force the state to respond. But the critical lessons of the settlement house for this volume are clear: the political economy of the Progressive era and the social struggles its contradictions produced heavily shaped the opportunities, choices, and support for a dominant form of communitarian, reform-oriented community organizing, the social settlements. And the example of the settlements reveals the early development in community organizing of an integrated practice that intentionally combined politics, service, and community building and organizing with local and national activism. But for the most part they did not pursue a more radical course or develop a more effective organizational structure beyond the local communities with which they were involved.

Depression Era Organizing

The Depression era of the 1930s presented a different context for organizers, occasioning a very different type of dominant form. In a nutshell, it was clear that the collapse of world capitalism created an urgency for both leaders and ordinary people and demanded more radical politics. In response, communities organized to harness the energy and anger that spilled over on a daily basis, in individual acts of defiance, social disorder, and organized resistance. The interaction of Depression-era conditions, radical local organizing, a vibrant and radical union movement, and New Deal federal policies all combined to create a dynamic and critical era in the history of community organizing.

While community efforts of the Communist Party, the Catholic Workers Movement, or Saul Alinsky, to name but a few, differed widely, these dominant models of the era were all characterized by militant strategies and tactics, a radical analysis of community problems and solutions, and expanded frameworks designed to mobilize more people and communities in resistance to Depression-era conditions and in support of democratic and just solutions. They organized at the local level because that was where people experienced problems on a day-to-day basis and where they could engage people to participate in social change efforts. But given the national and worldwide nature of problems in the 1930s—not only the failure of capitalism but the emergence of fascist regimes—the dominant forms of this era included a broad critique of problems that sought to take local residents beyond their own communities to see problems in a broader light and focus on developing organizational frameworks at the national level. This was certainly the case in Communist Party organizing, which used a radical analysis to catalyze community people and which saw local work as a means to build a national political party in the United States and further the international working-class struggle. But it was also true for the efforts of Saul Alinsky who, while suspicious of "ideological organizing," and while committed to community work for its own sake, also understood that his community efforts in the late 1930s were part of a broader ideological struggle against the fascist menace. He saw that "people's organizations" were needed nationwide in order to have more impact on a larger scale than the local community (Fisher 1994).

The local efforts of the Communist Party, highly controversial because of close ties to the Soviet Union, were best expressed in the Unemployed Councils, which formed to address community problems such as housing evictions, unemployment, hunger, and racism.

In addition to the radical militancy of the Unemployed Councils and the courage and ferocity of the organizers and activists who faced great personal danger, community efforts operated on multiple levels of practice. By connecting the multiple levels, the Communist Party hoped not only to organize new members and address local issues but also tie local activity and more particularized organizing to broader struggles on the national and international scale. On one level were the basic principles—such as a critique of capitalism, the nature of class conflict, and the need for working-class democracy—that undergirded all efforts and tied local efforts intellectually to the world beyond the community. The next level included the national campaigns and organizational forms that transcended community efforts—whether in Chicago, New York, or Birmingham, Alabama—and tied them to broader struggles and campaigns, such as campaigns for national social insurance and anti-lynching legislation, as well as support for the Scottsboro boys' trial and opposing the imprisonment of Angelo Herndon, two major national causes of the party opposing racist attacks on African Americans. The third level—the community level—was the site of the day-to-day activism of members to address local issues, whether an eviction of a neighbor, a local family's need for help from the relief bureau, or a protest at City Hall. At all three levels of organizing, theory and practice were deeply interconnected, designed to get people involved in local public life and use community organizing as a staging ground to address deeper systemic problems and broader struggles which could catalyze people's engagement (Fisher and Kling 1987; Nelson et al. 1981; Naison 2004). The crippling flaws in Communist organizing in the 1930s rested in the anti-democratic manipulation of local efforts in order to support ideological and international campaigns developed by or with the consent of operatives in the USSR. Despite a good deal of autonomous activism on the part of U.S. organizers at the local levels, their achievements were ultimately distorted and undermined by attachment to directives from the Comintern. That said, these efforts provide a vivid and provocative historical example which valued community as an organizing site, recognized its limits, and offered an organizational theory and practice to go beyond the limits of local efforts, especially the limits of local work in the face of national and international crises.

The efforts of Saul Alinsky began in Chicago in the 1930s amid the same conditions and radical fervor that legitimized and created opportunities for organizing efforts of the Community Party and the militant, democratic labor movement of the time. Alinsky's efforts in the Back of the Yards neighborhood are generally well known; therefore we will discuss his efforts and model briefly in terms of how they contributed to the critical lessons of organizing in this period: (1) the emphasis on militant, conflict tactics, and (2) the development of ideological and organizational frameworks that expanded the impact of community organizing. The former underscores how a context such as the Great Depression produced and legitimized conflict tactics. Now it was acceptable, if not encouraged, for organizations to protest contemporary conditions. The times seemed to demand it. This was no time to act polite, go through mainstream channels that had clearly failed, or build consensus with economic or political leaders who were seen as responsible for both the economic depression and the failure to end it.

The Alinsky method of community organizing learned its militant tactics and conflict approach to community organizing from the radical politics of the Communist Party and the nascent C.I.O., especially that of the United Mine Workers and its leader, John L. Lewis. The Alinsky method encouraged organizers to get community people in touch with their anger, to "rub raw people's resentments," to use any and all nonviolent tactics in order to publicize the issues and enable community people to win victories, and thereby see the power of collective direct action. Alinsky was a strong believer that the ends justified the means— that is, that almost any and all tactics were justifiable to protect democracy and advance the interests of working people, who were disregarded by the overall system. The more a tactic disturbed those in power, the better. Alinsky liked to say that "life is conflict and in conflict you are alive." Like great democratic leaders before him, he understood that power concedes nothing without struggle, and the more creative and unpredictable a community's strategies and tactics the more effective their efforts. Of course, Alinsky's theory and practice of organizing did not only use conflict. His efforts used a wide variety of tactics to achieve their goals, from negotiation and compromise to economic development initiatives and community-building efforts. But it was Alinsky's use of militant tactics, or at the least the threat of them, for which he is

best known. In the late-1930s, with so much at stake due to the dual
threats of both economic depression and the rise of fascist alternatives,
with the future of democracy uncertain, militant protest fit well with the
overall turmoil and conflict of society.

Like the Communist Party, Alinsky saw the value of organizing
beyond the local community, but he preferred to do so through
community-based "people's organizations" rather than a national party
apparatus with a mobilizing analysis of contemporary problems. To be
sure, Alinsky offered an overall analysis of contemporary problems that
would attract community residents. In the late 1930s, he saw himself as
a "professional anti-fascist," fighting the forces of reaction at the
community level and beyond. But Alinsky rejected explicit ideological
organizing. In fact, later on he emphasized in response to the New Left
that organizing must be "nonideological." Alinsky incorporated militant
conflict tactics from the radical activists of the early 1930s in Chicago,
but not the value of a structural analysis—the communists called it a
"line"—to galvanize constituents and help them make connections
between their local circumstance and those beyond their community.
He saw ideological organizing as fundamentally undemocratic, as contrary to community organizing. He was quite open about his populist
ideas and anti-fascist politics, but these were more personal than part of
an organizational program or vision.

Alinsky had learned from criminologist Clifford Shaw and others
that the locus of community should be an end in and of itself, that
community was the perfect site for democratic process. He sought to
counteract the limits of community by developing loosely connected
"people's organizations." To that end he secured help from Marshall
Field, the owner of Chicago's largest department store, to found the
Industrial Areas Foundation (IAF) and through the IAF he sought to
promote and spread his approach to community action. "Alinsky
efforts" since then have proliferated. They were curtailed by the rise of
the Right in the 1950s; they started slowly in the early 1960s and then,
on the heels of the southern civil rights movement, revived in organizing efforts in industrial cities in the north; and then continued in the
1970s and thereafter in the Southwest, where they found greatest
success, and elsewhere. But while his organizing theory recognized the
importance of building an organizational structure beyond the local

community and his personal views recognized the value of a critical political analysis, his militant, confrontational mode of organizing always emphasized the primacy of local work, the commitment to local people and the local community. Undoubtedly he did so in part because there were so many other social movement efforts at the time focusing on the bigger issues and working on a national scale. But he also did so because he was uncertain how to resolve the tension inherent in building a national organizational structure and broad intellectual framework while focusing on the specific needs and people involved in each local community with which he and his staff became involved.

Sixties Organizing

In the history of community organizing, perhaps the high point, the historical moment most central to the progressive canon of the history of community organizing, is the sixties. Extending approximately from 1960 through 1975, it is full of critical examples of progressive and left community-based efforts, all of them either produced or renewed by the social movements of the day. Any list would include civil rights organizations, which were part of the early civil rights efforts of this period such as the Montgomery (Alabama) Improvement Association; groups such as SNCC and, later, the Black Panther Party; the New Left and student movement efforts such as SDS; even the renewal of settlement houses in this period into more active and vibrant community service and action sites; not to mention the renewal of Alinksy's work. Also significant in this period are federal Great Society program efforts during the War on Poverty of the Lyndon B. Johnson administration, which actually for a time funded community-based efforts. This was administered out of the Office of Economic Opportunity and was committed to the "maximum feasible participation" of the poor and the development of community action agencies to advance and coordinate community interests at the citywide level. Finally, the movements of the sixties gave birth to the feminist movement of the early 1970s.

There are strong parallels in Canada with a New Left movement committed to local organizing on such issues as housing and welfare, anti-colonial movements in aboriginal and black communities, and a strong anti-imperialism often focused on the Vietnam War and Third World liberation struggles. As well, the Canadian federal government was concerned with poverty and the development of the welfare state. The differences between the countries included the emergence of the nationalist movement in Quebec and a strong trade union movement in Canada linked to a social democratic party. In both countries, it was certainly a heyday of community action, one that offers many lessons to contemporary organizing. Our necessarily limited discussion focuses on one central element, the importance of left social movements to progressive community organizing, a lesson that seems lost on many contemporary efforts since 1980.

The radical ferment of the sixties grew out of the civil rights movement. All efforts stood on the shoulders and used the models of the black struggle for equality after World War II. Civil rights efforts such as the Montgomery bus boycott in 1957 and other anti-segregationist community-based struggles before and after it helped lay the groundwork for Mobilization for Youth in 1958, the founding of SNCC (Student Non-violent Coordinating Committee) in 1960, and SDS (Students for a Democratic Society) and its community-based ERAP (Economic Research and Action Project) projects shortly thereafter. The Ford Foundation, NIMH (National Institute of Mental Health) and Kennedy administration followed in the early 1960s with well-funded community-based experiments in community organizing, committed to local control and citizen participation in service delivery and advocacy efforts. The Community Action Program began its support of Community Action Agencies in 1965. The Association of Community Organizations for Reform Now (ACORN) was founded in 1970, as were many other community efforts. The period was a heyday for the experiments and initiatives in community action and local democratic participation. As Jennifer Frost puts it, "During the 1960s a wide range of political, social welfare, church, labor, and government entities shifted their focus to the local and communal level. . . . The massive shift of organizing sites to the community contributed to what came to be called the 'backyard revolution' of the mid-1960s and 1970s." It also influenced gendered conceptions of the sites and agents of resistance and social change. "This understanding of the community as an important site for organizing more fully incorporated women's activism, challenged male-defined notions of 'workplace,' and revealed the community as a place of work for women" (Frost 2001, 23–24).

Admittedly, not all of the efforts were like-minded. Some were more interested in incorporating dissent and rebellion rather than fomenting it. One common ingredient was the renewed focus on community. Community-based efforts such as those of the Unemployed Councils and Alinsky were in the minority in the 1930s because the more obvious primary locus of change was the factory, not the community. By the 1960s, however, due in part to a growing conservatism among labor as well as the fact that the primary agents of social change in the 1960s—African Americans and college students—were not heavily involved in the industrial factory system, community efforts, whether in local poor communities or college campuses, began to replace factories as the primary sites of social change and the working class as the primary agents.

But what was truly distinctive for this period was the extensive role played by social movements in framing the type of organizing that occurred throughout the period. There was certainly broad interest in the local community, in and of itself, as the site of radical change and opportunities for democratic participation; but there was also a theoretical framework of community as inherently alternative and oppositional to mainstream society. Tom Hayden, SDS leader, called for "a politics of responsible insurgence rooted in community after community," reflecting "the felt needs of their locales" (Fisher 1994, 104). Charles McLaurin, SNCC staffer, confided that the experience of community work demonstrated to him and many others the power of poor people. At the community level people had the opportunity to get involved, to become "the true leaders. We need only to move them, to show them. Then watch and learn" (McLaurin n.d.). More like Alinsky-style organizing than the strategies of the Old Left, the emphasis was on "letting the people decide" and "immediate action" rather than developing "a full-scale program" (Payne 1966, 87). But sixties organizing was not about narrow conceptions of community. The central role of community was defined broadly to expand activism beyond the local and to offer a critique of mainstream society's anti-community features. Community was used as both a site and as an alternative. Efforts were focused on building actual community institutions as well as an overall sense of community. Movements politicized the struggle to defend community, as well as the search for it, by emphasizing features of the dominant system such as alienation and the hyper-competition of contemporary capitalism, which intentionally undermined community. "The desire for connectedness, meaningful personal relationships and direct participation and control over economic, political and social institutions on the basis of the needs of the individual and community, takes on radical meaning in a period such as ours" (Breines 1982, 7). From Martin Luther King, Jr. and the civil rights movement use of the vision of "beloved community" onward, community was both a strategic structural site as well as a critical oppositional concept and vision.

But there was also concern about the limited scale of communities, the structural limits of community organizations, and the relation of community organizing to social movement building. Social historian Lerone Bennett found SNCC to be "an organization in revolt against organization" (Carson 1981, 182). Kim Moody, an SDS leader, feared the narrow "localism of the poor" when the broader goal of ERAP was to build "an interracial movement of the poor" (Breines 1982, 35). What one can see throughout most community organizing efforts is "the anti-organizational impulse, stressing the movement before the organization" (Breines 1982, 50). Community leaders and members saw themselves more as movement activists than as organizers and their overall work as more tied to movement building, such as the civil rights, student, anti-war, or women's movement, than to community per se. This tension was downplayed, however. At the time "the notion that the movement represented a community which it had continually to regenerate and communicate to others can be traced from the civil rights movement" through ERAP, the student movement, and onward (Breines 1982, 48). Sixties organizing was almost always about blending community organizing with movement building, with an emphasis on the latter but with a deeply internalized conviction that community work was central to and inseparable from movement building.

Social movements have always been central to effective community efforts. The early work of Alinsky in Chicago would not have succeeded if it had not been for the militancy of the industrial labor movement. Similarly, in the 1960s, Alinsky organizing built on the strength of the civil rights movement. Social movements provide opportunities, direction, and support for such local efforts. Even more than community organization, they have the power to force claims, politics, strategies, and tactics onto not only the local but also the state and national political stage, thereby legitimizing and catapulting them beyond traditional barriers. Community initiatives are usually the product of or tied to broader social movements. In a society that relies so heavily on and is dominated by its economic system, social movements develop and can earn legitimacy to serve as vehicles for change and alternatives to the status quo. Rather than being aberrant "suprapolitical" phenomena, social movements regularly address domestic problems, voice claimants' issues, promote opposition, and force the state or private sector to respond. This is as true for the antebellum movement to end slavery as it was for farmers' and workers' movements at the end of the nineteenth century, women's movements over the past two centuries, labor movements especially in the 1930s, and movements of racial and cultural minorities, whether for black civil rights or for those of gay men and lesbian women, since the 1950s.

It is also true for phenomena that do not seem at first glance to be the result of or even connected to social movement efforts. For example, the contemporary movement of community development corporations (discussed in chapter 4), with its moderate goals and strategies and community economic development emphasis, appears devoid of movement animus or oppositional imagination. But community development corporations (CDCs) began on the heels of the 1960s as part of a community control movement, to address not only issues of civil rights at the community level but also economic empowerment. Without the civil rights movement, for example, without the broad demands for "participatory democracy" and community mobilization of the student movement of the era, CDCs would have had a very different origin and purpose. That said, none of the above is static. Movements decline and end. The context for organizing changes, and the form and success of community organizing efforts often change with it. In such moments, the reciprocal relationship between social movements and community organizing seems less obvious and can get lost. Our study of community organizing in the sixties reveals this contested relationship between social movements and local efforts.

Critically, history also demonstrates that local organizing gives birth to, galvanizes, and sustains social movements. The core issue is not organization versus movement building, but rather the content and structure of social movement organization and its relationship to local practices. Clearly there are tensions. Community organizing is premised on the assumption that building a relatively permanent structure with clear processes of delegation of power and roles facilitates longevity and democracy. Social movements tend to be by definition much looser. Groups mobilize for specific campaigns or actions and then disband. It is impossible to impose a single structure on a movement. Social movements are short lived and cannot be reproduced or channeled into traditional organizations. And yet, at all levels of social movement building, organizing, even local organizing, provides the activists, relationships, resources, and organization without which it is difficult for movements to emerge, be sustained, and develop. Just as community efforts need movements, movements do not develop out of or exist in a vacuum. The populist, labor, or civil rights movement, or the feminist movements of the past century, all developed out of local organizing and became, as social movements, far greater than the sum of their local organizational parts (Fisher and Shragge, 2007).

In conclusion, the progressive canon of efforts in the three historical periods discussed underscores that some of the most noted community efforts in the hundred years from the late nineteenth to the late twentieth centuries in the United States have been ones that understood and practiced key lessons. They understood that community efforts were political. They remained connected to and sought to build on their movement roots, benefited from a critique of the limits of the dominant political economy and culture, and understood that local problems were almost always caused by forces and decisions that rested outside of the community. They therefore sought to organize at both the local and national level, and used a broad range of strategies and tactics, including conflict tactics, which both reflected their times and sought to change them. And finally, they focused on issues of political economy, or at least linked work around cultural or social issues to those of class and economic democracy. In so doing they understood the contested nature of community as well as of political life, and fought hard to advance their agenda, their organizations, and their movement.

UNDERSTANDING THE ANTI-CANON

Research in the past and present of community organizing reveals an "anti-canon" (for this concept, see Primus 1998) which must be included in the broader history. The inclusion of the anti-canonical aspects of any canon are critical, not only because they are part of the history but also because their inclusion: first, acknowledges the existence of conservative and reactionary eras that help produce and support conservative and reactionary initiatives; second, challenges the liberal and uncritical blinders that conceal these underlying forces of reaction and conservatism; and third, serves as "negative reference points" from which future efforts can distance themselves (Primus 1998, 248). We argue in this book that the past, present, and future of community efforts cannot be effectively understood without examining the anti-canon, without understanding the place and persistence of reactionary forms of community and community intervention, and without understanding the role that reactionary contexts play in producing comparable forms of community action.

Community Efforts Are Not Inherently Progressive

Another lesson from the history of community organizing is that efforts take varied political forms. Despite the impression one would get from reading most of the literature on community initiatives, they are not inherently left-leaning or liberal; they are not intrinsically progressive in nature. They can be used for reactionary purposes such as keeping black or gay people out of a neighborhood, or for conservative purposes such as protecting property values and therefore limiting who lives in the community and how land is used. They can be formerly liberal or even left efforts that are moderated or incorporated by the pressures of a different context. The politics of a community effort depend on a wide variety of factors, including the reason(s) for organizing the group, the ideology and politics of the leaders as well as the members, the dominant social movements at the time, and, especially, the political economy of the era. There are certainly as many conservative and reactionary uses of community in U.S. history as there are democratic and oppositional ones, and we strongly doubt that the United States is an exception in this regard.

One reason for the narrowed view of the history of community efforts, for the myopia of the existing canon, which excludes reactionary efforts and eras dominated by a reactionary politics, is the failure to understand that all community initiatives are political, whether they see themselves as such or not. Most do not. Many of the social settlements did not; they were there to provide a service; they were there to address immigrant needs and promote social harmony, that is, to counter the disorder resultant from the unregulated capitalism of the prior Gilded Age. Most community-based service providers since the early twentieth century do not see their work as political, because "political" in the American context means tied to elections and political parties. Nevertheless, all of these groups are political in that they form to address a problem, or meet a neglected need, or help a specific group, all of which require power. They are usually extra-political, that is, outside of the political mainstream and formal structures, but they still are very much involved with influencing public and private decisions of who gets what, how, and why, especially why some groups and classes benefit at the expense of others. The failure to see them as political, that is, engaged in both local and broader struggles for power, induces a myopia that narrows community efforts to a romantic view that they are inherently on the side of expanding social, economic, and political justice. In fact, conservative and reactionary forms occur more often than their liberal or radical counterparts. They take a more virulent and dominant form in eras supportive of conservative and reactionary initiatives, but persist and develop under all conditions.

As noted earlier, the nature of the dominant forms of community action is connected to the broader political-economic context of any historical period. In eras of consensus, conservative and reactionary forms dominate. What is clear in studying community efforts in eras such as the 1920s, 1950s, and since 1975 is how the examples from the canon and those in the anti-canon are yoked in a historical continuum of conflict and change. Periods of conservatism and reaction are often just that, reactions against—backlashes that seek to undermine prior progressive gains, to moderate former progressive efforts, and to support conservative and reactionary ones. But these eras are not simply backlashes. They also represent deep currents and ongoing elements in American political life. Even a brief, highly selective study of community efforts in these periods demonstrates both the existence and nature of anti-canonical efforts in community organizing, ones that are all too important and prominent to be considered anything less than central to understanding community and community efforts.

1920s. The history of community organizations in the 1920s offers a stark contrast to the efforts in periods that came just before and just after it. The 1920s are an archetypal conservative political economy. With the close of World War I, right-wing repression against social activism and labor organizing, exemplified by the Red Scare of 1918, delegitimized prior reform projects and victories. The Red Scare was followed by a so-called return to normalcy, in which the business ethic of the 1920s replaced the social reform impulse of the Progressive era. Heightened individualism replaced concerns about social cohesion. A resurfacing of laissez-faire ideology replaced analyses of structural causation. Society receded from concern with social issues into more individualist and materialist pursuits. Right-wing community efforts and social movements resurfaced as well, such as religious fundamentalism, the Ku Klux Klan, and other nativist organizations. But, critical to our overall argument, the conservative context not only supported right-wing efforts but it also moderated and reconfigured progressive ones.

Whereas social settlement workers and other nascent social work forms of community organization were characterized by an integrated and pluralistic community organization practice prior to the 1920s—one committed to aiding individuals, building community, and changing society—after World War I, most community organization and social work leaders rejected having anything to do with social causes (Berry 1999). The political economy of the 1920s dramatically altered the practice of community organization. Settlements and other community efforts did not decline in numbers as much as they faded in significance and, for most at least, shifted their programming (Chambers 1963). Chief among the reasons for this was the conservative political economy, which gave these and other developments particular salience and legitimacy, not to mention support.

In place of the core settlement elements of collaborative practice, community building, and social action, the 1920s institutionalized a much more restrictive and confined practice. Jane Addams said that social work reflected the "symptoms of this panic and with a kind of protective instinct, carefully avoided any identification with the phraseology of social reform" (quoted in Lundblad 1995, 667). The atmosphere of social work thus changed in the 1920s. There was a new emphasis on being disengaged, that is, being objective experts rather than social reformers and focusing on the individual and recreational activities rather than collective needs and more politicized issues. Social work students in the 1920s were even said to scoff at the very idea of community service (Lubove 1975).

Not everyone dropped the idea of community. Many who were previously interested in community activism, now under pressure to change their ways, redefined community organization to be more professional and less activist, that is, to pursue interorganizational coordination and administration—building and managing federations of social service agencies that sought to bring greater order, efficiency, effectiveness, and power to voluntary sector welfare efforts (Trolander 1975; see also Brilliant 1990)—rather than working with the poor in immigrant slum neighborhoods. By linking charitable efforts, by developing a centralized mechanism for collecting and distributing charitable giving, by being more attentive to issues of funding and record keeping, this new emphasis in community organization, which resulted in the formation of precursors to the current United Way, fit closely with the business-minded, efficiency-seeking, and professional temper of the time (Fabricant and Fisher 2002). Earlier community-based and activist efforts were now rejected as romantic and naïve, unsystematic and unprofessional (Schwartz 1965).

Another direct impact of the change in political economy on community organization efforts was the loss of control over funding and, with it, a shift in organizational mission and practice. Once the Red Scare climate subsided and prosperity for certain sectors of the economy renewed, aggregate funding in the 1920s improved for voluntary associations such as settlement houses. But charitable giving became more circumscribed than before, with allocations for services such as educational and recreational activities but not for social advocacy or activism (Herrick 1970). Even the settlements found themselves refashioned, with funding streaming in for recreational services and Americanization efforts but not for labor organizing or resident mobilization.

Similar to the privatization and corporatization of community efforts in our own conservative context since 1980, in the 1920s many community efforts became increasingly dependent on formalized, business-supported sources of charitable funding, in this case local community chests. Chests reduced dependence on religious institutions by offering a potentially steady stream of stable, alternate funding. Community Chest support, however, also required standardized operations. For example, the early style of settlement voluntary work—autonomous, innovative, informal, passionate, and committed to the cause of social, economic, and political justice—gradually became more administrative, businesslike, bureaucratic, and heavily constricted in terms of its strategy, tactics, and programming (Trolander 1975; Walkowitz 1999). For organizations interested in social reform and social action, the whole decade was "a long hard struggle . . . uphill all the way" (Chambers 1992, 452). The broader political economic context thus had a powerful conservative impact on community-based efforts in the 1920s, fostering reactionary efforts and incorporating and moderating liberal and left organizations.

1950s. The most prominent form of community organizing in the 1950s was the neighborhood homeowners' associations that proliferated in outer cities and new suburbs. Whether called civic clubs, homeowners' or property associations, or neighborhood protective organizations, they all shared a twofold goal of protecting property values and building and maintaining community. We argue that these homeowners' associations are rarely considered part of the history of community-based efforts, as they have little in common with the goals and practices of other efforts such as the social settlements, Alinsky, or sixties activism, which sought to create a more inclusive, diverse, and egalitarian society. They are part of the anti-canon, in that they sought an exclusive, homogeneous conception of community designed primarily to maintain community and protect the value of house investments. To that end, community improvement associations did more than keep out "undesirables." They pressured elected officials or community leaders for service provision in the form of street cleaning and garbage removal. They helped enforce deed restrictions that regulated a wide variety of community planning and housing issues, including materials used in construction, setbacks, minimum sales prices, and uses of the house, even who could own or reside there (Plotkin 2005). In these organizations, community protection always went hand in hand with community maintenance. In the 1920s and especially the 1950s, homeowners' associations sought protection against their chief threat: racial integration.

Needless to say again, Americans have formed community associations and used community in many different ways. The proliferation and use of neighborhood improvement associations in outer-city neighborhoods or suburban communities in small towns was not restricted to the 1920s or 1950s, the two historical periods we are arguing helped foment, perpetuate, and foster reactionary uses of community. Centrifugal urban growth has been a long-term phenomenon rather than being limited to specific historical periods. Fogelson (2005), focusing on the origins of exclusive suburbs prior to 1930, sees suburbanizaton and the development of restrictive communities as a broad national phenomenon—not limited to a single city, region, or state—that cuts across historical periods. In fact, despite the beliefs of people in the United States, suburbanization began in Britain, and did so at the beginning of the nineteenth century (Fishman 1989).

Restrictive covenants speak to the core values and objectives of suburban community formation. As Fogelson (2005, 123) argues for affluent suburbs, "What was it about them that required the imposition of 'protective restrictions'? To answer these questions, it is necessary to look beyond the restrictions to the deep-seated fears that were embodied in them—fear of others . . ., fear of change, and fear of the market. A look at these fears reveals much not only about suburbia but also about American society in the late nineteenth and early twentieth centuries." These enclaves and their associations, not only in suburbs but also in outer-city neighborhoods, also speak to the conservative uses of community in a mobile, often rootless society (Garb 2005). Inherent in these communities, built by developers and defended by community associations, is the constant search for and re-creation of community so common to the American experience. "The result of this endemic restlessness was not only that Americans were constantly on the move and routinely settling in communities to which they had no 'local attachments,' but also that they invariably lived among strangers. . . . To put it another way, most suburbanites would have to create a community before they could join it" (Fogelson 2005, 148). And given that most were fleeing diverse and messy cities, communities they created emphasized order, stability, and homogeneity (see Sennett 2007).

The impact of these neighborhood improvement associations and deed restrictions on the conceptualization and formation of community in the United States has been profound. They are critical to understanding how "constructions of race and manifestations of racism" are tied to community formation (Gotham 2000, 629). But in racially tense urban environments, especially northern cities in the 1920s and 1950s after the great migrations of African Americans from the rural south to the urban north and south, homeowners' associations were focused mostly on racial exclusion rather than community formation (Plotkin 2001).

With the origins of the Cold War and initial civil rights initiatives in the late 1940s, the extent of segregation in the 1950s did not change. As Loewen notes, "of 350,000 new homes built in northern California between 1946 and 1960 with FHA [Federal Housing Administration] support, *fewer than 100 went to blacks*. That same pattern holds for the whole state, and for the nation as well" (2005, 128–129; author's emphasis). What changed was that in 1948, in *Shelley v Kraemer*, the U.S. Supreme Court, pushed by the NAACP, struck down racial restrictive covenants, which limited ownership and tenancy to "Caucasians and Whites only." Given the great migration of African Americans to northern cities during the Second World War; given the postwar housing crunch in these cities in the 1950s, aided and abetted by federal housing policies; and given the emerging urban crisis that began in the 1950s, not the 1960s, massive conflicts erupted between largely white working-class, Roman Catholic, single-family homeowners on the one side, and African Americans on the other. In Thomas Sugrue's pioneering study of Detroit in these years, most white residents in the outer-city neighborhoods close to the auto plants thought their economic interests and communal identities were threatened by racial integration. They turned to homeowner associations to defend their interests and their world (Sugrue 1996). Federations of property owner associations formed in the city to challenge any property owners and real estate brokers who "breached restrictive covenants" (1996, 221). When legal and extra-legal means failed, anti-communist rhetoric (it was, after all, the 1950s) and violence ensued. "White Detroiters instigated over two hundred incidents against blacks moving into formerly all-white neighborhoods, including harassment, mass demonstrations, picketing, effigy burning, window breaking, arson, vandalism, and physical attacks. Most incidents followed improvement association meetings" (1996, 233). Similar conditions of competition for space, housing, and community as well as similar uses of homeowners' and neighborhood associations were evident in Chicago (Seligman 2005) and other cities facing housing and economic pressures.

In the post–World War II era, the conservative cold-war political economy stifled progressive forms of community action and encouraged more anti-progressive forms of community development, both at home and abroad. Community efforts such as homeowners' and property associations have a long history. But conservative eras such as the 1950s tied this necessity for neighborhood associations to a reactionary politics. Segregationist goals were intertwined with community betterment, interconnecting the protection of property values with a politics of neighborhood exclusion and racism. This continued in the next reactionary political economy, the years since the late 1970s. Writing about Los Angeles, Mike Davis found affluent homeowner organizing to be not only the source of the anti-property tax initiatives in the late 1970s that foreshadowed Reaganomics, the most powerful social movement in southern California in the 1980s, but also a critical force behind the "deliberate shaping" of "fragmented and insular local sovereignties" that modeled suburban development throughout the United States (1990, 164).

Conservative and right-wing uses of community continue in our current era. The anti-canon is not an historical artifact. But its past and present are filled with lessons. Among the most important is that community action is not inherently progressive. More specifically, in conservative eras, first, the dominant form of community action adopts a conservative and reactionary politics; second, liberal efforts are moderated and incorporated; third, left efforts are marginalized and often repressed; and fourth, reactionary community efforts are unleashed.

POST-1975. In the neoconservative decades after 1975, the impact of a conservative, arguably reactionary, global and national context on local organizing continued to be enormous. Other forms of organizing arose in the years since 1975, ones that were much more explicitly reactionary, focused on social rather than political/economic issues. Prominent examples could include groups such as Restore our Alienated Rights (ROAR) in Boston, opposing busing; anti-abortion groups picketing women's clinics, harassing women seeking abortions, and even leading to the murder of doctors performing abortions; and Christian fundamentalists organizing at both the national and local level to advance their fundamentalist vision and issues. It is easy to argue that the New Right movement, which developed and heavily influenced politics since at least 1980, has been the most successful social change initiative since then. The fusion of disciples and proponents of free-market economics and anti-communist/cold war politics, on the one hand, with leaders and congregation members of Christian fundamentalist churches—including Roman Catholics, but mostly Southern Baptists and evangelical Protestants—on the other, resulted in the most powerful political grouping of our era. Many of their efforts were at the national level, and most of it was top down rather than bottom up. But a great deal of what has become known as the New Right was also focused on mobilizing people at the grassroots, in their local communities. In the 1970s, in fact, many campaigns, such as opposition to the Equal Rights Amendment, came out of grassroots, community efforts. While a more detailed analysis of New Right grassroots organizing awaits in chapter 4, suffice it to say here that New Right efforts were successful primarily because they straddled critical divides evident in the left/ progressive canon of community organizing. They blended issues of both political economy and culture. They used conflict strategies and tactics against their enemy targets—the forces of radicalism and liberalism. They understood the value of community-based organizing, but they understood even better the importance of national organizations, in concert with local efforts, fighting for state power. They always saw themselves as part of a broader social movement. And they always focused on blending local work with electoral politics, a blend avoided by most progressive forms of community organizations since Saul Alinsky's efforts in the late 1930s (Fisher and Tamarkin 2009). The anti-canon is thus filled with lessons not only for students of the history of community organizing but also for current academics and activists.

Of course, since 1975 a wide variety of efforts continued to promote democratic resistance and left insurgency. A new left populism, reflected in the work of groups such as ACORN and countless neo-Alinsky efforts (discussed further in chapter 5), occasioned claims of a backyard revolution. Nevertheless, the neoconservative political economy that largely determined the direction of most community organizing since 1980 has moderated most of them, pushed them away from oppositional strategies, and even adopted left-populist practices in right-populist grassroots efforts. As we demonstrate in chapters 3 and 4, the load shedding of public responsibility by the national government foisted new burdens as well as opportunities on local groups. The dramatic increase of nonprofit organizations in the past three decades, including but not limited to community-based efforts, is a manifestation of this national policy. Clearly the proliferation of progressive community work since the late 1970s should be seen as an outgrowth of 1960s activism and a growing desire for democratic participation. But the proliferation of such community work must also be understood as a byproduct of neoconservative politics and policies, the result of the interaction of community concepts and practices, on the one hand, with the broader national political economy, on the other (Fisher and Shragge 2007). Rinku Sen agrees, when she argues that three contextual trends have had a major impact on progressive organizing since the late 1970s. These are "the resurgence of conservative movements and the power gained by such movements in the United States since the early 1970s; the character and organization of the new economy, which is distinguished by the rising use of neo-liberal policies and contingent workers; and the continued and unyielding role of racism and sexism in the organization of society" (2003, 1). It is to this current context, and how it has shaped community organizations and community efforts, that the book now turns.

CHAPTER 3

The Market, the State, and Community in the Contemporary Political Economy

NEOLIBERALISM PLAYS a constitutive part of community practice in the contemporary Anglo-American world. More specifically, there are two principal forces of neoliberalism that pertain to community-based efforts—the primacy of the market and the decentralization of the state. First, in contemporary community-based efforts there is an acceptance of the market as the principal arbiter in the allocation of goods, services, wealth, and income in society. Even within the current context, with its greater recognition of market failures, there is relatively little appetite to theorize other, or alternative, kinds of economic relations in society. Most striking about this embrace of the market is that it is evident not just among free market ideologues (Porter 1997) but also among many left pragmatists (most notably Shuman 2000; Shuman and Fuller 2005) who see the market as the only viable mechanism to improve the lives of all citizens. This embrace of the market is evident in its application in such diverse practices as the Community Economic Development (CED) industry/movement in Canada, the privatization of council housing in Britain, and the prominence of the "social economy" in all three countries.

Second, there is a rejection of large-scale (that is, national-scale) bureaucratic interventions or policies. This rejection has been most explicit in the work of Giddens (1998, 2000) and Osborne (1990; Osborne and Gaebler 1992), but is true more broadly. The devolution of state powers from the national to the local level (including communities) is a process embraced by most theorists of the role of community and practitioners in the field. These decentralizing processes are seen in such policies and practices as the contracting out of social services in the United States, or the high profile of community-focused public sector initiatives in Britain (such the New Deal for Communities). And the processes of privatization and devolution are closely intertwined in both theory and practice. Even with the new strategies of state intervention in the economy in the current crisis, these two forces of neoliberalism work in tandem to transform the context in which community theory and practice occur—thereby transforming the theory and practice themselves.

Before we begin to discuss these theories and practices, several clarifications need to be made. First, and as we argued in chapter 2, practices in communities do not emerge like Athena from Zeus's head—autonomously and fully formed. Instead, they do so in the context of larger sets of public policies, and the ideologies and theories that partially constitute those policies. Community-based policies and practices converge in the United States, Britain, and Canada (Fremeaux 2005; Brodie 2002), and these, in turn, have been shaped by comparably convergent ideas about community, the state, and the market. Second, although these theories and practices may appear to be disparate and disconnected, we outline common themes that run through them.

THE MARKET AND COMMUNITY INTERVENTIONS

Although we have already introduced the concepts and practices of neoliberalism, it is worthwhile to briefly restate here its connection to the market. As David Harvey has usefully defined it, "Neoliberalism is in the first instance a theory of political economic practices that proposes that human well-being can best be advanced by liberating individual entrepreneurial freedoms and skills within an institutional framework characterized by strong private property rights, free markets and free trade. The role of the state is to create and preserve an institutional framework appropriate to such practices" (Harvey 2005, 2).

The promotion of an entrepreneurial strategy or "market-based community development" builds on this description and has reshaped priorities and practices of organizations working in local communities. This embrace of the market has, in many ways, been developing over time. In the American context, it has its roots in the ambivalence of the earliest community development corporations (CDCs) in understanding the causes of "the urban crisis" in the 1960s (this was particularly true in the debates around "black capitalism" in the late 1960s; see DeFilippis 2004, ch. 2). This ambivalence has over time moved toward a clear, overarching perspective that reliance on the market is *the* way to develop inner cities for the benefit of those living in them. No matter what the policy or strategy, the central idea is that local economic development will create wealth and jobs, and thus act as a way to ameliorate inner-city problems such as affordable housing, unemployment, and poverty.

Most support for the use of the market has come from those taking an openly neoliberal position. Perhaps the most high-profile work has been that of Michael Porter. Porter argues that "a sustainable economic base can be created in inner cities only as it has been elsewhere: through private, for-profit initiatives, and investments based on economic self-interest and genuine competitive advantage" (Porter 1997, 12). But Porter and his organization, the Initiative for a Competitive Inner City, are far from alone, and the political content of the promotion of the market is not narrowly defined. In fact, the breadth of support for the market-based perspective has made it the dominant understanding in community development work in the United States (see, for instance, Bendick and Egan 1991; Berger and Steinbach 1992; Carr 1999; Community Development Partnership Network 2003; Grogan and Proscio 2000; Nowak 1998; Peirce and Steinbach 1987; Weissbourd and Bodini 2005). A Brookings Institution paper stated the logic most nakedly when it argued:

> To address poverty, create wealth.
>
> Wealth is created by investing in assets.
>
> The economic mechanism for asset investment is the market.
>
> Therefore, to increase wealth in poor communities, expand market activity to the assets of those communities. (Weissbourd and Bodini 2005, 5)

There is perhaps no clearer expression of how hegemonic the logic of the market has become than the growth in the "social economy." Some on the Left have argued that the market and entrepreneurial strategies can be used instrumentally to promote greater equality and justice. For example, Shuman and Fuller (2005) argue that U.S.-based community development corporations, rather than being dependent on philanthropies and government subsidies, should create for-profit organizations that generate revenue to support the nonprofit initiatives. And the social economy has become a mantra for many liberals. In the British context, this is closely related to the issue of social exclusion, and in both Canada and Britain the social economy is often discussed in the context of the transition of welfare to workfare. Thus, it is agreed upon that poverty must be addressed at the community level, through the market, and the organization of programs for individuals via workfare.

Just as important as the embrace of the market to improve low-income communities is the way in which the logic of the market has infiltrated and permeated the logics and understandings of community-based efforts. More and more, community-based not-for-profits are expected to understand the world like for-profit businesses—and behave accordingly. Efficiency, accountability, the bottom line, cost-saving, worker productivity, and entrepreneurialism are the watchwords in contemporary not-for-profit governance. This is often a perspective driven by the funders of community-based efforts, who have increasingly argued that community-based organizations should think and behave as businesses. Corporate logic and prerogatives dominate community-based efforts almost as much as they do for-profit efforts. There has even been a push among some foundations and intermediaries for community groups to use business marketing techniques to "sell" their communities to investors. As the Local Initiatives Support Corporation (LISC—one of the primary intermediaries supporting community-based efforts in the United States) put it in a report promoting the use of marketing by community groups, "The essential marketing approach is creating an identity for the community that will entice investors, entrepreneurs, lenders, and families to invest" (Beck and Higgins 2001). But it is probably James Carr, then senior vice president of the Fannie Mae Foundation, who made the most explicit comments when he argued that communities needed to market themselves to investors, and in order to do so, "some of these places could be treated as urban blank slates, where the development takes on an image the investors choose" (Carr 1999, 22).

We now turn to a discussion of how the market has been expressed in practice in the community, with the understanding that these practices have been promoted by state agencies and private foundations.

PRACTICE IN THE TIME OF CHOLERA

Just as the intellectual justifications for the primacy of the market in community efforts take various different, if related, forms, so too do the practices. There is a myriad of different ways in which community-based practice is market centered. These practices, while apparently disparate, have much in common with each other, and it is often hard to know how to categorize them. In this discussion we will describe Community Economic Development (CED) in Canada; the business and market-centered work of Community Development Corporations (CDCs) in the United States; the social economy, social enterprise or social entrepreneurs in all three countries; and workfare and community-based workforce development in all three countries.

Community Economic Development emerged in Canada as a strategy at the local level, to combat deindustrialization and related high unemployment at the end of the 1980s. It was quickly embraced and supported by many of the provincial governments as well as at the federal level (Shragge and Toye 2006). There is a wide range of traditions and practices associated with this strategy, from those that explicitly attempt to create democratic alternatives to capitalism, to those that act as very limited service providers shaped by the policies and ideas discussed above. Haughton (1999) discusses three approaches to what he calls local economic development: restructuring for capital, renewal and repair, and restructuring for community and ecology. The first is linked to reducing state intervention, and relies on local wealth creation and the trickle-down approach to combat poverty. The second is pragmatic, involving consultation with local people, and is based on expert intervention to plan and implement programs. The third is concerned with participation of citizens in economic and social regeneration and aims to create economic alternatives that are equitable and ecological. Charland and Toye discuss the difficulties in locating a single definition of CED in Canada:

> The range of these definitions, from CED as a strategy for increasing wealth through balanced growth, to CED as an alternative to conventional economic development, is an illustration not only of the liberal to progressive range of definitions that exist, but also of the pragmatic requirement of CED promoters to define their approach relative to the dominant development paradigm: economic

development. The degrees to which CED either, on one hand, strengthens economic development or, on the other, seeks to replace conventional economic development, reflects the range of practice across the country, and the vision underlying those activities. CED can be undertaken as part of a transformative social change project (building on the community development approach), it can be applied to support an orthodox economic development process (the liberal local economic development approach), or it can fall somewhere in between those two extremes. (Toye and Charland 2006, 28)

These definitions reflect the tensions in theory and practice as well as the competing underlying values and politics. The question then becomes, which practice is dominant and what is government's role in shaping these definitions of practice? One important contrast is between CED and social enterprise or the social economy. In theory, the former has an assumption of a geographic base and has an integrated strategy to improve the total area, and with it a related process of democratic participation of citizens. Regardless of the underlying politics, this is a shared assumption. In contrast, social enterprise or social economy is linked to more limited collective or individual entrepreneurial efforts, mainly with social aims. The difference is that the process involved, the community-based holistic approach, is diminished. Kay (2006) describes social enterprises as not-for-profit organizations that seek to meet social aims by engaging in economic and trading activities. They have legal structures which ensure that all assets and accumulated wealth are not in the ownership of individuals but are held in trust and for the benefit of those persons or areas that are intended beneficiaries of the enterprise's social aims. Additionally, they have organizational structures in which full participation of members is encouraged on a cooperative basis, with equal rights accorded to all members. There is thus an overlap between traditional business development and social enterprise. In Canada there has been a clear shift away from the broader and politically challenging components of CED and toward the more constrained social enterprise perspective—paralleling the growth of state support for these practices (Shragge and Toye 2006).

In Canada, the United States, and the United Kingdom, much of the practice has followed a narrower route than CED. In Canada and

Britain, supported by government in various ways, the direction is toward creating community-based services and training programs for the "excluded" (Gough et al. 2006; Toye and Charland 2006). In these countries, despite the "spirit of entrepreneurship," most of the practice has been supported by a variety of government programs, particularly at its early stages. For example, in Quebec there are government-funded organizations that provide start-up money, loans at reduced interest rates, and technical support for new social economy businesses, as they are called there (Shragge 1997). Thus, even with the practices that have created alternatives, or that have radicalized CED practice, the dominant practices are linked to an entrepreneurial vision, pushed by state and related private foundation funding and programs. The more radical practices become marginalized and isolated in the process, with exceptional organizations able to balance the demands of the state or private foundations while maintaining elements that challenge the dominant system. In contrast, the dominant practices tend at best to be led by professionals with the technical skills necessary for the economic components of these forms of development.

Similar to the experience and practices of CED in Canada, CDCs in the United States have become increasingly oriented toward economic development activities. In a sense, this is a return to what CDCs had done in their formative years in the late 1960s and early 1970s, before affordable housing construction became the dominant activity. But the turn to the market has never been more pronounced in American community development than it is has been since the turn of the twenty-first century. Rodney Fernandez, the CEO of Cabrillo Economic Development Corporation (California) was sympathetically quoted in *Shelterforce* magazine—the trade journal for the American community development industry/movement—"I think in order for us to remain a not-for-profit, we have to make a profit" (quoted in Getter and Vazquez 2007, n.p.). Similarly, Janaka Casper, president and CEO of Community Housing Partners Corporation (Virginia) told *Shelterforce* that the key to organizational strength for CDCs was "Don't let emotion and mission let you make bad business decisions" (quoted in Walsh and Zdenek 2007, n.p.). It is worth noting that both of these statements were made in *Shelterforce*'s special issue on "Community Development at 40"—an issue devoted to a discussion of the state of the field in 2007, and with particular emphasis on what CDCs are doing, and need to do, in the contemporary context. According to the most recent census of CDCs in the United States, almost 40 percent of CDCs engage in small business development—and one-fourth of CDCs actually own their own businesses. And these numbers are dwarfed by the rate of CDCs that provide technical assistance to businesses (70 percent) and training for entrepreneurs (52 percent) (National Congress for Community Economic Development 2006, 15).

Perhaps it is unsurprising that the United States has most heavily embraced the market as the vehicle for community-based interventions. This is evident in a motley mix of government policies that have been enacted since the 1980s, which share the central premises both that public policies should work through community-based organizations and that the community-based organizations should work through the market. These policies began in 1986 with the creation of the Low-Income Housing Tax Credit, and continued with a CDC tax credit program to do economic development in 1993, the passage of the Federal Enterprise Zone/Empowerment Communities legislation in 1993, the passage of the Community Development Financial Institution Act in 1994, and finally, in 2000, the enacting of the New Markets Tax Credit program. All of these policies tie market prerogatives and practices to community-based efforts, all situating housing and inner-city rejuvenation as privatization initiatives. It is not surprising that the aforementioned Michael Porter was in communication with President Clinton and Vice President Gore, because his theories are clearly embodied in the policies and practices of New Markets Tax Credits (see Rubin and Stankiewicz, n.d.). And these policies, because of the money attached to them—limited as it might be in the broad sweep of American public sector spending, but significant compared to what community organizations have to work with—have certainly pulled community organizations with them, and contributed to the embrace of the market. But they have also, by virtue of the limits of their funds, further contributed to the embrace of the market by community organizations. Community groups, in short, are pulled toward market solutions by public sector initiatives, but then need to continue down the road of private sector investment because of the limits of what the public sector is actually providing.

As we already indicated, there has also been the growth of what people call the social economy or social enterprise. Although there is no clear definition of what is included in this category (see the discussion in chapter 1 of Nicholls 2006), generally speaking, the social economy refers to businesses that operate with the famous "double bottom line" of both social and economic goals (*triple* when you include environmental goals). They can be either not-for-profits that own and operate for-profit businesses themselves, or, in some cases, socially motivated for-profit entrepreneurs. Famous examples (in the United States) abound, but they get mentioned repeatedly, which perhaps magnifies the impression people have of their size. For instance, HousingWorks is an advocacy/service provision organization that works with residents of New York City who are HIV positive and funds much of its work through its thrift stores and coffee shops. The market that the social enterprise businesses are serving is itself often a social service—and this is particularly true in the realms of subsidized child care and home health care, industries where many of the service providers are affiliated with not-for-profits. This sector has grown dramatically in the United States since the early 1990s. Much of the growth has been driven by foundations that saw such business ownership as a way for community organizations to continue their core mission and work once the foundations withdrew their funding. As one foundation program officer put it, "One of the big appeals of social enterprise is that it aims to be self-sustaining after the initial foundation investment. This is a funder's dream, because you won't feel guilty after you stop funding" (quoted in Seedco Policy Center 2007). Despite the attention and growth of social enterprises in the United States, there is a lack of data on how many social enterprises there actually are—or even how to distinguish social enterprises from other businesses and not-for-profits (see Rangan, Leonard, and McDonald 2008). The data are better in the United Kingdom, which is unsurprising, since the growth of social enterprises has been particularly strong there (see Nicholls 2006). As of 2006 there were an estimated 55,000 social enterprises in the United Kingdom (Social Enterprise Coalition 2009).

Finally, community organizations have become increasingly involved in issues of workfare and "workforce development." These activities were certainly part of community-based organizations' efforts prior to the period of welfare reform in the 1990s (see Harrison and Weiss 1998), but they have grown significantly since then. With these changes, the focus of policy has moved from one based on rights to one that emphasizes individual responsibility. For example, on the subject of unemployment, David Ranney states: "employment is as much a form of moral behavior as a way to make a living. Everyone now has a personal responsibility to get and hold some kind of employment" (2003, 166). Jamie Peck uses the concept of a "workfare regime" to describe an approach to social policy that prioritizes the linking of income support to labor market integration. He argues: "functionally, workfarism implies an ascendancy of active labor-market inclusion over passive labor-market exclusion as workfarism seeks to push the poor into the labor market, or hold them in a persistently unstable state close to it, rather than sanctioning limited nonparticipation in wage labor in the way of welfare systems" (2001, 12).

Linked to these regimes are "business/employment service codes and norms for the job-ready; [and] remedial services for 'unemployables'" (Peck 2001, 12). Moreover, workfare regimes are "a rolling forward of new institutions and new norms of regulation" (16). Workfare has to be understood as an approach that is more than work for welfare. It is a basic change in the income support system which assumes that an individual's right to income support is subject to some kind of work-related measure. Regardless of the conditions of the work itself, the goal is to push people into a job. As a consequence, recipients are encouraged to be part of the labor market, even if the work makes them worse off financially than they would be receiving social assistance. Employability is a social construct, not an objective measurement of skills; it is the outcome of strategies of various intervenors as well as changes in the institutions of employment, the family, and social assistance. "Employability thus concerns the condition of those men and women who society believes have a duty to be employed" (Morel 2002, 13).

Institutions and programs are needed to make changes in these groups so that they can be successfully integrated into the economy, either as flexible workers or as small-scale producers. Such programs vary by the mixture of carrots and sticks—incentives and punishment. This ideology incorporates far more than the immediate administration of social benefits. It structures the expectations for those receiving social aid. It pushes recipients to a variety of institutions and organizations to seek programs that augment their benefits or keep their eligibility. Both the employability programs and many of the organizations supported by them provide these services. They act as a compliment to administration of social aid, and reinforce the pressures of a workfare regime. Part of the role of community organizations in the context of these policy changes is to develop the programs for employability and work readiness for social assistance claimants.

In Britain, Gough et al. argue that the social economy as "conservative interventionism" is a decentralized form of "enabling a passage into normal wage work" (2006, 192), and it is "a stepping stone for individuals to improve themselves and escape poverty" (198–199). In Canada, driven by a variety of government funding programs, the second most important area of CED practice is in human capital development and training (Toye and Chaland 2007). An example of these practices in Quebec is the network of "entreprises d'insertion" or training businesses. These began in the 1980s, but their growth and their network developed rapidly in the 1990s with the increasing role of the community sector in employment programs for the poor. These organizations provide short-term training in a socially oriented business for those receiving social assistance. The businesses are mainly in the service sector such as food production, recycling, and so forth, and move people from social assistance to employment (http://www .collectif.qc.ca). The jobs that follow tend to be unstable and low-wage. These examples indicate the role played by community organizations in the government policies that push social assistance recipients from welfare to work.

PROBLEMS IN THE EMBRACE OF THE MARKET IN COMMUNITY WORK

While the turn to the market in community work is well established—and thus so are the critiques—we think it is still worth remembering the problems evident in this theory and practice. It is also worth noting that we would not object to the embrace of the market if we thought that the market could be the vehicle to realize social and economic justice in communities. Unfortunately, it does not appear to be so, and the critiques remain compelling—in fact, they are a significant part of why we are writing this book, and therefore warrant some discussion here.

There are three primary problems with community-based efforts embracing the market as their organizing framework. The first is the simple reason that there are fundamental differences between for-profit and not-for-profit organizations that get lost in embraces of the market. Obviously theorists and practitioners are well aware of this; there has been much discussion of the "double-" or "triple-bottom lines" (of people and profits; or of people, planet, and profits, respectively). But this still misses the point; that is, the goals of the market are clear and simple, and they are different from those of equity or justice or the public good. The classic free market economists are, of course, largely dismissive of notions of social enterprise or the double bottom line. As Milton Friedman famously put it, "there is one and only one responsibility of business—to use its resources and engage in activities designed to increase its profit" (Friedman 2002 [1962]). There is no place in the market for concerns relating to community, equity, or anything else. But in this sense, Friedman was simply echoing the thoughts of Adam Smith—the patriarch of free-market economists—who, comparably famously, put it: "It is not from the benevolence of the butcher, the brewer, or the baker, that we expect our dinner, but from their regard to their own interest. We address ourselves, not to their humanity but to their self-love, and never talk to them of our own necessities but of their advantages. Nobody but a beggar chooses to depend chiefly upon the benevolence of his fellow-citizens" (Smith 1998 [1776], 22).

While the first problem of the turn to the market is that the goals of businesses are not transferrable to community-based not-for-profits, the quote from Smith raises the second, and perhaps more serious problem with the use of the market. The market does not do many of the things that community organizations want done—which is why the public sector or the not-for-profit sector does them. We are being a bit glib here, and there are certainly reasons why "market failures" might occur (first among them being imperfect information—a nearly bottomless black box of vital importance in economic theory). But there is no getting away from the fact that the public sector's provision of basic social services emerged (albeit in different ways, and at slightly different times, in the three countries discussed here) due to the failure of the market to provide them. Similarly, most community-based efforts emerged either to force the public sector to fulfill its responsibilities or to provide those public services as contracted agents. Thus, the embrace of the market by community organizations represents a fundamental misunderstanding of the nature of problems in communities. As Herb Rubin put it, perhaps deliberately trying to invoke (and mock) the specter of Adam Smith, in his discussion of how we should properly understand community development, "There aren't going to be any bakeries here if there is no money to afford jellyrolls" (Rubin 1994). In other words, more serious problems such as poverty and unemployment cannot be solved through limited business development at the community level.

The third problem with the embrace of the market in community-based efforts is that community itself is undermined by the market. This is so for two different reasons that both result from the role of capitalism in producing urban space. The first is that communities are divided into a set of use and exchange values, and many of the basic components of community life—schools, parks and other public spaces, houses of worship, rental housing, health care, and so forth—are all defined for the people in communities by their uses, not by their potential exchange value. They are, in short, parts of life that are not viewed as commodities or investments by those using and experiencing them. Capital, however, interacts with communities in different ways, and is interested first and foremost, in the commodification of social life, and conversion of what people need into profit. A landlord does not view a multifamily rental property that he or she owns in the same way that the residents of the property do. The goals are structurally different—and, we should add, at least partially structurally antagonistic. This is not a new critique (see, for instance, Logan and Molotch 1987; Mollenkopf 1981; Stoecker 1997), but its validity is not undermined by its lack of novelty. And despite having been made before, the point clearly needs to be made again, since its meanings and implications have not been properly understood by the theorists or practitioners of community development and other community-based efforts.

The second way communities are undermined by the market is that communities, in order to be meaningful realms for the people within them, need to have some kind of stability—so that relationships can be built and trust established. Communities do not need stasis, and this is certainly not an embrace of the conservative views of community that resist change in and of itself. But communities cannot be constantly undermined by the fluidity and rapaciousness of the market while also maintaining stability. Community organizations cannot function if the market for residential housing in their neighborhood leads to a turnover of population that is too rapid to allow for the organization to maintain its membership. An embrace of the market threatens to unleash forces that undermine the community itself. The currently vast landscapes of foreclosed properties in American inner cities, which are doing so much to undermine the decades of community development work, stand as a stark reminder of the power of unregulated market forces to destroy communities.

COMMUNITY AS DECENTRALIZED SOCIAL POLICY

While the market has assumed a hegemonic position in the thinking and practices of community-based efforts, there has been a closely related set of theories and processes involved in the devolution of the state and the emergence of community as a central arena for state interventions into social and economic relations. There has been, in short, a shift away from the nation-state's role in social provision and development toward more localized and community-based forms of social policy and governance in Canada, the United Kingdom, and the United States. The ideas promoting these shifts have emerged in various forms, and, theoretically at least, there is no reason why a decentralization to the community scale should be closely aligned with privatization. Community as social policy has prospered as a framework for governance under center-left regimes in all three countries. But although there are promoters of devolution from across the political spectrum—particularly in North America, but less so in Britain—only a relatively narrow set of agendas have been enacted in practice. In the United Kingdom it has become a staple of the thinking of New Labour, and perhaps because of the differences between the federal political structures of North America and the centralized structure of the state in Britain, the conversation of decentralization and devolution has been much more vocal and public in the latter than in the two other countries discussed here. Loud, public statements by representatives of New Labour on the importance of communities in the governance of social policy have been commonplace since 1997. As Hazel Blears, secretary of state for communities and local government put it, "there are few issues so complex, few problems so knotty, that they cannot be tackled and solved by the innate common sense and genius of local people. With the right support, guidance and advice, community groups and organisations have a huge, largely latent, capacity for self-government and self-organisation. This should be the hallmark of the modern state: devolved, decentralised, with power diffused throughout our society" (Ministry of Communities and Local Government 2008, iii). These sentiments merely echo the words of Tony Blair and Gordon Brown, the political architects of New Labour, and Anthony Giddens, its intellectual totem. But it would be too simple to state that the emphasis on community in the contemporary United Kingdom is a function solely of New Labour. And it is worth noting that the Single Regeneration Budget program (discussed below), and the central role of community in that program, was a creation of a Conservative government.

In the United States, the hostility to centralized government has long been a staple of the Right, and some segments of the Left, but both were joined by the center-left with the emergence of the New Democrats in the early 1990s (anticipating New Labour by half a decade). This is most notable in the writings of David Osborne on "reinventing government" (Osborne and Gaebler 1992), whose book *Laboratories of Democracy* (1990) contained a foreword written by then Governor Bill Clinton. But it is not just Bill Clinton (or Hillary Clinton, whose book on her philosophy of social policy was that "It Takes a Village"), rather it is the broad sweep of the center-left in the United States since the 1980s that has embraced community as the scale of government interventions. And this is certainly true for Barack Obama, who famously began his political education as a community organizer in Chicago.

The development of these policies through the 1990s has some parallels with practices and demands of the New Left that emerged in the 1960s and 1970s. In this sense, the Left in the United States was part of the broad rejection of the centralized state that was evident in the 1968 uprisings in places as varied as Paris, Mexico City, and Prague. Although the diversity of the political projects evident in 1968 belies any notion of a "global movement" (and actually reinforces our argument that a decision over the political scale of social policy is not, in and of itself, a politically left or right decision), in the American context it surprisingly

came from the Left. The old liberal Left stood for expanding the powers and reach of the centralized state in order to promote the general
welfare and curb the excesses of capital. But the New Left was much
more suspicious and critical of large, centralized government. The argument at the time for devolution of the state was nicely summarized by
Midgley when he observed that it was "a reaction against the centralization, bureaucratization, rigidity, and remoteness of the state. The
ideology of community participation is sustained by the belief that the
power of the state has extended too far, diminishing the freedoms of
ordinary people and their rights to control their own affairs" (Midgley
1986, 4). Similarly, Jane Jacobs, a writer and activist whose politics are
not easily categorized, would make this argument through the 1970s and
1980s from her perch in Toronto after her famous departure from New
York. For her, the issue was more about decentralizing from the citywide scale to the community, rather than from the national scale to the
community. A typical statement of Jacobs' was, "the governments of
large modern cities are not only incomprehensively complex today, but
also their direct effects on citizen's lives are now so ubiquitous that they
cannot help but fail when their functions are centrally organized. Many
functions must be decentralized and brought under direct, continuing
control of local communities" (quoted in Repo 1977, 48).

This is a tradition on the Left that continues to this day, as many
leftists in the United States (Shuman 2000; Williamson, Imbroscio, and
Alperowitz 2002), United Kingdom (Hines 2000), and Canada (Torjman
2007) continue to advocate for more decentralized forms of social policy
(see chapter 4). To be sure, the old and new Right in the United States
has always been harshly critical of public-sector interventions in the private market, when business did not want it. Therefore, the Right has
almost always taken the lead on arguments for and policies on devolution
and decentralization, even at the same time expanding state power abroad
and pursuing social issues such as anti-abortion. But the "surprise" from
the liberal Left on the nature of the state came not only with New Left
emphasis on community and decentralization but also with the Democratic regimes first of Jimmy Carter and then of Bill Clinton, the latter
boasting about "ending big government as we know it."

In short, we are currently experiencing a flourishing of support for
the decentralization of government. And this is support that not only

cuts across the political spectrum in the Anglo-American world but also has itself become a globalized process. As a World Bank report on cities in the Global South put it:

> Decentralization has quietly become a fashion of our time. It is being considered or attempted in an astonishing diversity of developing and transitional countries . . . by solvent and insolvent regimes, by democracies (both mature and emergent) and autocracies, by regimes making the transition to democracy and by others seeking to avoid that transition, by regimes with various colonial inheritances and by those with none. It is being attempted where civil society is strong, and where it is weak. It appeals to people of the left, the center and the right, and to groups which disagree with each other on a number of other issues. (Quoted in Montgomery et al. 2003, 372)

The implications of the changes presented here set up both possibilities and limits for community organizations. The possibilities include expanding their visibility and importance and the role they can play in the wider society, particularly in relation to the state. At the same time, however, expansion has had the impact of narrowing their mandates as the state begins to shape community organizations through a variety of policies.

COMMUNITY AS SOCIAL POLICY

Government policies have directly contributed to the growth of community organizations, as well as to the composition and programmatic activities of those organizations. In general these can be divided into two closely related parts: the contracting out of increasing amounts of the public sector to private not-for-profit organizations, and the devolution of the state from the national scale down toward the regional, provincial, state, municipal, council, and, ultimately, the community scale. Thus, when these two processes are brought together, there are simultaneous transformations in the scale of public intervention and in the realm through which that public intervention takes place. All roads, it seems, lead to community-based organizations. Community has rightly been called "the institutional fix" for the problems of social services and social policy in the Anglo-American world (Macmillan and

Townsend 2006). Community organizations, however, have not simply been passive recipients of this transformation. Instead, they have played an active role in the creation of this "shadow state" (Wolch, 1990), and they have, as "entrepreneurial" actors sought out the state and its resources (Marwell 2007). There are four components to the shift to community as decentralized social policy that are important to us here. These are:

1. the retrenchment of the state;
2. the devolution of state functions, and the shrinking of the scale of state intervention;
3. policies that redirect and restructure activities to community-based nonprofits; and
4. community-based practices that adjust and respond to the state policies and market imperatives.

Together, these transformations have led to the not-for-profitiza-tion of the state. We will address these transformations in the order presented above, but this is not meant to imply a chronological sequence or hierarchy of causality, whereby state retrenchment simply and unidi-rectionally causes the growth of the community-based not-for-profit sector. Rather, the processes are interrelated and mutually constitutive. This is not to deny that the actions of the government carry significantly more weight than those of any community-based organization, given the obvious differences in institutional capacities and embedded power relations. Instead, it is to recognize that community organizations them-selves make demands on the state for recognition and have promoted the agenda for greater community participation in service provision and local development.

Since the late 1970s and early 1980s, there has been a significant shrinking of state resources for low-income people and communities in the Anglo-American world. To be clear, this does not mean that the organizations in low-income communities have seen less public money come their way—depending on the nonprofit, many have seen increases due to the contracting out of public services discussed below. Instead, this means that the overall amount of public sector spending in low-income communities has decreased. Perhaps emblematic of this have been the processes of welfare reform that all three countries have undergone since the 1990s. But the withdrawal of national monies for poor people in the three countries extends beyond just welfare reform. For instance, in the United States, the Department of Housing and Urban Development, which is responsible for federal government programs in low-income urban neighborhoods, shrank from 7 percent of the total federal budget in 1976 to 1 percent in 2005 (National Low Income Housing Coalition, 2004). Similarly, Community Development Block Grants, a staple in federal funding for development in low-income communities, declined by 48 percent in real dollars from 1977 to 2003 (National Low Income Housing Coalition, 2004).

Related to the retrenchment of the state, there has been a process of devolution from the national governments down toward the province/region/state levels of the three countries. Such devolution, however, has continued farther down the scale, and it is cities that become increasingly responsible for, or saddled with, the provision of public goods and services—that is, the means of social reproduction that have often defined the very essence of local government. Importantly, this has occurred at precisely the moment at which local governments have themselves turned away from the provision of such services, in a transformation David Harvey (1989) famously referred to as one from "managerialism to entrepreneurialism." These "New Urban Politics" have local governments becoming much more centrally involved in the realm of economic development, often as risk-taking entrepreneurial actors themselves. In short, the process of devolution has occurred simultaneously with, and interrelated to, the process of state retrenchment. Thus we have witnessed localities taking on more responsibilities at precisely the moment when they are increasingly unwilling and unable to meet those responsibilities.

Regardless of the institutional capacity or willingness of local governments, the devolution of social welfare and services has been a dominant feature in "the rescaling of statehood" (Brenner 2004). In the United States, this began under the Nixon administration in the early 1970s and has continued largely uninterrupted in the thirty-five years since (see Bockmeyer 2003; Eisinger 1998; Goetz 1995). In the United Kingdom, the devolution has been primarily to Scotland and Wales, and to a lesser extent, the regions, rather than to the local councils. However, there has also been a resurgent interest in localized Area Based

Initiatives since the 1990s. This has probably occurred most notably through "single regeneration budget" areas—of which there were more than one thousand in the program's six rounds of funding (DTLR 2002). But this has also included the very high-profile New Deal for Communities cases, which have attracted political and academic attention beyond their limited scope (as they only apply to thirty-nine areas) (see Lawless 2006). To be clear, Area Based Initiatives are not a new policy lever in the United Kingdom, or in any of the three countries discussed here. But what is new is the extent to which communities, or more accurately, community organizations, are expected to participate in the urban regeneration processes as "partners." This means that community organizations are expected to, as Julie MacLeavy (2009, 850) put it, "pull in every local service—from schools, health centers, social workers, police officers, housing departments and Jobcentre Plus." Finally, since 2006 both New Labour and the Conservative Party have been promoting a policy framework of "double devolution"—a movement of responsibility from the central government toward local councils, and from local councils down to the communities that they represent. Although it does not appear that in practice much has actually occurred, beyond the usual movement of public services to community-based voluntary sector organizations, there is a "taken to its logical conclusion" component to the policy makers' conversation that makes it worth noting (see Jordan 2007).

As the state has been withdrawing, and rescaling, the community-based sector has grown significantly in all three countries—thus bringing us to the third component of the nonprofitization of the state. Much of this growth has come from organizations trying to fill the gaps the government left behind, but more of it is probably a function of the increasing role of the community-based sector in the provision of social services—often with public monies. This has been accomplished through a dense network of contracting and subcontracting chains. In the United States, this contracting out of government services grew dramatically in the 1980s (although it certainly predated that decade—see Wagner 2000). The 1980s marked a period of significant growth in the contracting out of public services as the Reagan administration deliberately used this method as a way to undermine the public sector, a process described by Gibelman (1995, 1999) as follows: "In this respect, POS [purchase of service] and privatization have been viewed as ideologically compatible, with POS representing one means to accomplish public divestiture. It represents a midpoint between predominantly government provision and total privatization." Ruthie Gilmore usefully describes the processes involved in the growth of community-based nonprofits:

> Legislative and executive branches transformed bureaucracies into policing bodies, whose role became to oversee service provision rather than to provide it themselves. This abandonment provoked a response among organizations that advocated on behalf of certain categories of state clients: the elderly, mothers, children, and so forth. It also encouraged the formation of new groups that, lacking an advocacy past, were designed solely to get contracts and the jobs that came with them. . . . Thus, for different reasons, non-profits stepped up to fill a service void. (2007, 45)

The size of the not-for-profit sector demonstrates this growth. In Britain, the number of active general charities grew by more than 70 percent from 1991 to 2004, with most of this growth coming from small charities with incomes of less than £100,000 (National Council of Voluntary Organisations 2007). These data, it should be noted, do not include either independent schools or housing associations—two components of the sector that have grown dramatically in Britain in the last twenty years (see Kendall and Almond 1999; Mullins 2006).

Similar growth is evident in the United States, which has witnessed a doubling of the number of organizations in the "independent sector" from 1981 to 2006, to more than 1.5 million organizations, the vast majority of which are the 501(c)(3)s that provide social and health services among other activities (The Independent Sector 2009). Clearly, some of this growth masks a very complex transformation of the voluntary sector. Smith and Lipsky (1993) argued that the "growth" in contracted public services resulted in part because nonprofit agencies could hire employees at cheaper rates and with fewer public sector regulations, not to mention use volunteers to deliver services. The data on community-based organizations reflect this transformation and proliferation. The numbers of community development corporations (CDCs)—the most common and important institutional form taken by community-based organizations working to improve their neighborhoods in the United States—have grown dramatically. As recently as 1994 there were between 2,000 and 2,200 CDCs nationwide in the United States, but by 1998 that number had exploded to 3,600—itself a number eclipsed by the 4,600 in operation in 2005. CDCs, which have historically been most concerned with affordable housing construction, have also become more diversified in their activities, with over 50 percent of them now providing some kind of education or job training program, and over one-third offering youth programs (National Congress for Community Economic Development 2006).

In Canada, the research has used the term "nonprofit" or "voluntary" sectors to include all of the not-for-profit organizations. Stone and Nouroz (2007) state that there are more than 160,000 of these types of organizations employing more than two million people. It is one of the fastest-growing sectors of the economy, accounting for 7 percent of the gross domestic product in 2003. A Statistics Canada report (December 3, 2008) contributes the following information: core nonprofits, which are smaller organizations closer to what we are discussing in this book, contributed $31 billion to the GDP in 2005, approximately 2.4 percent of the nation's economic activity. They represented 33.1 percent of the total nonprofit sector in 1997, increasing to 35.6 percent by 2005. During the nine-year period of this study, these organizations grew at an annual rate of 7 percent, compared to 5.8 percent for the economy as a whole. The overall growth in these types of organizations is reflected in the emergence of CED organizations. In a survey conducted in 2002–2003 of 294 organizations across Canada, two-thirds were founded after 1989. It is clear that community-based, nonprofit, and voluntary organizations have grown rapidly in Canada over the past twenty years, and play an increasingly significant social role.

Since communities are the realm in which social reproduction occurs, and housing is arguably the focal point of social reproduction, it is not surprising that community-based organizations in the Anglo-American world have become central players in the provision of housing for low-income people. In the United States, within the context of the pronounced withdrawal of the state, the provision of housing has come primarily via CDCs. Community development, as an industry, has been more about the production and maintenance of housing than any other single activity or set of activities. CDCs have built or rehabbed more than

1,250,000 housing units in the United States since the 1970s. And the rate of CDC production of housing has grown dramatically, averaging more than 86,000 units per year from 1998 to 2005, more than three times what was being produced in the early 1990s (National Congress for Community Economic Development, 2006). Often, the housing provided by CDCs and other community-based housing nonprofits has been administered in collaboration with the state. Nonprofit housing efforts have developed more than 22 percent of all housing constructed with Low Income Housing Tax Credits (introduced in 1986). This share has grown over time, as the nonprofits increased their capacity to get the deals done (Schwartz 2006, 90), and HOME grants (a federal affordable housing subsidy program) and community development block grant monies are often utilized by nonprofit housing developers. Thus, to the extent to which housing policy in the United States still maintains some focus on the supply of affordable housing, it has been through the nonprofit sector that this supply has been provided (see, for instance, Swanstrom 1999). One point to emphasize about these organizations is that they have emerged as both market players and public entities— building in the market, but with public monies. This is a very different experience from that in Britain, where the growth of the community-based sector in housing has been driven primarily by organizations participating in the privatization of formerly council (public) housing.

The privatization of council housing began in Britain in the 1980s under Thatcher in two distinct ways. First, tenants were given the right to buy their council flats, and thereby the privatization was direct from the state to the household. It was estimated that more than a million council units were sold in this way in the 1980s (Kleinman 1990, 85). But more important for us here was the second transformation of social housing in Britain, which has been a process moving the stock away from councils and to not-for-profit housing associations. This began in the early 1980s, has continued ever since, and has occurred through both new construction of social housing by housing associations rather than councils (Hoggart 1999), and, perhaps more important, through "stock transfer" from councils to associations. The largest of these occurred in Glasgow in 2003, when the city council's entire housing stock was transferred from the council to a new Glasgow Housing Association, which is now Britain's largest social landlord (McKee 2008).

Along with the shifting of housing away from the public sector and onto the community-based sector has come a similar shift in the provision of services. This has included the growing number of community-based organizations creating and operating charter schools in the United States (see Martinelli 2004), and the proliferation of foundation trust hospitals in the United Kingdom since 2004. It is, perhaps, in the realm of welfare reform and workfare, however, that the shift of services from the state to the community is most evident. In some cases the offloading has been dramatic, for example in Milwaukee, Wisconsin, where the county social service agency contracted out virtually the entire welfare-to-work program (see Kaplan 2000). The important implications of this for us here are that the programmatic activities of community-based organizations shift or adjust in the context of having to directly meet the needs of their community members (with government money) and simultaneously handle the pressures of corporatization and public control while trying to meet community needs.

PROBLEMS WITH THE COMMUNITY
AS DEVOLVED SOCIAL POLICY

Devolution of social services to the community scale has undermined the overall provision of public services in the three countries being discussed here. These processes have left certain people and communities in relatively favored positions, and (re)marginalized others through the uneven landscape of community organization density and representation (see Lake and Newman 2002). These are fair and important concerns, but are not the lines of critique we wish to pursue here. Instead, our concerns are principally with the impacts on community-based organizations themselves and how the transformations of social policy have impacted them and their capacities to be agents in efforts for social change and greater economic and social justice in cities. We see four interrelated problems with the current political economy of community as social policy.

Theoretically, the growing set of interactions between community organizations could have enabled community groups to increase their legitimacy and visibility—and therefore their political strength and influence—vis-à-vis the state. We do not see that as an impossible scenario, and recognize that, as Trudeau (2008) bluntly puts it, "Government funding is both an enabling and limiting resource" for community organizations. However, this brings us to the first problem we see with the current reality, which is that too often the relationship between community-based organizations and their government funders is so asymmetrical that the argument for empowerment via government contracts is difficult to sustain. In their study of community-based service providers, Fabricant and Fisher (2002) see the community-based efforts as "under siege." Jennifer Wolch, in her debate with leading nonprofit authority Lester Salamon, describes the relations between government and community-based nonprofits as one of relatively powerless communities confronting a state which itself is under assault from the forces of global capitalism. Her analysis of the dynamics between the community organizations and the larger political economy is thus: "David was just lucky; Goliath usually wins" (Wolch 1999, 26).

While Wolch's summation may be a bit glib, we are broadly sympathetic to her point. The relationships between community organizations and the government are usually structured in such a way that community organizations are in a position of being responsible for the provision of social services, but not in a position of control over those services (see Trudeau n.d.). It is the government that sets policy goals, rules, targets, and so forth, while it is the community organizations that have to meet them in order to both have services provided in their communities and obtain the contracts to do the providing. Although there is a strong rhetoric of partnership or empowerment in the context of community organization involvement in public services, the state usually exhibits little understanding or regard for localized processes and traditions, and it assumes that all communities have both the capacity and the will to follow policy decided from the center. Lesley Hodgson uses the concept of "manufactured civil society" to refer to this process, and she argues that rather than maintain direct control from the center, government "steers from a distance" (2004, 156), drawing upon the interaction of local actors who usually are outside of traditional government circles. In this top-down process, those local groups that buy into the government and foundation programs are rewarded, and groups and organizations that do not, or are too small to do so, become marginalized.

Our second critique emerges from the first. The government's hiring of community organizations not only steers, with its Requests for Proposals, the kinds of services provided (and all the particular rules, targets, and so forth that go with that), but also influences the trajectory of the organizations themselves. A burgeoning literature has emerged on how public contracting has pushed community organizations to become both more professionalized—and thereby divorced from their communities—and more businesslike in how they operate and understand their roles. As the funding requirements for different kinds of services are complex, contradictory, and often baffling, community organizations have increasingly come to be run by individuals with professional degrees—and those are MBAs, rather than social work degrees. There has thus emerged a minor industry in nonprofit management which provides training and professional certifications and qualifications for "executives" in this field. This professionalization and business orientation has been evident for quite some time (see Smith and Lipsky's excellent *Nonprofits for Hire*, 1993), but has certainly become more pronounced. Trends that were emergent in the 1980s and 1990s, and represented a break from the past, have become normalized in contemporary practice. It is not coincidental that Nicole Marwell's (2007) detailed ethnographic look at community-based service providers in Brooklyn, New York, has the subtitle, *Community Organizations in the Entrepreneurial City*.

The third problem we see is that the shifting character of community organizations, in turn, has limited the ability of the organizations to demand social change as a core part of what they do. This is true for three distinct reasons. First, because the organizations are dependent upon government funding for their revenues, their capacity to challenge the government has become compromised. Simply put, being dependent upon government, it becomes hard to engage in the often contentious, confrontational, and, sometimes embarrassing (to politicians) processes of community activism. It is, as the old saying goes, difficult to bite the hand that feeds you. The second reason is that the organizations put themselves in the position of arguing for services that they themselves are providing. Thus their demands for greater funding, for instance, can easily be dismissed as mere self-interest by those unsympathetic to their efforts. The retort to demands for greater funding for services is the obvious, "sure, you're asking for more money for your organization, so what?" The last reason is that by being the provider of services, the capacity of community organizations to mobilize the community has become compromised because the members of the community too often interact with the organization from a position of dependence, rather than from a position of strength. Service provision need not entail disempowerment and client status, but too often it does.

None of this is to say that activism, and making clear demands on behalf of the larger community, cannot or does not occur by organizations receiving government contracts. Clearly it often does. But government contracts make such efforts much more difficult than they would otherwise be. Every stage of the mobilization process, from the strategic targeting, to the framing of the issues, to the mobilization of the people, becomes more difficult for community organizations that are in the position of service providers.

Finally, the last critique of the role of community organizations is that by becoming the provider of services, the organizations contribute to making the state less responsible. In short, by accepting the process of contracting out, we have enabled the state to withdraw from the provision of services. And in the eyes and imaginations of the public, we have furthered the notion that the state should not be the provider of social services to people and communities. There is a double withdrawal of the state operating here—one now, in the form of the contracting out of services to community organizations, and the other (hypothetically) later, since the state need not be the provider of such services. It makes it nearly impossible to target the state, which has become invisible to the public, which only deals with the local community agency. The community organization cannot target the state, not only because of conflicts of interest with its funding source, but also because the state poses as no longer responsible for—no longer in the business of—meeting social need. That is the community's responsibility. In addition, the nation-state no longer has a direct responsibility to local citizens. The community cannot turn with any success to a state that is no longer responsible, and it cannot turn on the local organizations or local governments, which are already under siege by corporatization and devolution—by both the embrace of the market and devolution of responsibility to the local. Democracy is doubly undermined, at the local and national level, and the market and community reign supreme.

Throughout this book we demonstrate that context heavily influences practice, but it does not completely determine it. It would be incomplete to argue that the forces presented in this chapter—market and decentralization—only lead to community-based practices that fit into this dominant perspective. Some community organizations have been able to take advantage of the context during the neoliberal period to promote an alternative practice, integrating radical politics with service provision or economic development. Within this process, some organizations have been able to develop services that engage in a more politically oriented direction or are democratic places where citizens can find ways to work on social questions. Some have described these as "alternative service organizations." These organizations differ from traditional service delivery along the following dimensions: the types of activities, the means of provision, the governing structure, the emphasis on professional employees, and their links to wider social change efforts (Shragge 1990). The following are examples of two organizations that have used economic development strategies as a means of responding to issues faced by particular groups that would traditionally be addressed through an incorporated service strategy.

Co-operative Home Care Associates (CHCA) is an employee-owned company providing training and employment in the home health care field. It was founded in the South Bronx in 1985 in a neighborhood in which there was widespread poverty and unemployment. At the same time, there was a growing crisis of home care as hospitals were sending many people back into the community who were not able to take care of themselves. Home care workers can be characterized as "the 'temp' workers of the health-care industry" (DeFilippis 2004). Workers were disproportionately women and black, often recent immigrants from the Caribbean. The cooperative has two related goals—to create good jobs for home care workers and provide decent services. By 1990 it became majority worker-owned, improving working conditions—wages and benefits—and introducing both training and a job ladder. The decision-making structure involves a board with the majority of its members from the ranks of the workers along with a workers' council and a management structure. There have been some tensions in this area, with debates about whether or not to unionize. CHCA has exported its model to other cities, with three worker cooperatives in operation. By 2007, CHCA had anchored a national cooperative network generating over $60 million annually in revenue and creating quality jobs for over 1,600 individuals (CHCA Web site, http://www.chcany.org/).

In addition, it has established a policy and advocacy organization, Paraprofessional Healthcare Institute (PHI), affiliated with its three cooperatives. This body supports worker participation and empowerment in long-term care, providing workers with education and support so that they can more effectively participate in the governance and policy making of their agencies. It also organizes conferences for "direct-care" workers to foster leadership development, as well as training to lobby politicians on questions of wages and benefits for home care workers. PHI has organized policy action groups to educate members about issues related to work and ways of improving working conditions. There is also a center for research and analysis and a resource center for people concerned about the workforce crisis in long-term care (PHI Web site http://phinational.org/).

This example demonstrates several important possibilities for services. First, it is possible to democratize the ownership and management of a service organization, helping employees learn about cooperative structures and related forms of participation. Second, these innovative forms of organization can work on a larger scale, demonstrating that democratic forms of ownership and decision making need not be limited to small organizations. Third, services such as home care usually provide precarious and low-paying work without benefits. CHCA is an example of an organization that has made gains in combining services that are accessible and finding ways to provide decent pay and benefits, good working conditions, and a job ladder. Finally, as seen in PHI, advocacy and organizing on policy and service delivery issues can be integrated with a service organization, thus challenging one of the limits affecting many of these organizations.

A-Way Express is a courier company in Toronto, founded in 1987 by people who have experienced directly the psychiatric system as patients, describing themselves as "psychiatric survivors." As a business it offers reliable courier service by public transportation to customers throughout Toronto, and provides meaningful and supportive employment to these survivors of the mental health system. Its main goal is to provide permanent, flexible employment within a not-for-profit organizational structure. It has established a solid reputation as an effective business with continuing growth of its client base. However, the social objectives are more important than the economic. A-Way Express provides an opportunity for those generally excluded from the labor market to have a job, and build a strong social network through work. A-Way combines an income-generating revenue with government grants and donations. Many of the couriers receive social assistance but are able to earn what is called allowable earnings above that. Most of the workers continue on social assistance because the medication they take is expensive and covered as part of their benefits. The organization has an equal number of employees and nonemployee-allies on its board of directors, and its management staff are psychiatric survivors (A-Way Web site, http://www.awaycourier.ca/).

A-Way is an example of an organization that uses economic development as a strategy to respond to a specific social issue—in this case, the exclusion of psychiatric survivors from the labor market. The social solidarity formed among workers is a strong attribute of the organization. It is also involved in policy debates and has advocated for positions favorable to its employees. A-Way has become part of a wider movement of psychiatric survivors and a network of similar businesses. It serves as an example of a business that has social goals, has grown out of and continues to be linked to a wider movement, and has become a social center for its employees. A-Way has redefined what it means to be a psychiatric survivor, emphasizing that people affected by mental illness can work and manage an organization. It contributes to building collectivity and solidarity, and defines people who have been through the psychiatric system as capable of working and contributing to the management of an organization (Church et al. 2008).

These examples of alternative not-for-profits are exceptional insofar as they begin with the idea of collective action as a key element through which workers have control over the organization; that is, they have a democratic participative structure. In addition, they serve as advocacy organizations for issues related to their businesses. They do not separate service/economic development from the longer-term processes of social change. These two organizations are exceptional in their ability to expand and advance social change in the context of privatization and devolution. However, they are not alone in their desire to be more democratic and autonomous or in their pursuit to be free of the constraints and burdens inherent in a system of privatization and devolution. As we will see in chapter 4, the pressures to adapt and conform to these structures, and to modify community practice accordingly, are intense and pervasive.

IN THIS CHAPTER, we have argued that the combination of increased use of the market—that is, commodification—and decentralization have shifted the primary activities and roles of community organizations in a time of neoliberal restructuring. We have presented examples of practice and policies that have shaped community organizations in the three countries, as well as illustrated the convergence in areas such as the social economy and housing. The consequence has been an expanded role of community through local organizations. However, these processes have narrowed the practice priorities to fall more in line with market and state-defined goals. In the next chapter, we pick up this trend by expanding on the dominant ideas that have shaped community practice.

CHAPTER 4

"It Takes a Village"

COMMUNITY AS CONTEMPORARY SOCIAL REFORM

WHILE THE CONTEMPORARY TURN to and romance of community is grounded in the neoliberal ideas and policies discussed in chapter 3, not all ideas about the importance of community, or new strategies and programs reflecting these ideas, are designed to perpetuate the unbridled free market or the decentralization of organizational forms. In fact, many have specifically denied that the turn to community is related to the neoliberal retreat of the state. Xavier de Souza Briggs, one of the most prominent of the contemporary writers on community, has explicitly stated that his embrace of community as the solution to social problems is "not the same as saying the urgent problems of our time demand smaller or less regulatory government . . . [or] to substitute extensively for more money and other types of capital, as in 'more community, less public funding'" (Briggs 2008, 38). (It could be argued, of course, that when you ignore the context in which you are working, you cannot see that people hear "more community, less public money," whether you mean that or not.) A broad range of concepts and strategies related to community—from neocommunitarian theory to strategic conceptualizations such as social capital, asset building, and consensus organizing—appear at first glance to have little or nothing to do with neoliberalism. Neoconservative ideas of the 1980s focused almost exclusively on the individual as the cause and solution to social problems. When those policies failed, policy makers and foundations turned to the family as the cause and solution to social problems. When that failed, the next step was a turn to community, picking up on the concept that "it takes a village to raise a child." Community became the contemporary village, the most appropriate collectivity to address social problems, and theoreticians, strategists, and practitioners brought forth old and new ways of affecting change at the local level. While all of these efforts are directly or indirectly a product of (and now a co-producer of) the contemporary political economy, their ideas, tone, and form seem removed from debates and conflicts over the nature of the broader political economy, the role of the state, and the neoliberal reassertion of class power. Their emphases, in fact, tend to promote a form of community that is essentially depoliticized and inward-looking, essentially absent of tensions, let alone deep differences. In sum, what developed in many varied concepts, strategies, and programs in the contemporary turn to community were relatively unproblematized theories and interventions that seemed to offer an alternative to an unbridled neoliberalism, but in reality fit all too neatly within that context.

During the past generation, as power concentrated increasingly in the hands of a global economic elite, ideas and forms of community appeared that depoliticized local space, turned it away from the political-economic causes of community problems, and sought cultural, consensual, and parochial responses to concentrated power. This chapter addresses the most widespread ideas about grassroots organizing and best-funded efforts working at the community level. These efforts have become a critical part of the contemporary turn to community, and not only in a single nation. These ideas, policies, and practices about community converged in the United States, Britain, and Canada (Fremeaux 2005; Brodie 2007) despite several distinct schools of thought and approaches.

All of these conceptions, strategies, and programs gained initial credence as moderate alternatives to the general onslaught of harsh "reforms" under the governments of Reagan, Thatcher, and Mulroney in the 1980s, which emphasized individual competition and the dominant role of the market in the context of a soon to be post-Soviet political theory. Community theorists sought to redefine and reinvigorate community-based efforts, refocusing social change to the grassroots, community level. Earlier theorists, such as Berger and Neuhaus (1996), writing in 1977, proposed the value of what they called "intermediary institutions" as an alternative source of social change, one different from "dependence" on government programs. In the 1980s, neoconservatives jumped on the bandwagon, seeing such ideas as a powerful intellectual contribution to their goal of undermining the welfare state (Dionne 1998). But the "turn to community" really took off with the elections of Clinton, Blair, and Chretien, which offered openings at the national level for new ideas and concepts of community that emerged to redefine a middle ground or "third way." This third way was built on the concept of "intermediary institutions" and later reframed as "civil society." These new ideas of civil society were differentiated from older, statist models of social change, whether Keynesian or socialist. With the passage of years, these newer community approaches have come to dominate how communities and local organizations understand the role they should play in social and economic development.

As emphasized in chapter 3, the dominant forms of community-based efforts maintain the supremacy of the market as they promote decentralized forms of collectivity distinct from the state. Community becomes the intellectual and programmatic vehicle for this policy direction, that is, a social policy direction in which the state intervenes and often controls but does not provide ("steers, but doesn't row" is the often-heard metaphor). This keeps responsibilities and commitments low while maintaining the "gains" made in opening up markets under right-wing administrations, but the policies of these administrations ultimately polarize society. In contrast, the third way administrations wanted to build a social consensus, with the ideals of community playing a key role in the process. Our argument is that the promotion of these contemporary ideas and practices of community building did not bring about any fundamental changes from the neoliberal economic and political agendas discussed in chapter 3. The ideas did result, however, in a different strategy, one that emphasized community-based social reform, albeit with less confrontation and a softer rhetoric.

As the credo "It Takes a Village to Raise a Child" replaced "If You're Not a Millionaire It's Your Own Fault," the overall logic, structure, and policies of neoliberalism became refashioned elements of communitarian thought and community-based social reform strategies. Or if neoliberal ideas were not eagerly embraced, social reform efforts reluctantly adopted some of the moderating and conservative strictures of neoliberalism in order to win modest goals in what was seen by theoreticians and practitioners as required adjustments in a very hostile context. We will now

turn to some of the basic ideas, beliefs, social analyses, and va\
underpin the contemporary "turn to community" which, in addit\
the policy initiatives emphasized in chapter 3, have become the 1.
marks of social change in the past three decades.

COMMUNITARIAN THEORY

Communitarianism is a broad theoretical umbrella for those interested in exploring the value of community and civic efforts at the community level. In the United States, for example, communitarians range
from those on the left, such as Michael Walzer, to those on the right,
such as William Schambra (Dionne 1998). The communitarian perspective posits the community and its organizations—often referred to as
"civil society"—as the focal point for society and all social relations.
As Ed Chambers, the lead strategist for the Industrial Areas Foundation,
among the most significant community organizing efforts in the United
States, put it, "civil society is the most important level of institutions. Its
power is generational. It's where values and traditions are instilled and
fostered. The state and the market came later and exist to support it.
Civil society trumps the state and market in value, but most people
don't think of it that way. . . . Civil society is the political conscience
and benchmark of democracy" (Chambers and Cowan 2005, 61). Bill
Bradley, a former U.S. senator and candidate for president, put it similarly:
"Neither government nor the market is equipped to solve America's
central problems: the deterioration of our civil society and the need to
revitalize our democratic process" (Bradley 1998, 108).

Proponents argue that civil society is not only a third way alternative to the state and the market, but the true way to both improve and
advance democratic renewal. The emphasis on civil society situates the
local community as the site and solution to social problems, with asso-
ciational bonds providing the social foundation upon which a democratic polity rests. Logically, therefore, societal problems are seen as
resulting from the disappearance of community, trust, interpersonal connections and cooperation, and civic virtue, as well as a lack of strategi-
cally appropriate initiatives at the community level. Authors such as
Robert Putnam and Amitai Etzioni argue for the rebuilding of "social
capital" as a means of recreating civil society. The emphasis is on the
local as a way of creating participation of citizens in socially oriented

networks. Such an inner-directed, consensus-based community strategy supports internal processes as ways to ameliorate social conditions. It assumes that local communities, even very poor ones, have the resources to address problems, that everyone in a community shares similar values and interests, and that the private sector is a likely partner in community building and community renewal.

To their credit, communitarian theories seek to move right-wing discourse away from the deficits and failings of individuals and families to more collective conceptions at the community level. Communitarian theories respond to a clear decline of collective behavior since the mid-1970s, and seek to counter the extreme individualism and privatism of the past generation with ideas and practices that emphasize the value of public life and greater public engagement. Moreover, they focus on developing participation and enabling people to take control of their lives and communities. These are useful interventions. But while the new communitarians respond to the destruction of community caused by neoliberal programs and policies, their emphasis on community is both adaptive and system-maintaining. For example, Amitai Etzioni, one of the foremost neocommunitarian theorists, has had a major influence on the emergence of a communitarian approach both in the United States and Britain. His writing focuses on reweaving the fabric of society by building community more broadly, proposing an alternative to the emphasis on the individual inherent in the social justice theories of John Rawls and others.

But a close reading of Etzioni and other communitarians reveals a primary focus on social order, not social change. Community becomes a collective form to address societal needs and, critically, to promote social stability, adjustment, and consensus. Etzioni sets out his agenda in his book *The Spirit of Community*. The beginning problem for him is actually not the market-based individualism of the 1980s, but rather the lack of a societal moral center, which he argues has waned since the 1960s. "As rights exploded and responsibilities receded, the moral infrastructure has crumbled, so did the public interest" (1995, 14). In addition, in the 1960s old values were challenged but not followed by affirmation of new ones, leaving "rampant moral confusion and social anarchy" (24). Critically, communities become the means to provide the dos and don'ts, the guides toward this new moral agenda—"the moral voice" (53). In order to enhance community as a solution to the problems faced in the United States, Etzioni calls for increased social order and consensus on basic values, and for greater individual responsibility in the context of a renewed communal order. For example, in his discussion of child rearing, there is reciprocity between parents' obligation to raise their children responsibly and the wider community's responsibility to enable parents to do so. The places where the building of communitarian values play important roles include the basic social institutions such as the family, schools, neighborhoods, working their way out to the nation. The underlying assumption is that there are both common interests and common values. This is what we would call a fundamentally system-maintaining, social-order approach, encouraging community as a means of establishing a moral order for a society that has lost its moral center. It is thus a fundamentally conservative (in the Burkean sense, and as we refer to it in chapter 1) understanding of community and society, where change is, by definition, a problem, and stability a desirable goal.

This social order dimension of civil society theory is very attractive to neoconservatives, who see dependence on the welfare state and personal irresponsibility as corrosive to order. Neoconservative Gertrude Himmelfarb (1998, 122) argues, for example, that this should be "precisely the function of civil society: to encourage moral behavior and discourage—which is to say stigmatize—immoral behavior." William Schambra, who worked in the Bush White House, sees the welfare state, what he calls "national community," as the source of problems. He sees voluntary associations at the local community level as the conservative alternative. When considering civil society or participatory democracy, Schambra and other conservatives envision "dutiful citizenship within traditional, local institutions like the church, neighborhood, and voluntary associations" (1998, 47).

In Britain, a different form of communitarianism has emerged from a separate set of theoretical and political starting points. Importantly, in the final analysis it too comes back to community as the way to address social disintegration and the lack of social order. Perhaps the most significant proponent of a communitarian approach in Britain has been Anthony Giddens (1998, 2000), whose work has had a direct influence in the shaping of New Labour. He argues that the shift to community was a compromise within the Labour Party. In contrast to Thatcher, who saw society as made up primarily of individuals, and who tried to dismantle a centralized state, New Labour wanted to have an approach that talked about society but did not want to revert to a centralized state. Community became the way to achieve these goals. Giddens argues, for example, that "the consolidating of communities and civil society as a whole, are to overcome the social disintegration brought by the dominance of the marketplace" (63).

Giddens's project is much less conservative than that of Etzioni, Himmelfarb, and Schambra, and also much more explicit in its theorizing of the state, market, and community relations. The United Kingdom was not the first to look to the right. Giddens argues that New Labour followed suit after the renewal of the Democratic Party in the United States, particularly under Clinton, who abandoned big institutional government and embraced the aspirations of the right to abandon the welfare state altogether, particularly as a force for progressive social development and change. The desire was to rewrite a social contract with cornerstones of "equal opportunity, personal responsibility, and the mobilization of citizens and community" (Giddens 2000, 2). The central role of community under New Labour redefined how it would rule and how it would develop social and economic policies. As Levitas (2000) explains, "'Community' is used as a deliberate alternative to 'society,' in order to signal difference from both the neo-liberal New Right and from the forms of socialism dependent on intervention by the state" (191).

As opposed to the general political system that is based on conflicting interests and majority rule, most communitarian forms of civic engagement build on a conception of social consensus. They focus on what is assumed to be shared—values, beliefs, and goals. There is an emphasis on the importance of participation, assuming that through these processes civic bonds are forged and succeed when people see these as democratic obligations. Politics is brought down to the proper human level in community, the level of person-to-person encounters. Place is equated with community, and place should be turned into community. Frazer argues that communitarians "see strong localities, together with strong families, well-ordered institutions like schools, hospitals, and firms all linked together by the relation of community, as the proper social infrastructure of the modern state" (1999, 143). Reinvigorating community is seen as a means to reorder society in a more humane form, one that considers problems at the local level and encourages people to come together and resolve them. Again, this is a direct response to what was seen as the hyper-individualism and exclusively market-focused political economy of the 1980s. Of course, not all communitarians are so conservative. Michael Walzer (1998, 123) sees civil society as a "space of uncoerced human association" and as a corrective not only to the capitalist market but also to the socialist state. Jean Bethke Elshtain (1998, 28) does not see civil society as a cure-all for solving social problems per se, as much as a means to promoting public citizen institutions. Nevertheless, she sees civil society as superior to social movements because civil society builds "ties of trust, reciprocity, accountability, and mutual self-help over time." On the other hand, as Theda Skocpol argues, moderate communitarians such as Elshtain and Putnam and left ones such as Michael Sandel all "privilege local community and interactions among family members, friends, and neighbors" in an almost Jeffersonian antipathy to national government and politics (Skocpol 2003, 9). Communitarian views of civil society, spanning across the political landscape, from right to left, see it as an alternative to the market and the state, one relatively free of macro problems and certainly without the need for conflict.

SOCIAL CAPITAL AND COMMUNITY BUILDING

The concept of social capital is central to the communitarian call to rebuild community. The central argument of social capital theorists is that community has declined dramatically and that this lack of connection between people has undermined civil society, which is the core sector for civic engagement. Accordingly, reviving community and social connections will produce the capacity to solve social and economic problems at the local level. The literature on social capital, both academic and popular, is sizable, as are the examples of practices that have adopted social capital concepts. Equally critical, there are a number of well-financed foundations, such as the Ford Foundation, that support social capital initiatives. Even national governments and global institutions such as the World Bank use this concept to shape policies impacting the development and roles of communities and local organizations. "Social capital has become the 'missing link' in development discourse, exhorting the poor and the disadvantaged to be active on their own behalf" (Powell and Geoghegan 2004, 13). For the purposes of this discussion, we do not systematically review this vast literature, but instead we examine its core ideas and implications for community development and organizing and provide some examples of its uses, virtues, and limits.

Social capital concerns relationships between individuals, and between individuals and organizations in local communities. Social capital emerges from "connections between entities and is further developed through trust, mutual understanding and through reciprocal actions based on shared norms and values" (Kay 2006, 162). It consists of resources within communities, which are created through the high levels of trust, reciprocity and mutuality, shared norms and behavior, shared commitment and belonging, both formal and informal social networks and effective information channels. These resources may be used by individuals and groups to facilitate actions to benefit individuals, groups, and/or the wider community. Moreover, social capital needs to be understood as a "relational construct" (Field 2003, 139). Individuals have access to resources when they have created ties. Thus relationships are central not only to building communities and reweaving their social fabric; but positive outcomes emerge from these relationships. Community building is about residents communicating and acting with other community members, establishing relationships that form the basis of civil society, the arena of society deemed essential to democratic life and social change.

The work of Robert Putnam (most notably, Putnam 2000) is probably the most influential, not only for his conceptualization but also for its adoption at the level of policy (Field 2003; DeFilippis 2001a). He argues for the rebuilding of social capital as a means of recreating civil society or community. The emphasis is on the local as a venue for creating participation of citizens in socially oriented networks. Putnam's work emphasizes, even more than that of others, the importance of the relationships, trust, and cooperation that are inherent in civil society, and which can make or break, in economic and political terms, democratic societies. Putnam refers to social capital "as the norms and networks of civil society that lubricate cooperative action among both citizens and their institutions" (Putnam 1996). He argues that "an impressive and growing body of research suggests that civic connections help make us healthy, wealthy, and wise. Living without social capital is not easy, whether one is a villager in southern Italy or a poor person in an American inner city or a well-heeled entrepreneur in a high-tech industrial district" (Putnam 2000, 287).

Perhaps not surprisingly, as with Etzioni's analysis of the causes of community decline, Putnam identifies the decline in social capital, at least in the United States, as beginning in the 1960s. For Putnam, issues confronting society become transformed into questions of individual versus collective "values," that is, whether or not citizens join associations or groups. Community becomes a good unto itself, a form of social capital, to be used to regenerate society. Social capital, for Putnam and others, makes democracy work; political renewal rests in "the values and institutions that sustain community" (Warren 2001, x). People's desire and willingness to join associations and groups—their sense of civic virtue—will build connections that provide the social glue for future initiatives (Joseph 2002, 11). In addition, Putnam emphasizes that the quality of democracy and the vitality of economic life depend to a large extent on the "degree to which its people enjoy social capital" (Mayer 2003, 112). Thus, social capital is responsible for both the strength and vitality of democracies. The economic well-being and development of a democratic nation and its people rest on local community interactions and connections. In addition, while most social capital exists among people who are more alike than different ("bonding capital"), Putnam and others recognize, at least in theory, the need for building connections between people who are different across some critical dimension, such as race and gender ("bridging capital"). Clearly social capital theory, as both a theory of social problems and a strategy for social change, is a leading concept and model in the contemporary turn to community.

The essence of social capital formation is to rebuild community. In Rothman's (1968) model of community organizing types, what he called locality or community development would now be best labeled as community building. Unlike other organizing approaches that essentially deliver community-based services (such as a soup kitchen or domestic violence shelter) or engage in social action (such as the civil rights movement or the group ACORN—see chapter 5), the community building approach essentially seeks to develop or redevelop a sense of community by bringing community members together to decide— usually in a democratic grassroots process—their identity, goals, strategies, and tactics. They could choose to provide a social service, engage in a social action, or just strengthen community connections and supports. For long-time community organizer Bill Traynor, another high profile proponent and practitioner of social capital development and community building, the basic goal of community building is to create a "functional civic infrastructure" (2008, 215). Community building begins with "connecting people to each other" (216), building common values, and encouraging people's participation in public life. This is an important part of all community work, arguably the basis of any kind of organizing. But we would argue the reasons for this community participation are heavily influenced by a conservative interpretation of the nature and uses of community, clearly one whose limits must seem highly constrained to good organizers such as Traynor. In a neoliberal age, Traynor argues for a community of connection, a paradigm for belonging that has its roots in the market and not in the political sphere. The basis of community is connections between people, their engagement toward local mutual problem solving by viewing, in Traynor's language, community as a "marketplace and community building as a market making strategy" (221). One of the departures of community building from other traditions is its emphasis on connections of individuals that can build networks and then community. "Networks can act like a consumer collective and use its collective demand to shape the services that are available to struggling families" (224). Underlying these ideas is the view that communities are not only essential sites but ones somehow autonomous from the wider society. This leads to adopting a model of community self-help based on networks and markets.

An excellent example of the flexible adoption of social capital and community concepts, and, ipso facto, some of the inherent weakness as well in the social capital concept, is its broad use across the political spectrum, from liberals seeking to transform urban neighborhood schools, improve community health, and develop effective community-based public safety efforts, to religious conservatives who seek to build social capital (now referring to it as "spiritual capital") within and between churches and other religious institutions. According to DiIulio (2007), religious institutions and individuals represent about half of the existing stock of social capital in the United States. Moreover, religious conservatives were very willing to have the national government support their efforts at community building through "faith-based initiatives" sponsored by the public sector's Office of Faith-Based and Civic Initiatives under President George W. Bush. Similarly, community-building efforts are seen as a means to strengthen families, not just communities. According to Morrison et al., there needs to be a direct relationship between building social connections and supporting families. They state: "This connectedness should be encouraged and promoted so that the individual 'silence' and isolation that tolerate and sustain neighborhood problems and sabotage mobilization efforts are curtailed. While rebuilding community structures, families can be supported and 'rebuilt' as well" (1998, 108).

Of course, social capital theory, strategies, and practices are not limited to projects that are market-oriented, faith-based, or family-focused. They range broadly from neighbors coming together to form community anti-crime and anti-violence teams, to anti-poverty and inequality efforts, to efforts by community-based nonprofit settlement houses in New York City that struggle to survive under the strictures of a neoliberal contracting system (discussed in chapter 3). At the same time that these community-based service providers reach out in a democratic fashion to service recipients, they also provide both a safe and supportive haven for them and encourage users to build community and take action on their own behalf (Saegert et al. 2001; Fabricant and Fisher 2002). Conceptions of social capital and community building are broadly popular and widely adopted by efforts that span the political spectrum and range widely in terms of locales, populations, and community needs. But there is little doubt that all forms of social capital and community building—theory, strategies, and practice—are heavily influenced by the conservative context in which the ideas and strategies emerged. Intentionally or not, social capital and community building help to bring neoliberalism to the grassroots as organizations seek to survive by figuring out how to adapt to neoliberalism's global hegemony.

One of the clearest examples of the fundamental conservatism of most efforts focused on social capital and community building is their primary attention to "bonding capital." It is rare that community-building efforts expand beyond the parochialism inherent in most communitarian conceptualizations of local social change. One good example of an exception is the work of the United Community Centers (UCC), a community-based nonprofit service delivery effort in New York City, whose efforts around HIV prevention built connections with taxi drivers to promote awareness about HIV and AIDS and engage them in planning activities (Hirota et al. 1997). The taxi drivers were open to the relationship because the UCC had previously supported them in a fierce taxi strike and in the founding of their own association. Over time, additional opportunities for collaboration created significant bonds between the UCC and the taxi drivers' association (Fabricant and Fisher 2002). While the norm in communitarian thought and social capital conceptions and practices is to focus on the internal community, not all social capital efforts are so internally focused that they do not understand the need for public funding; a significant number, according to Cnann (2006), would welcome government assistance to expand social programs and services. But while they might look outward when seeking funding, it is rare that they look outward to build solidarity with politicized groups that engage in conflict.

It is this contextual myopia of most community-building theories and strategies which we find most disconcerting. We certainly agree that building relations and community are critical elements in any grassroots democratic initiative. We understand that economic globalization requires community building to provide both stability and identity in a global economy that undermines both. Building community becomes a means to address the antisocial aspects of economic globalization. But a myopic version of community building ignores the broader political economy. It ignores the role of economic globalization and its decision makers in both undermining community and pushing social reformers into forms of change which, while addressing some needs, primarily support the overall system of neoliberalism (Fabricant and Fisher 2002).

BUILDING COMMUNITY FROM THE INSIDE OUT

Communitarian and social capital concepts and initiatives all operate with the largely implicit and unrecognized assumption that people in communities share a set of values, interests, and goals. There has emerged, in turn, a body of conceptions of community practice—somewhat lower-order theorizations of practice—that share those assumptions and theorize "good" practice accordingly. These are called asset-based (or capacity-based) community development and consensus organizing. They too have become very popular, not only among academics and community practitioners but especially among funders such as Kellogg, Ford, Annie Casey, and others. The Ford Foundation, for example, is an enthusiastic supporter of the asset-based concept and strategy. A description of one of its programs reads as follows:

> The Asset Building and Community Development program helps strengthen and increase the effectiveness of people and organizations working to find solutions to problems of poverty and injustice. Thirty-one program staff focus grant resources in two program units in New York and abroad. We support people who are building human, social, financial and environmental assets that enable people and communities to expand opportunities, to exert control over their lives and to participate in their societies in meaningful and effective ways. (Ford Foundation 2006)

One of the attractive features to funders of asset-based and consensus approaches is that both position themselves, in theory and practice, as alternatives to prior models of social change that focused on conflict or opposition. They represent contemporary alternatives to older conflict models that sought to mobilize or engage people in confrontations against the powers that be. They stand as alternatives to Saul Alinsky's organizing, which encouraged rubbing raw community resentments and mobilizing community residents to demand social justice and economic redistribution on behalf of the working and middle classes and against economic and political elites.

The shared characteristics of these approaches emphasize local participation, leadership development, mobilizing local resources, and minimizing social conflict. Each emphasizes the inner strengths of community and its residents, but the asset-based approach tends to maintain an inward focus. With the assets approach, community has both the responsibility and the possibility of resolving social and economic problems locally, or at least reducing poverty. In the consensus approach, however, there is a recognition that such resources also rest outside most poor communities and it is the task of the local community, leaders, and organizers to convince the wealthy to help them. The assets-based approach, by far the better known and better funded of the two, assumes that communities possess the resources to address their own problems.

John McKnight (1995) pioneered this approach in his writing in the 1990s, and it has had, and continues to have, a major impact on the orientation of private foundations and some community practitioners. He has written extensively and consulted widely with a large variety of organizations and people with power to influence community practice, such as foundations that support these activities. His work is complex and combines both a radical and a conservative vision. This is not dissimilar from how communitarians first distanced themselves from the hyper-individualist Right but then offered a highly moderated form of community work that corresponded to the strictures of contemporary neoliberalism. McKnight's radicalism comes in the form of a fundamental challenge to the power of professionals, particularly those who work in the community, such as social workers and a wide variety of the so-called helping professions. He locates one of the most significant problems facing the United States as the growing control of all aspects of daily life by those professions, which as a consequence have eclipsed the democratic life of the community. He writes, "It is clear that the economic pressure to professionalize requires an expanding universe of need and the magnification of deficiency. This form of marginal professional development can only intensify the ineffective, dominating, and iatrogenic nature of the professional class as they invade the remaining perimeters of personhood" (23–24).

McKnight's task is to find a way to "dissolve the 'professional problem'" (McKnight 1995, 25). From here he constructs a perspective that is based on citizenship, as opposed to client status, and on assets, as opposed to deficiencies and pathologies. He argues for a practice that strengthens the capacity of people to control and manage their lives through a vibrant and democratic community. The radical veneer begins to peel off the surface, and the conservative core of his perspective emerges, however, once community is understood as a relatively self-contained unit and change as an inward-looking process.

With their asset-based model of community organizing, McKnight and Kretzmann argue that the solution to impoverished inner-city communities in the United States cannot be found by focusing on deficiencies and problems. Instead they counter with a different starting point—a clear commitment to a community's capacities and assets. They focus on existing community strengths, that is, those community organizations and individual skills already present in the community. (In social work this is referred to as a "strengths perspective." It is worth noting here because much of McKnight's work distances his approach from social work and social service approaches.) According to this conceptualization of McKnight and Kretzmann, traditional community organizing practice identifies problems and then constructs services as a solution to them. This then creates a dependency and reduces people from their status as citizens to that of clients with a reliance on outside experts. This "needs-based strategy can guarantee only survival and can never lead to serious change or community development . . . this orientation must be replaced as one of the major causes of the sense of hopelessness that pervades discussion about the future of low-income communities" (1999, 5).

McKnight and Kretzmann propose an alternative that they call "capacity focused development." Their position has two central ideas. First, significant community development can only take place when local people commit themselves to identifying and investing their resources and efforts, thus avoiding a top-down or an outside-in practice. Second, the prospect for outside help is bleak because of budgetary constraints and weak job prospects. The basic goal is to mobilize assets to build community by involving "virtually the entire community in the complex process of regeneration" (1999, 345). The basic solution to the professional service problem is to use existing assets pulled together within the community to create networks of self-help and support. Again, as with social capital conceptions and community-building strategies, the primary issue is seen as simply finding and connecting existing community components. Capacity-based models emphasize that "identifying the variety and richness of skills, talents, knowledge of people in low-income neighborhoods provides a base upon which to build new approaches and enterprises" (160). McKnight and Kretzmann recognize, however, some of the limits of what can be achieved locally and argue that low-income neighborhoods should "develop their assets and become interdependent with mainstream people, groups and economic activity" (171).

Melvin Delgado (2000) explains capacity building as a community-based model that can be incorporated into traditional service programs such as tutoring, life skills, recreation, and family support. An asset perspective represents a fundamental way of conceptualizing individuals and communities, regarding their potential for growth and contributions to society. "Community building often involves mapping out the resources in a community and meeting needs through strengthening those resources through local action" (Hess 1999). Once assets have been identified and harnessed, the community produces a "capacity inventory," which provides the necessary information for people to become producers rather than problems. McKnight identifies two sources of assets and capacities: those of individuals and those of organizations or associations. His asset/strength perspective is focused on community regeneration and development and offers a new conceptualization of community building.

One oft-noted example of the asset-based approach is Jody Kretzmann's early experiment in the Rogers Park community on Chicago's North Side. A nonprofit affordable housing group, Peoples Housing, sought to renovate a theater space in one of its buildings. The Kretzmann-led group surveyed 1,080 residents regarding their vision for the arts center and their potential contribution to it, that is, what assets they could bring to the effort. Initially the surveyed residents responded that they did not have anything artistic to contribute. But when asked more specifically what artistic skills they had, such as rapping or storytelling, "people began to realize they had a lot to offer. People need to be reminded of their own talents. . . . If you say, 'You have some skills and resources,' people can take action from that." Ultimately 42 percent of surveyed respondents said they would actively participate, and more than 8,500 got involved in some capacity. And their next project explored the potential for economic development, creating business opportunities for the hand-painted tiles they created (Bardone, 1996).

This very delimited model has also been exported to Canada. The Ontario Prevention Clearinghouse (currently named Health Nexus) seeks to enable communities to promote health and enhance well-being, thereby reducing demand on health care and the social service system. It does this by building capacity, connecting communities with resources to form partnerships, and advocating for related change (see Health Nexus). These efforts occur in a context of program cutbacks by the provincial governments, which provide health and social services. The Clearing House defines community capacity building as "the identification, strengthening and linking of your community's tangible resources, such as local service groups, and intangible resources like community spirit." It proposes that while definitions of community capacity change as the community grows, "it is basically the infrastructure of networks, organizations, attitudes, businesses and core values that a healthy community is built upon. Community capacity will allow you to get done what needs to get done" (Health Nexus).

Another form of asset-building community development in Canada is Vibrant Communities. With support from the McConnell Foundation, totaling approximately $11 million over the period 2001 to 2011, and in partnership with the Tamarack Institute and the Caledon Institute, six communities received matching funds to implement poverty-reduction initiatives. In the second phase, which began in 2006, the number of communities involved increased to eleven. Vibrant Communities focuses on identifying and mobilizing local capacity and assets to pursue goals related to poverty reduction through creating partnerships that mobilize people, organizations, businesses, and government (see Tamarack Institute). The programs also include a strong learning component and sharing across communities. Underlying this approach is a belief that poverty can be reduced by concerted local action through building community capacity. An asset-based conceptualization of poverty structures the local initiatives (Leviten-Reid 2004). Within the shared framework, there is variation in practice among participating communities. For example, in the British Columbia capital region, social marketing is used to engage the community in tackling sustainable income (jobs rather than benefits) and housing for low-income residents. In Halifax, Nova Scotia, priority is given to improving collaboration between inner-city residents and government structures that would support their initiatives. In some Canadian communities, there has been success in mobilizing support from the business community. The common thread of asset-based community work in Canada is the belief that poverty reduction can be achieved through local work that builds a consensus with broad-based community participation. There is no attention to or analysis of why poverty is present, what the role of the market and state is in poverty creation and prevention, or whether a sustainable income should be a right (Leviten-Reid 2004).

Not too dissimilar from the Vibrant Communities initiative is the work of other disciples of McKnight and Kretzmann's model who disregard the radical challenges in this conceptualization of community organizing and pull out those parts that fit nicely into an acceptable practice for the neoliberal 1990s, and then professionalize it. For example, Mark Homan, in a widely used textbook, presents a summary of the elements of practice that follow from this perspective. The starting point is the recognition that the existing assets of a community are those factors that give it energy to take action. Teaching individuals a variety of skills builds on their capacities. Connecting people and building relationships allows individuals to share their talents, through linkages with existing community resources. He states: "Whenever you connect resources, you create investors. . . . You extend ownership and participation" (1999, 37).

The next step in the process is to create or increase community resources—bring something new into existence. A pillar of this process is establishing community ownership of the direction, actions, and resources. Community members create the plans, not just approve them. Community members are also expected to do much, if not all, of the work if possible. At the same time as building on a community's internal capacity, beneficial external relations are also necessary, with allies, other communities, and sources of public support. The fundamental goal is to foster community self-reliance and confidence. This can be achieved through self-sustaining organizations, effective mechanisms for community decision making, and a renewal of leadership. These steps are intended to enhance the general quality of life. The question of who will support these initiatives and provide the resources for them is ignored, including the dicey relationship between local organizations and those who fund them. In addition, such an inner-directed, consensus-based community strategy supports internal processes as ways to ameliorate social conditions without challenging the causes of these problems. As noted before, it assumes that local communities, even very poor ones, have the resources to address their own problems and that the private sector is a likely partner.

CONSENSUS ORGANIZING

Michael Eichler, a promoter of the concept and practice model that he calls consensus organizing, believes that the conflicts of the past are no longer useful. "Today's organizer must be seen as a skilled practitioner, a potential asset to everyone in the community wishing to be involved in civic action. . . . Through the possibilities of partnership and . . . collaboration . . . the organizer must build cohesion and trust among all constituents" (Eichler 1998, n.p.). Eichler goes further, however, in his model of consensus organizing. He sees four types of community organizing, with consensus organizing being the most evolved. The four models include: (1) Saul Alinsky and conflict organizing, (2) women-centered organizing, (3) community-building approach, and (4) consensus organizing. The essence of consensus organizing is to bring together interests within a neighborhood with those of the rich and powerful outside of it. "The consensus organizer recognizes the value and power of mobilizing honest and dedicated people from both groups—the community and the power structure" (Eichler 2007, 8). By power structure Eichler means elite individuals and groups in the private, not public, sector. Eichler proposes that consensus organizing runs "contrary" to the conflict model, and shares more in common with the other two, specifically their openness to "power sharing." But the idea of power sharing in the women-centered and community-building models is very different from the emphasis in consensus organizing on partnerships and shared interests with economic elites. Eichler's model offers a set of core beliefs that challenge the limits of some other models, including the parochialism inherent in those models which argue that communities have the resources to address their own problems. Consensus organizing, while ultimately more conservative than asset-based approaches, actually improves on that model when it underscores the limits of a romanticized and exaggerated view of community capacity.

Eichler's model of consensus organizing takes on more meaning when it is applied. Eichler got his start in the Monongahela Valley outside of Pittsburgh, which was once the core of the United States steel-producing industries and by the mid-1980s was a deindustrialized shell of its former self. To address this problem, Eichler, once a fan of Saul Alinsky's conflict approach, saw the conservative writing on the wall, and, as he tells it, got a job working with the Allegheny Conference on

Community Development (ACCD), a powerful group of corporate CEOs from such businesses as U.S. Steel, Westinghouse, and Mellon Bank. Eichler sought to help both sides; the workers and families that remained in the Mon Valley communities, on the one hand, and the corporate executives who were confronted with the immense problem of addressing deep economic and social problems, on the other. His strategy sought to build consensus, connection, and a sense of mutuality between the two groupings. Consensus organizing emphasized their common ground—a devastated economy—rather than their antagonistic interests.

Eichler did the same, more or less, in Houston, where he secured support for his consensus organizing model from the Local Initiatives Support Corporation (LISC), which had played a role in the Mon Valley efforts. LISC was now seeking to expand its program to twenty cities, and Houston was one of them. In Houston, Eichler developed a a board of directors composed of business leaders from major corporations, an organizational model similar to the ACCD project in Pittsburgh. Eichler and his staff, supported by LISC and the Houston business group, identified six neighborhoods in need and set out to work with residents there. In some ways, consensus organizing fit laissez-faire Houston perfectly, at least from the perspective of the elites. Almost everything of substance that happened in Houston was decided, more or less, by the business community, and Eichler discovered a good deal of support for his consensus organizing model. LISC ultimately adopted consensus organizing more broadly, especially preferring its emphasis on nonconfrontational methods (Gittel and Vidal 1998, 2).

There are two critical elements to keep in mind about this approach to community. First, consensus organizing distinguishes itself from almost all dominant progressive forms of community organizing by its explicit focus on building partnerships with the wealthy and powerful, usually from the corporate sector. Once seen as key opponents to progressive social change, the wealthy and powerful are now refashioned as allies with whom the community can build consensus and find resources. There is an assumption of shared interests between community people and private elites outside the community, though Eichler clearly cautions that "a consensus organizer seeks agreement on a solution to a problem and does not attempt to reach agreement on the cause" (Eichler

2007, 93). Discussions of causes could clearly lead to fissures in the cross-class coalitions Eichler and LISC built. Such ideas of consensus clearly and explicitly deny that conflict of interest and unequal power relations are central to the problems that exist in poor communities.

What is also different about the consensus organizing model is that, unlike the asset-based approach, it does not view the community as being able to resolve its own problems through the use of its own resources. Instead it realizes, to its credit, the need to look beyond community borders for additional resources. In a neoliberal context, Eichler determined that those resources were no longer available in the public sector, be it at the national, state, or local level, and that relationships and partnerships must therefore be built with supportive foundations and corporate economic elites.

As with the asset-based approach to community building, consensus organizing assumes that local communities will and should find partners in the upper echelons of the private sector, that is, among the major proponents of neoliberalism. Instead of directly confronting the forces of neoliberal capitalism, and the individuals and businesses that benefit from it, consensus organizing builds partnerships with economic elites. It assumes that the inner-city poor and the rich and powerful have overlapping mutual interests and needs. Furthermore, consensus organizing emphasizes consensus and collaborative strategies, deemphasizes community tensions, and ignores the causes of most community problems. The deemphasis on conflict, evident in almost all communitarian, social capital, capacity building, and consensus approaches reflects the preference of global capital for consensus. Ironically, contemporary capitalism pushes people back into communities and steers their efforts away from oppositional strategies, while simultaneously global capital concentrates power and competes furiously on a global stage. Consensus organizing fits very nicely in the equation that economic progress requires social peace at home.

COMMUNITY AS
PROGRESSIVE OPPORTUNITY

Not all proponents of contemporary community-based strategies are as conservative as supporters of the asset-based and consensus organizing models. One of the central features that makes these models fundamentally conservative is they either ignore or adapt to the broader political economy. But there is a growing body of literature and related practice that promotes the idea of community-based alternatives as a vehicle for progressive social change. Unlike communitarian and community-building theorists discussed above, or asset-based and consensus conceptions and local practices, the promoters of a redefined progressive community understand the drawbacks of neoliberal politics and policies and the need for intervention between community and the broader political economy. We have selected a few examples of recent theorizing and strategizing to illustrate this position. For example, Christopher Gunn (2004) argues (as we do in chapter 3), that the ideological tendency in the United States was to restrict state activity (except warfare and policing), which contributes to both privatization and devolution, which in turn have created opportunities for both for-profit and not-for-profit organizations in areas such as service provision or training. Williamson et al. (2002), identify the triple threat as urban sprawl, internal capital mobility, and globalization.

As a response to these shifts, Gunn, Williamson, and others define the challenge as anchoring capital in a specific community. The community needs to be strengthened in two ways to do this: by ensuring the capacity to exercise meaningful governance over economic fortunes and by opening up new possibilities for more egalitarian, inclusive politics and policies at the local level. It is the latter point that differentiates this group of writers from the romantic communitarians; the commitment to local processes acts to counter social and economic inequality. For this to happen, government programs and initiatives from all levels are necessary to support community practices. This redefinition of the role of the state is significant in that it argues that, in contrast to conservative communitarian conceptualizations of a "third way" alternative to state and market, the state has to play a redistributive role and support the local as the progressive alternative to free market capitalism.

Similarly, Michael Shuman (2000) begins with a critique of the impact of the global economy and competition for investments on local communities. He argues that the way forward for communities is to increase their reliance on local resources, workers, and capital. The localism he advocates acknowledges the presence of large corporations alongside local initiatives; therefore, Shuman stresses the importance of community alliances and popular movements to strengthen alternative practices. He promotes community corporations, local consumption, and the use of local inputs in production as tools for "going local." Communities are not to be isolated and can have wider relationships as long as they retain a degree of control. There are thus differences among those that have a progressive outlook in their democratic participatory form of organization and in some of the content of their activities, but they still fall within the limits of working locally, with an inward focus.

So far, the return to localism among progressive promoters of community emphasizes alternative participatory forms of local development. However, along with this trend, the return to the local represents an opportunity for expanded democratic practice. Hillary Wainwright (2003), and Archon Fung and Eric Olin Wright (2003), have conceptualized these forms of democratic practice. Wainwright argues that the social movements of the late 1960s and 1970s "provided a glimpse of the need for deeper forms of democracy" (2003, 185). These new forms challenged the notion that democracy was limited to the state, and argued that local groups built their legitimacy through a wide range of activities that were transparent and involved citizens directly in their operation. The community organizations are the means that citizens have for "elaborating the detail of how broad policy commitments are carried out" (186). Wainwright uses the term "embedded bargaining power" to capture the essence of these processes. A key element is the ability of representatives of community organizations to negotiate with state institutions and representatives, and one of the conditions under which they can succeed is if the state respects the autonomy of their participation. Thus, a related condition is the openness of the state to share decision making. Democracy through instances of local control coexists with the pull toward institutionalization, with the state shaping the boundaries of how much control is exercised externally.

Fung and Olin Wright use the concept of "empowered participatory governance" (EPG) to describe recent attempts and successes in building local democracy and negotiation between local and outside groups such as government bodies. It is participatory because it relies upon the commitment and the capacities of ordinary people to make sensible decisions through reasoned deliberation, and it is empowered because discussion is tied to action. For these authors, there is a direct and planned involvement by state institutions in these processes of deliberation. EPG is defined as a form of collaborative governance that distinctively combines popular participation, decentralized decision making, practical focus, continuous deliberation and engagement, and cooperation among opposing parties and interests that frequently find themselves taking different sides of political and social questions (263). The concepts of "embedded bargaining power" and "empowered participatory governance" describe the extension of democratic practices into local relations between community organizations and state institutions. In both definitions, local organizations have been able to effectively negotiate or bargain with representatives of government, either administrators of programs or politicians. The shifting structures of local governance have been an important part of increased local democracy gained through these processes. However, these tend to be locally limited and to reinforce the legitimacy of the local community as the primary locus of action.

WHAT'S WRONG WITH CONTEMPORARY CONCEPTS AND STRATEGIES?

The essential point of this chapter is that no community effort—from those on the Right, to social capital initiatives, to Left-oriented ones—was immune to the reactionary political-economic context of the past generation. New Right efforts capitalized on the supportive context, achieved extraordinary successes (including effecting state power between 2000 and 2008), and opposed progressive ideas, policies, and programs. The context, pushed and fueled by New Right efforts, heavily affected the practices of a wide variety of identity politics in community-based activism, especially but not limited to efforts by women and gays (Fetner 2008). And the broader context—with its limits and opportunities—even shaped the well-known, once radical, and now well-established community organizing networks, such as the Industrial Areas Foundation (IAF), that were increasingly pushed away from radical activities into more moderated forms. Reflecting a trend common to other progressive, not-for-profit organizations, the IAF, once known for its conflict tactics and its willingness to "rub raw people's resentments," began to focus, as did most other progressive, congregation-based community organizing efforts, not only on values and community building but also, for example, on civic renewal work in public schools. Commentator and organizer Mike Miller noted in the early 1990s, tongue-in-cheek, that whereas in the 1940s Alinsky had written *Reveille for Radicals*, a book on the contemporary IAF would more aptly be entitled *Reveille for Moderates* (Miller 1992). To be sure, some of this was by choice, but much of the shift was the result of the organization trying to figure out how to progress and advance social and economic justice in a context vehemently hostile to both. To its credit, the IAF did not drop its oppositional tone and tactics, but the organization took on a different form. While still progressive and impressive in its work, nevertheless the work of the IAF and other community organizing networks was clearly delimited and redirected—just like the other examples of theory and practice of community-based efforts we have been discussing—by the political economy of neoliberalism (Fisher and Shragge 2007; Fisher 1994).

In this chapter and the one before, we have argued that contemporary ideas, policies, and practices of community-based work reshaped many of the key directions of local work, narrowed both conceptions of community and the strategies and tactics used by community organizations, and passed policies and supported programs to further goals antithetical to the long-term solution of serious social problems. The changes have brought community work in line with the general policy orientations of the transition to neoliberalism, and they do so at the expense of building opposition through local organizing. We have critically examined some of the key concepts and ideas that are acting to shape community-based practice in the current context, but many of the actual practices per se are not as problematic as the way in which they are implemented, that is, in their impact on the direction and function of community organizations. For example, the idea of building connections (social capital), or developing skills for involving citizens as leaders (capacity building), or creating citizen-run services or economic initiatives is neither new nor problematic. The problem is how these activities are used and understood in a neoliberal context and in the related goals set by local organizations (and often goals set for them by their funders, either government or private foundations and trusts). In other words, community has become a way to organize social provision, social control, and social reform in a time of restructuring the relationship between government and communities under an ideology of increased individual, family, and community responsibility for managing social problems. The consequences have been a romancing of community as well as a narrowing of practice.

The community-oriented ideas, policies, and practice we have been discussing on first reading might seem like a "common sense" perspective. After all, what is the problem with concepts that support the building of strong local communities? Or building consensus with the wealthy? Or moderating strategies and tactics in a reactionary context? Our basic position is that there are neither the resources nor the capacities at the local level to solve major community problems such as poverty, poor education, insufficient affordable housing, and so forth. These problems require broad and systematic state policy and programs, often with the redistribution of resources to low-income communities. In other words, starting with the fundamental social and economic inequalities based on class, gender, and race, we do not believe that it is either desirable or possible to address these issues through local programs alone. Of course we do not promote a naïve reliance on the public sector. Communities need to build power to make demands on both government and corporations. Contemporary concepts of community and strategies for community-based social reform, discussed earlier in this chapter, push away from sole reliance on community efforts and require state policies and support.

We are not the first to offer such a critique. Theda Skocpol is a sharp and caustic critic of myopic conceptions of community building such as social capacity. "Many who worry that the United States is no longer a nation of voters and joiners hope that civic revitalization can occur apolitically and from the bottom up. Perhaps citizens can redress the nation's ills while organizing children's soccer games; perhaps foundations can solve national problems by dribbling tax-exempt grants to local community groups. But a more accurate picture of America's past suggests the need to think in new ways about contemporary civic dilemmas" (Skocpol et al. 2000, 542). While her earlier work trumpeted "putting the state back in" to discussions and policies addressing social problems, Skocpol's more recent work emphasizes the limits of both local-only and national-only models of social change. Her research on nineteenth- and twentieth-century voluntary organizations, for example, reveals the value of an alternative model that transcends the limits of community by situating grassroots efforts within a national organization. She argues that such an institutional infrastructure was the norm for voluntary efforts from the mid-1800s through the first two-thirds of the twentieth century, and that our current bifurcated organizational models that privilege grassroots efforts and national advocacy groups are not as effective as a national membership federation. She argues against grassroots groups operating alone as "just scattered local creations." But Skocpol is also sharply critical of centralized advocacy efforts run by "self-appointed professional advocates operating out of Washington D.C. or New York City" and detached from the grassroots. In their place, Skocpol calls for "well-institutionalized national networks that used membership dues to support *elected* leaders who had authority and incentive to organize large numbers of fellow citizens" (Skocpol et al. 2000, 542, author's emphasis).

Our multidisciplinary approach to and synthesis of contemporary community initiatives agrees with Skocpol's criticism of romanticizing community and promotion of translocal national organizations that go beyond the limits of local work. Our analysis, however, focuses on the workings of contemporary capitalism rather than Skocpol's more institutional emphasis. Accordingly our critique of the "turn to community" shares even more in common with an analysis known as the regulationist perspective. The work of critics such as Mayer, Dixon, Jessop, Peck, Gough, Katznelson, and others has been fundamental to our understanding of contemporary community efforts. John Flint, for example, emphasizes the social ordering that occurs in communities and through community organizations. "Appeals to the collective moral values of citizens are sited within communities through which informal social controls enable the primacy of a law-abiding consensus to be asserted. Community is to be utilized as the sphere in which re-engaged active citizens will enforce re-established, universally held moral values" (2002, 252). Dixon, Dogan, and Sanderson (2005, 14) argue that the fundamental premise that all in a community share the same values and interests, that there is a social consensus to build or rebuild, is inherently flawed. "If human aspirations do vary, . . . then communitarianism has an inherent weakness in its naïve conception of community as a social construct." For Ash Amin (2005, 618), "Third Way localism suffers from a romance of local community." Mike Raco, focusing on the relationship between neoliberalism, community, and "the new localism" in the United Kingdom, argues that the expansion of "community" in urban policy there has not been primarily about handing power to community organizations. In part these policies represent a challenge to the bureaucratic welfare state. Mostly, however, "community empowerment has been re-established in a context of shifting relationships between state and civil society, with community representing a convenient territory of action to be mobilized, shaped, and activated in the pursuit of a broader agenda" (Imrie and Raco 2003, 242).

Margit Mayer, perhaps the best-known critic of the incorporation of community efforts, sees that with the apparent failure of both the market and the state as means of social provision, social reform efforts at the community level become a way to connect the economic to the social through the incorporation of local organizations.

> In terms of institutional reorganization, consequences have been the growing role of sub-national levels as well as the growing inclusion of non-state actors, the emphasis on "good governance" including civil society forms of self-organization, all held together by the "activating" state. . . . By focusing on the marginalized and excluded themselves and not on the causes of inequality and marginalization and by defining them as agents of their own survival, it mobilizes these groups toward their own (re)integration into the labor market (whether it's the low-wage sector, micro-enterprises or into the social economy) where market productivity replaces the social rights and welfare state criteria that used to apply to them. (2003, 123–125)

Furthermore, the emphasis on moderated forms of community undercuts interest in oppositional forms, so that it is not surprising to discover that "new types of urban activism and movements involving protest and other forms of disruptive repertoires do not appear on the radar screen of most social capital scholars and never on that of policy discourse" (2003, 117).

At the same time, however, we are also critical of those who use a Marxist or regulationist analysis when they too quickly dismiss community as being solely part of the neoliberal project. We may challenge what have become dominant orientations and mediated practices, but we do not emerge from our analysis with a deterministic viewpoint. The Marxist and regulationist critiques are important because they situate the shift to community-based social reform policies and ideology in the context of important political and economic transformations. There are several problems with their position, however. They assume a uniformity of political orientation of community organizations and do not examine their diversity, histories, and traditions. There is confusion at times between what can be described as state policy to incorporate and use community versus community as a diverse and complex set of practices. Many organizations have been drawn into the orbit of the state and play the role described by the left critiques; however, the relationship between community and the state is more conflictual than they argue. To see all community efforts as the same is problematic. Some community organizations contest, mobilize, and politicize, while others, for a variety of reasons too complex to address here, are well adapted to provide services and adjust to the sociopolitical relations of the neoliberal context.

In addition, the regulationist critiques often lack an understanding of the limits of the choices faced by community organizations. The funding options in the current context narrow the possibilities. However, as we will describe in later chapters, many organizations simultaneously live with new forms of social regulation and draw on older traditions of opposition and organizing. The strong contribution of the recent Marxist and regulationist writing is to situate the challenges of community in their immediate political-economic context. Their limit is that they fail to take into account not only the broad diversity and political range of community initiatives but also the traditions and human agency that allow the contradictions and tensions to emerge in the daily practice of organizations. Although it has been difficult to sustain and it involves swimming against a strong current, local work can be oppositional and progressive. It can build an active base of residents and both make demands on local resources and build coalitions on wider issues. Further, it is impossible to envision any kind of broad-based progressive movement without a local base. Communities can contribute to this movement through local organizations. But they can do so even more effectively by linking grassroots efforts to a national organization

with a mobilizing ideology, electoral strategy, and social-movement orientation that extends social change efforts beyond the local community.

WHAT'S RIGHT WITH THE ANTI-CANON

The critical lesson of organizing both with and beyond the local
community comes from strategic conceptualizations and examples of
practice on both the Right and the Left. Here we offer a recent historical example from the Right, from the "anti-canon." In the next chapter we offer examples from the Left, when we discuss the work of
ACORN and other efforts. Despite antithetical goals toward democracy
and human rights, in both cases—Right and Left—we discover successful organizing efforts which, unlike the dominant moderated approaches
discussed in this chapter, reject depoliticized approaches that avoid tensions and conflict. Moreover, unlike most other community efforts since
the 1980s, they embrace local organizing but situate it in a model of
organizing that also includes a strong national organization and electoral
activism. In terms of the Right, there is also much more emphasis than
in ACORN or any other efforts we address in this volume on the
importance of a mobilizing ideology and social-movement building.

One of the central lessons from studying the anti-canon of recent
community organizing in the United States is the successful use of local-
oriented, grassroots organizing in the 1980s and especially the 1990s by
groups such as the Christian Coalition. According to Left critic William
Grieder, "In this era, the Christian right is clearly the most successful
political movement to arise from the ranks of ordinary citizens" (2009,
295). To be sure, not all groups on the Right, whether economic or
social ultraconservatives, have embraced local organizing. The Moral
Majority, arguably the most important organization on the Christian
Right in the 1980s, ignored the grassroots potential of evangelical and
charismatic Christian churches. Instead, the Moral Majority, led by tel-
evangelist Jerry Falwell, focused on national issues, a nation-centered
organizational structure, and a national-oriented technological device—
direct mail—to help build a Christian Right movement. But in the late
1980s, Pat Robertson, both through his own presidential bid and the
help of Ralph Reed, built a more effective Christian Right organization
by turning to the grassroots and combining a more local-oriented perspective with their national focus. The Moral Majority was a Baptist-led

organization "strongly managed from the top." The charismatic Christian movement, based in local churches, which Robertson and the Christian Coalition tapped into, represented a preexisting, grassroots constituency. Robertson, Reed, and the Christian Coalition picked up on the turn to community that was widespread in the 1980s, and became among the first on the Right to organize the strength of the grassroots evangelical minority (James Wright, conservative activist, cited in Harrell 1987, 222).

From its outset in 1989, the Christian Coalition focused on mobilizing this grassroots constituency. Ralph Reed was hired by Robertson to propose a strategy to organize conservative Christians. Reed's plan for the Christian Coalition emphasized using conservative Christian values and arguments for expanding Christianity in American public life. In Robertson's and Reed's view of things, democracy and conservative Christianity went hand in hand. As Reed put it, "The case for democracy is that the rights of government derive from the consent of the governed, and the surest antidote to tyranny is a free people that believes it owes allegiance to a Higher Power, not the government. The consent of the governed rests upon faith in a sovereign God to which government itself is subject. In this greater moral context, faith as political force is not undemocratic; it is the very essence of democracy" (Reed 1996, 8–9). But the memorandum Reed submitted to Robertson on how to organize a successful movement emphasized a different organizational structure, proposing "the new group focus on building a state-by-state, county-by-county grassroots organization that reached all the way down to the neighborhood level." It also advocated "teaching those pouring into the political process how to be effective citizens by launching an ambitious training program" in grassroots organizing (Reed 1996, 13).

The organization Reed and Robertson built in the 1990s followed suit. It is rare to read anything published by the Christian Coalition that does not promote this turn to community. For example, Robertson emphasized that "The mission of the Christian Coalition is simple. It is to mobilize Christians—one precinct at a time, one community at a time—until once again we are the head and not the tail, and at the top rather than the bottom of our political system" (IFAS 1995). As Ralph Reed argued, "the Christian community got it backwards in the 1980s. We tried to change Washington when we should have been focusing on

the states. The real battles of concern to Christians are in the neighborhoods, school boards, city councils, and state legislatures" (Watson 1997,
63). One community at a time, the Christian Coalition mobilized political campaigns to get conservative Christians involved in grassroots politics, usually local Republican party or school boards, to advance their
"Christian" agenda and the Christian Right movement.

Greider is right about the success of their organizing effort. By late
1990, the Christian Coalition claimed 57,000 members, 125 local chapters, and a $2.8 million annual budget. In a study of the 1992 elections,
People for the American Way reported that the Religious Right won 40
percent of the state and local elections it entered (Wall 1993; Bradley
1992). By 1993, Ralph Reed claimed there were 4,000 religious conservatives sitting on America's 15,000 school boards (Reed 1994, 191).
In 1994, evangelical Christians constituted one-third of Republican
voters (Marley 2007). In 1994 alone, Reed said, the Coalition had raised
and spent $1.4 million to defeat Clinton's health care plan. In 1995,
probably at the top of its strength, when it was building on the reactionary congressional victory of the Contract with America and its own
Contract with the American Family campaign, the Christian Coalition
claimed 1.6 million members, 50 state affiliates, 1,600 local chapters, and
a $25 million annual budget. One year later at the Republican National
Convention, the Coalition claimed that 500 of the approximately 2,000
delegates were coalition members, probably the result of a $2 million
expenditure (Watson 1997, 54, 64). Michael Lind, a sharp critic of the
Christian Coalition, concluded in 1996 that "without the support of his
[Robertson's] Christian Coalition, it is unlikely that any Republican can
win the nomination for the presidency" (Lind 1996, 99). The Christian
Coalition fell short of Robertson's prediction that it would become "the
most powerful political force in America by the end of this [1990s]
decade," but in a relatively short time, from 1990 to 1996, the Christian Coalition had built a powerful organization of national leaders and
grassroots chapters and activists. Marley (2007, 204) calls it "a time of
unprecedented power for American evangelicals," one that placed Pat
Robertson and the Christian Coalition as the leader and at the center of
the Christian Right (IFAS 1995).

But the success of the Christian Coalition, and the primary lesson for
including this anti-canonical effort in this chapter on contemporary

practices, is not only that the Right, too, discovered the grassroots and turned to community in the 1990s and after. Rather a critical lesson is that the anti-canon of the Christian Coalition did not replicate the romance of community. For our purposes, the lesson of the Christian Right in the 1990s is not only how the Christian Coalition developed a strategy for grassroots organizing and implemented it with much success but that they also understood from the outset that this grassroots strategy was part of a broader movement building plan that linked the local to the national, linked local organizing to a national organization. In the 1990s, that meant intentionally building a strong movement infrastructure that "allowed the right to train the firepower of the entire movement on the political work of the smallest grassroots right-wing effort" (Hardisty 1999, 13). Kim Fellner, former head of the National Organizers Alliance (NOA), understands the existence and threat of the anti-canon in community organizing. She argues that "Organizing is not inherently progressive. There are a lot of right-wing organizers who do this, too" (Szakos and Szakos 2007, 8). But what the Christian Coalition did that most community-based efforts did not was build an organizational infrastructure that blended both the local and the national, that is, it went beyond community to build a federated national organization which Skocpol and others see as a much maligned but valuable model. A Christian Coalition manual, used in its Leadership Training Schools, highlights this integrated model of organizing at both local and national scales.

> The Christian Coalition is a grassroots organization, and every organization must have structural soundness in order to succeed. While it is true that the foundation for the success of the Christian Coalition is local, a system of coordination must be in place to insure that each part of the organization is working together. No grassroots organizations can succeed if all authority is concentrated at the top. Likewise, no grassroots efforts can succeed if all authority is exercised at the local level. Consequently, an organizational structure has been devised to support the local grassroots organization and provide uniformity. (Fisher 1993, 3.1)

The national organization, led by Robertson and Reed, articulated and legitimated a conservative worldview, which tied religious beliefs and actions to public life and politics. It emphasized that the organization, with both national and local components, was part of a broader cause, a social movement. "By carefully attending to the many aspects of movement-building," Jean Hardisty suggests, the Christian Right created "an overwhelming force that swept the right to power and swept away liberal reformism in fifteen short years" (Hardisty 1999, 13). More specifically, to achieve this end the Christian Coalition provided training sessions that offered technical skills for engaging in the local political process, while at the same time it developed a powerful national organization that mobilized the Coalition's power nationally and locally. This organizational structure provided a most effective transmission belt for building the Christian Right movement (Burghardt 2009). Furthermore, the model fits well with the theories of Theda Skocpol and her critique of myopic communitarian models of community discussed previously, and with the example of ACORN, whose similar local/national organizational infrastructure will be discussed in the next chapter. We are not suggesting, of course, that simply adopting an organizational structure of a strong national organization and an active grassroots network made the Christian Coalition successful. It is not even clear how deep the Coaltion's grassroots went. As Hardisty (1999, 13) reminds, "The contemporary right is a well-financed and well-run movement that combines shrewd strategic planning for political success with a rigid set of ideological principles, backed by certitude and based in implicit and explicit religious beliefs. It has an exceptionally strong 'movement infrastructure,' made up of membership organizations, networks, think tanks, media outlets, campus publications, coalitions, interest groups, PACs, and funders." But we do propose that the movement infrastructure illustrated in the Christian Coalition example, rather than a narrow community focus, is a critical dimension to effective organizing.

THE NEXT CHAPTER examines the underlying assumptions, strategies, and tactics in some local organizations that have not gone the way of the majority of community-based organizations. They work for expanding economic justice and human rights, not unregulated capitalism and social conservatism. Even within what has become the dominant practice and orientation of community work, there are organizations that do "work the contradictions." For example, they build power at the local and national scale, do both service and action, include conflict in their strategic repertoire, work on local development, help create democratically controlled alternatives to market forms of economy and housing options, and so forth. Within the framework of neoliberal capitalism, many community organizations have become important actors in maintaining social order, through the implementation of programs funded by government and foundations. However, as we will see in the two chapters that follow, some organizations still engage in conflict with a vision for social justice and consciously fight against the strictures of neoliberalism.

CHAPTER 5

What's Left in the Community?

Up to this point, our book has examined the limits and virtues of community-based organizations. Our central argument has been that over the last thirty years the shrinking of political goals of these organizations has been accompanied by a narrowing of the frame of reference in community-based efforts to a focus on the community in and of itself. But despite the larger tendencies of weakened political demands and shrinking perspectives, there are still significant efforts in Anglo-American communities that have not lost sight of the goals of social and economic justice for their communities. There are still community-based efforts that recognize that justice within communities can only come from changes in the larger political economy. They organize in ways that extend beyond the community in order to try to realize greater justice within the community. They help people build power through collective action in order to enlarge democracy through nonparliamentary means.

With the organizational examples that follow, we illustrate possibilities that run against the grain of the dominant trends discussed in chapters 3 and 4. Although we write here about specific organizations, the focus will not be on traditional case studies. Rather, we emphasize themes or issues, with each illuminated by more than one community-based effort. This necessarily shifts the focus away from local particularities within communities—the limits of case studies—toward larger-scale sets of issues and processes that affect a host of North American and British cities, albeit in very different ways. Each of the organizations selected challenges the dominant models of moderated contemporary practice and acts in opposition to the wider trends in the current period shaped by neoliberalism. The organizational efforts serve as examples of effective, if imperfect, community initiatives.

Moreover, the organizational examples that follow are chosen primarily because they reflect broader themes and practices which illustrate contradictory connections between communities and the larger world, and because they provide alternative analyses and practices that stand outside of and often in opposition to the current mainstream. The general theme of this book is that it takes much more than a community to advance economic and social justice. In this chapter we discuss select contemporary organizations that not only advance these goals but also address the limits of the dominant contemporary approaches to community-based work.

What other criteria distinguish our examples from the dominant modes of contemporary community practice? While all of the organizations discussed in this chapter contribute to concrete improvements in the lives of their members and the wider community, at the same time they all work to extend and protect social and economic rights. They also believe that the power to do this is through organizing people either within their own group or through wider alliances, including social movements. The organizations are outward-looking, insofar as their efforts have a focus that includes and goes beyond the local. Integrated into their practice is an analysis of the broader context of their work. This includes an understanding of the changing political economy as establishing new barriers as well as providing opportunities to advance the causes of their organizations. Their goals include increasing social and economic equality of their members or constituency. Critically, all of the examples see conflict as central to their practice. They all understand that organizing is fundamentally a means of addressing basic inequities of power. To that end, they all offer an example of practice grounded in a political analysis that guides their commitment to progressive social change through popular mobilization. There are other themes, of course, that unite the examples and distinguish them from the dominant practices of the past thirty years. And there are many other examples we could have chosen to illustrate our points. But the ones we selected are organizational examples that we have watched, studied, evaluated, and in some cases worked with for years.

The three organizations we selected, and the themes we emphasize in each of the examples, are: (1) the Fifth Avenue Committee in Brooklyn, New York, which highlights the potential connection between community development and organizing models; (2) the Immigrant Workers Centers in the United States and Canada, with an emphasis on efforts in Montreal, which, among many issues central to this study, provide a critical example of organizing on labor issues at the community level; and (3) ACORN (Association of Community Organizations for Reform Now), a United States-based mass organization known largely for its protest tactics that also offers an organizational model which ties local organizing to a national organization and focus. Because each organizational example raises questions of contributions and contradictions, our analysis of these models of community action is simultaneously encouraging and critical. But although we are simultaneously critical and supportive of these efforts, we have selected them because we see them as exemplary. It is important to look at successful alternatives and how they have developed over time. "Success" for us includes recognizing both the achievements and potential as well as limitations of community-based efforts. It includes their ability to work effectively to alter the larger social relations that constrain those efforts and the efforts of other people and organizations in other communities. The use of exemplary but imperfect organizational examples enables us to look at real-world organizations that point toward a radical understanding and strategic analysis of community-based initiatives, one elaborated in the book's final chapter.

COMMUNITY DEVELOPMENT AND COMMUNITY ORGANIZING

One of the central problems with much of the work that has been written on community is its tendency to fall into dualistic thinking: organizing or development; consensus or conflict; community or labor; local or larger-scale. Perhaps the most significant dichotomy in contemporary community practice is the divide between confrontational community organizing and community development. The key issues are about forms of community organizing that are confrontational and conflict-oriented, rather than the more consensus-oriented forms of practice that have become prominent in the last twenty to thirty years. It is the former that is understood to be incompatible with development, while the latter is not.

In many ways, this is not a new dichotomy. One long-time organizer/developer states that in the 1970s it was common for organizers to think that "organizers and organizations that migrated to community development work were 'impure,'" while developers thought that "organizers and organizations that did not expand to practice community development were 'immature'" (Capraro 2004, 154). But the period since the 1970s has not fundamentally lessened the supposed dichotomy. There has been, certainly, a renewed interest in community organizing among CDCs in the United States since the late 1990s—as opposed to the period of the 1980s and most of the 1990s, when the focus was very narrowly on bricks-and-mortar development. But, like Randy Stoecker (2003), we would argue that most of that "organizing" was of the consensus organizing/community building type which, as we discussed in chapter 4, consciously and purposefully rejected the confrontational tactics and power-taking focus.

Some authors have argued that organizing and development are not simply different, but the goals are contradictory. Stoecker, an author whose writings we are certainly sympathetic to, has argued that organizing is rooted in a conflict model of society, while development is rooted in a functionalist model (that is, tending toward equilibrium) (Stoecker 2001). The two forms of practice therefore have fundamentally different goals because they understand the world in different, and mutually exclusive, ways. Paul Grogan, the former CEO of the Local Initiatives Support Corporation (LISC—probably the largest and most significant of the intermediary organizations that support community development in the United States) agrees with Stoecker and sees the decline of organizing as a good thing for community organizations— even taking the time to ridicule organizing by stating, "The community organizing and planning of that period [the 1960s] was soon squandered on divisive or extremist political tactics, including the in-your-face style of protest that Tom Wolfe famously dubbed 'mau-mauing'" (Grogan and Proscio 2000, 66). It should be noted that perhaps the only thing that people like Stoecker and Grogan agree on is that organizing and development are incompatible goals, and that development has long since overtaken organizing in the work of community organizations in the United States and elsewhere—with the former lamenting this, and the latter celebrating it.

We have argued that not only is such thinking counterproductive, in terms of limiting the potential scope and range of community-based efforts for social change, but also misunderstands community. In short, these views are politically limiting precisely because they understand the possibilities of community in ways that are too limited. We are not alone in this critique, and organizations certainly exist that work in several different arenas and in a variety of ways. They organize and do development. They can be collaborative and consensual, but they are not afraid of conflict and civil disturbance. And they act at a set of different scales, ranging from the community to the city, state, province, and globe. They do so because they understand that the nature of community is one of complex relationships that manifest themselves in different kinds of local interactions, and also transcend the community. Organizations such as People United for Sustainable Housing (PUSH) in Buffalo, New York; Alliance to Develop Power in Springfield, Massachusetts; the Northwest Bronx Community and Clergy Coalition in the Bronx, New York; and, perhaps most famously, the CDCs associated with the Ricanne Hadrianne Initiative for Community Organizing (RHICO) in Massachusetts (see Greenberg 2004; Winkelman 1998) have managed to transcend the barriers to doing development and organizing at the same time. One organization that does development while maintaining a commitment to social justice-focused organizing is the Fifth Avenue Committee in Park Slope, Brooklyn (New York).

FIFTH AVENUE COMMITTEE

The Fifth Avenue Committee (FAC) emerged in the 1970s in Lower Park Slope in Brooklyn, New York. Lower Park Slope, unlike its wealthy neighbor Park Slope to the east, faced the same problems of systematic disinvestment and decline that were evident in many urban neighborhoods in the United States in the 1970s. A set of meetings took place in 1977 that attracted about four hundred people from the Fourth and Fifth Avenue corridors in the neighborhood, and out of these meetings FAC was formed to address the issues of tenant rights, housing abandonment, vacant lots, and crime prevention. It was incorporated in 1978, and its first project was the conversion of a few vacant lots to community gardens in 1979. From these rather typical and modest origins, FAC has emerged into one of the largest and most dynamic community organizations in New York City. Its work reads like the kind of motley mix of services, housing construction, and retail development that any large and mature CDC in the United States would have undertaken—albeit with a greater emphasis on organizing than most.

For our purposes here, the key issues to be addressed are housing development and organizing, the connections between community organizing and labor, community and criminal justice laws, and the growing immigrant rights organizing that is community-based in the context of a community that is transnational, that is, transcends community.

Before we discuss the particulars of FAC, however, we need to emphasize that the organization, despite thirty years of growth—which has made it a large, multipurpose not-for-profit organization, and a player in the politics of development in New York City—has never lost sight of the goal of social and economic justice. Its mission remains to "advance social and economic justice in South Brooklyn," even if its staff know that they can not possibly realize social and economic justice in one neighborhood. It is this unapologetically politicized view of what they do, and how they do it, that led Howard Husock of the conservative Manhattan Institute to argue that CDCs are not mainstream organizations—as they claim they are—and that you should not "let CDCs fool you" (Husock 2001). We would argue, however, that Husock's conclusion that CDCs were radical organizations masquerading as mainstream efforts was a result of his picking the wrong organization to examine. FAC is radical, not CDCs.

The biggest issues involve housing development and organizing. Like many CDCs, housing is probably the largest component of the work of FAC. FAC developed its first housing, a rehab, in 1980. Importantly, in the year before, FAC first began its campaign to address issues of displacement of low and moderate income tenants from the neighborhood. FAC, in Lower Park Slope, is on the edge of Park Slope, which is one of most intensely gentrified neighborhoods in New York City, and is second only to Brooklyn Heights in the borough of Brooklyn in terms of the quality and prices of its housing stock. This has meant that FAC has long had the shadow of gentrification hanging over it, and since the late 1990s, that shadow has swept down over the area and overwhelmed the organized resistance to displacement that has long existed in the area. But we are getting ahead of ourselves. First we will discuss the housing development that the organization has done, and then move on to its housing organizing.

FAC has developed a set of properties in its neighborhood since 1979, and now manages over six hundred units of housing. This housing has largely been in the form of mutual housing association (MHA) or limited-equity co-op, both of which have two central features. First, they allow the development to be sheltered from the vagaries of the flows of capital that constitute the real estate market, and thereby partially decommodify the properties. Second, they both have built into their governance structures a significant amount of resident control. FAC has also done a set of supportive housing projects for the formerly homeless.

The development of housing has been taking place alongside a set of housing organizing struggles. FAC first began to address issues of displacement pressures due to rent increases and gentrification in the late 1970s and early 1980s, but as the process of gentrification accelerated in the second half of the 1990s, these efforts became a more coherent and organized campaign. The "Displacement Free Zone" (DFZ), as the campaign is known, is a roughly one-hundred-block area that is larger than the immediate neighborhood of Lower Park Slope—a recognition that the pressures facing the neighborhood are shared by those adjacent to it. Tenants in the zone who are facing evictions due to rent increases contact FAC (there are signs posted on streetlamps and garbage cans that indicate the turf and its boundaries). The first step is negotiation with the landlord; when that does not work, the "negotiations" become increasingly noisy and confrontational. This often includes bringing vanloads of people to the landlord's house to picket or have a street party (or both). FAC has also been known to turn out its community when it needs to fight explicitly with politicians. In 2007, FAC and its supporters were described by the local media as "storming a hearing" with the Brooklyn borough president and the city's Planning Commission to fight for a supportive housing facility for the mentally ill homeless (Rizk 2007). It was a fight that FAC won, and the facility was approved and up and running eighteen months later.

While FAC organizes confrontationally, it is also working with members of the state legislature to pass a bill that would offer landlords a tax credit if they own a building that is not governed by rent regulation laws and they agree to rent their units at below market rent to a low- or moderate-income household. "The Community Stability Small Homeowners Tax Credit," as it is called, has passed the state assembly a couple of times, but has not yet passed the state senate—a typical problem for progressive legislation in New York State. Finally, FAC also engaged in a protracted fight in the early 2000s to have the rezoning of Fourth Avenue provide inclusionary zoning specifications, which would require some portion of rentals be within reach of people with low to moderate incomes. In this effort FAC failed. But importantly, FAC has since played a major role in similar fights in Williamsburg/Greenpoint in Brooklyn and Chelsea in Manhattan, and in both cases of rezoning, there were inclusionary zoning components. Despite not being in either of these neighborhoods, FAC was vital to the success of these efforts (although those inclusionary zonings were, themselves, weaker than most advocates would have liked). Although none of these development projects or organizing tactics are going to alter the basic character of domestic property as a commodity in capitalism, they do alter the logic that governs the commodity exchange.

Housing is a typical part of what CDCs do, but FAC is also involved in issues of labor, labor markets, and workplace justice. First, in the issue that perhaps hits closest to home for CDCs, FAC has been leading an effort to build a collaboration between labor unions and CDCs to insure that the affordable housing that CDCs construct is built with union labor and pays prevailing wages. This has almost never been the case, and the fact that most affordable housing in New York has been made affordable on the backs of the workers doing the construction has been called affordable housing's "dirty little secret" by *City Limits* magazine (Ciezadlo 2003). FAC's efforts in this area have begun with its own development in Red Hook (an adjacent area, which is not yet gentrified, and thus has cheaper site acquisition costs), which, through an agreement with the building trades unions, is being done by neighborhood workers, who are also unionized. This strategy is borrowed from the public housing residents' alliance, which has been working with the building trades unions for years to have maintenance work on public housing be done by public housing residents, who have been apprenticed into the union.

Second, in the 1990s, as "welfare reform" was occurring in Washington, a particularly punitive interpretation of the law was being imposed on low-income New Yorkers by then mayor Rudy Giuliani. Organizing efforts sprang up around the city in opposition to the mayor and his welfare policies, and one of the primary ones to emerge from

this came from FAC and its splinter organization "Families United for
Racial and Economic Equality" (FUREE). FUREE is a group of
women on, or formerly on, public assistance, organizing for economic
justice in the realm of public welfare policy. Their most significant campaign at the point of this writing puts pressure on the city government
to improve the pay and working conditions of the workers taking care
of the children of the women leaving welfare for employment. This
child care, which came as part of the welfare reform package in 1996, is
paid for by the government at abysmally low rates—$105 per week—to
take care of a child under the age of two. FAC is also a cofounder of a
statewide campaign to shift public economic development subsidies
away from the corporate retention deals (read, corporate welfare) that
have dominated the city and state's policies, and toward "high road"
policies that create living wage or better jobs that come with benefits. It
has similarly been a central player in the "One City, One Future" coalition that has been spearheaded by Jobs With Justice, the National
Employment Law Project, the Pratt Center for Community Development, and FAC. One City, One Future has brought together an amaz-
ingly diverse coalition of more than sixty organizations from around
New York City to demand that economic development be equitable
and just.

Problems and Tensions with the Fifth Avenue Committee

There are several issues that have arisen with FAC, and our discussion of the organization would be incomplete if we did not address them
directly. The first is that if the metric used to assess success of the organization's anti-gentrification work is the extent to which gentrification
and displacement have slowed down or been halted, then the organization has certainly not succeeded. Gentrification has, in short, continued
apace in the neighborhood—and largely swept away the poor and working classes (except those lucky enough to be in subsidized housing—
much of which would be FAC-built). As an FAC staff member once
joked to one of us, "we're going to be an organization with a staff of
forty in a neighborhood with three poor people." FAC, despite its
efforts to reach beyond the scale of the community in its organizing
campaigns, has been limited by the fact that it is, and remains, a community organization at a time when communities are being made and

remade by forces that extend well beyond those communities—in this case, the spectacular growth of securitization of residential finance, and its driving of an explosive boom in gentrification in the last ten years.

The second issue is one that is related to the first, but has a longer history. As with many community organizations, there have been moments when FAC has struggled with its connection to the larger community, and this was certainly true in the late 1990s—at the tail end of a period of rapid growth for the organization. FAC began a discussion of whether or not to become a membership-based organization. But after much debate, it decided against that course of action, for two reasons. First, becoming a membership organization ran the risks of newcomers to the neighborhood and organization (read, white gentrifiers) transforming the organization and its mission by virtue of their membership. Becoming a neighborhood improvement organization that promotes gentrification is something the organization has worked tirelessly to avoid. Second, the organization is a service provider, and as such, its ability to provide services might be compromised by members who might want preferential treatment in the administering of such services. This would undermine the organization's legitimacy in the larger community. In the end, the organization decided that it would have "FAC activists" (there are about five hundred of them currently), who would sit on committees and take action for the organization and build the organization's strength and connection to its constituency, but would not be "members."

IMMIGRANT WORKER CENTERS: COMMUNITY-LABOR ORGANIZING

It is estimated that there are approximately 130 community-worker centers across the United States (Fine 2006). These are mainly in immigrant communities and work with those closest to the bottom of the labor market. These centers are an important innovation in the field of community organizing, focusing on issues of labor outside of the workplace. Gordon describes these centers as seeking "to build the collective power of their largely immigrant members and to raise wages and improve working conditions in the bottom-of-the-ladder jobs where they labor" (2005, 280). Fine, in her overview of these centers, states that they use a combination of the following approaches: service delivery, including legal representation on issues such as wages and status; advocacy, including research that exposes working conditions and lobbying for policy or legislative change; and organizing, including the development of leadership in immigrant communities in order to take action on their own behalf. As opposed to traditional labor organizing along craft or industry lines, these centers build on identification with race, ethnicity, and place as key elements (Fine 2006; Tait 2005). In addition, they have tended to use direct action and lobbying as strategies, rather than union and specific workplace organizing. Fine (2006) argues that the success of these centers in improving working conditions for immigrant workers is derived from two sources. First, because of the limited power of immigrant workers, there are no other organizations that have succeeded in direct economic intervention on their behalf. Second, given the existing industrial structures and prevailing employment practices, only comprehensive changes in public policy can make a substantial difference. To understand the emergence of these centers, some elements related to their context will be examined, followed by an example of one center in Montreal. We will conclude with lessons that emerge from practice.

Context Faced by Immigrant Workers

The growth of worker centers is a response to several factors. The transformation of the labor market has been influenced by global economic restructuring, including the shift of industrial jobs from North America to the Southern Hemisphere. At the same time, the changes in economies in the south have pushed millions of people out of their countries, migrating to where they hope to find better conditions. However, many of those new immigrants end up in nonstandard employment and "under once extinct forms of labor-management relations" (Ness 2005), mainly in the service sector. Immigrant workers, like many others, are vulnerable to precarious and unstable working conditions, and few avenues are open for them to protect themselves and to improve working conditions. Short-term production, service sector work, and temporary labor have become the new forms of employment, especially for immigrant workers. It is difficult to organize workers in small factories and in unstable jobs with high turnover. Precarious labor, and exploitation of undocumented workers without secure immigration status are common features. These conditions have made it difficult for trade unions to organize these workers (Tait 2005; Lawson 2003). Despite all of these barriers, however, some immigrant workers have been able to organize through unions (Waldinger et al. 1998), with the support of unions in the community (Ness 1998; Needleman 1998), and through innovative means. Ness remarks in relation to case studies of immigrant workers in New York: "It is remarkable that despite the seemingly insurmountable obstacles, transnational workers in New York are engaged in substantial organizing efforts" (2005, 4). Two examples illustrate the innovative attempts to bring workers in specific sectors together to fight for improved working conditions. The New York Taxi Worker's Alliance, previously mentioned, is an example of an organization that has organized one sector and challenged the city to improve working conditions, building on grassroots relations between drivers (Mathew 2005). The Restaurant Opportunities Center New York (ROC) is an example of an organization that used multiple strategies in fighting for improved conditions in one of the sectors that is most difficult to organize. It uses methods of targeting employers for issues such as nonpayment of wages and poor working conditions, researching and documenting the conditions in the sector, working on broader campaigns, and offering services such as training for its members. It has also expanded into several other cities in the United States (Restaurant Opportunities Center New York). This organizing approach bridges issues related to labor and immigration. It works locally, but in the case of ROC has affiliations in other cities. And it has a strong grassroots base that is the source of its strength.

These community-labor organizing organizations are not the first type of nonunion worker organizing. Historically, there were movements of immigrant workers outside of the workplace, such as Mexican Mutualistas and the Chinese Hand Laundry Association. These were organized in response to racist policies of the labor movement, which excluded nonwhite minorities in the early twentieth century (Louie 2001). The contemporary local place-based initiatives have been a response to changed historical circumstances, including the decline of the power of trade unions, so that immigrant workers have been drawn into movements centered on race and ethnicity, gender, and community politics, rather than labor and class exclusively. Their strategies have

been influenced by the traditions of the civil rights movement demands
for economic justice, feminist organizing demands for gender equity and
voice, and welfare rights and other poor peoples' movements demands
for a social and economic safety net (Tait 2005). The community
worker centers discussed below are another important example.

The Immigrant Workers' Centre, Montreal

The Immigrant Workers Centre (IWC) in Montreal is a relatively
new example of the community labor approach being put into action in
Canada. It was founded in 2000 by a small group composed of Filipino-
Canadian union and former union organizers and their allies of activists
and academics. The idea of the center grew out of the experience of the
two founders, who had worked as union organizers. They observed that
much of their recruitment and education to support a union drive had
to take place outside of the workplace and, apart from personal homes,
there were few places where this could happen, particularly in a collective way. Thus the idea of the center was to provide a safe place outside
the workplace where workers could discuss their situation. Further, they
had a critique of the unions themselves, arguing that once they got a
majority to "sign cards" and join the union, the processes of education
and solidarity built into the organizing process were lost as union
"bureaucrats" came in to manage the collective agreement. In its first
year, the organization was able to secure a grant from the social justice
fund of the Canadian Automobile Workers to intervene on labor issues
in the community. The IWC focused on providing education and critical analysis that goes beyond the specific role of unions, as well as finding ways to address worker issues outside of the traditional union
structures.

The activities of the IWC cover individual rights counseling, popular education, and political campaigns that reflect the general issues facing immigrant workers, such as dismissal, problems with employers or,
sometimes, inadequate representation by their unions. Labor education
is a priority, targeting organizations in the community and increasing
workers' skills and analysis. Workshops on themes such as the history of
the labor movement, the Labour Standards Act, and collective organizing processes have been presented in many organizations that work with
immigrants as well as at the IWC itself. The Skills for Change program

teaches basic computer literacy, while incorporating workplace analysis and information on rights. The goal is to integrate specific computer skills while supporting individuals in becoming more active in defending labor rights in their workplaces. There is also an ongoing link between the struggles of immigrant workers and other social and economic struggles; building alliances is a priority. In addition, the IWC supports union organizing in workplaces where there is a high concentration of immigrant workers.

Campaigns are viewed not only as a way to make specific gains for immigrant workers but also a way to educate the wider community about the issues that they face. For example, the first campaign, in 2000, was to defend a domestic worker, under the Live-in Caregiver program, against deportation. In addition to winning the campaign, the issue of importing labor as "indentured servants" was brought to public attention, and many community organizations and unions became involved in this issue.

Because many immigrant workers do not work in unionized shops, the Labour Standards Act provides one of nonunionized workers' few recourses against their employers. Along with many other groups in Quebec, the IWC became involved in a campaign to reform the Labour Standards Act in 2002. The IWC brought to the campaign specific concerns, including the exclusion of domestic workers from this act and the difficulty in accessing information on workers' rights. The IWC actively contributed to the campaign, using the campaign to educate, mobilize, and organize immigrant workers. In 2003, several victories were achieved, including the coverage of domestic workers by the reformed Labour Standards Act. However, despite the reforms won in this provincewide campaign, the act still has many inadequacies in protecting workers in precarious and irregular jobs.

The IWC has also initiated a campaign on issues related to the north-to-south relocation of production, and the resulting job loss and factory closures in Montreal. The spring of 2003 saw the closing of three recently organized factories employing immigrant workers. Using union-busting techniques, the companies laid off workers who then came to the center for help. Actions to sensitize workers and the wider public were initiated. One of these actions was directed at the Montreal Jazz Festival, a large buyer of T-Shirts manufactured by one of the companies, Gildan. The IWC demanded that the festival adopt an ethical buying policy in response to Gildan's labor practices, both locally and in their factories relocated in Honduras. The goal was sensitization to the common struggle of workers north and south. The campaign was part of a wider campaign against Gildan, led by the Maquila Solidarity Network in Toronto, which resulted in some improvement in the conditions in factories in Honduras.

As the IWC has become better known, workers come for advice and support on specific problems and issues. The center sees this as a way to encourage and support people in standing up against their bosses, but also as a basis on which to build wider campaigns. The case of a live-in domestic worker, who became ill in her employer's house and unable to work, was the beginning of the center's most recent campaign. This worker was accompanied to make a claim with the CSST, Quebec's workplace health and safety agency, to ask for compensation while she could not work. She was told that under provincial CSST legislation, domestic workers do not fit the definition of "worker" and therefore are not covered by the CSST. The IWC's research found out that three provinces in Canada (Ontario, British Columbia, and Manitoba) protect domestic workers from workplace injury or illness. In conjunction with PINAY, a Filipina women's organization, and the Association des Aides Familiales du Québec, which represents and serves domestic workers, the IWC launched, in March 2006, a campaign demanding that these workers be covered. It has been supported by over seventy organizations, including the large union federations.

Another aspect of the IWC's work has been its contribution to the organizing of cultural events with political content. The first was an International Women's Day event organized in 2001. A coalition of immigrant women of diverse origins organized a cultural event, panels, and a march to emphasize the concerns of immigrant women and international solidarity. This event has become an annual event, and through its success has increased the profile and the issues faced by immigrant women within the wider women's movement in Quebec. The first MayWorks events, a community/union festival celebrating labor struggles through the arts, were launched for May Day of 2005. The festival was initiated by the IWC and found collaboration from trade unions and the wider activist community.

Overall, the IWC is a place of intersection between the traditions of the labor and community movements. Work-related issues have been the concern of the labor movement, acting on the assumption that the best way for workers to have a strong voice is through the union movement. However, the IWC, along with other organizations, sees that this is limited because of the difficulties in organizing workers. In the current context, new forms of labor organizing that include support both for and from the trade union movement are required. The IWC works on both fronts, with the goals of serving, organizing, and educating those who are not unionized. At the same time, it supports workers' efforts to unionize and to help them get adequate services from their unions. The union-community relationship is developed through many activities of the center, including building alliances with younger union activists, supporting immigrants in organizing, and in helping them negotiate conflicts with their trade unions.

Through its work, the IWC has formed new alliances and has become a meeting place for many groups of social activists. The core of the organization is a group made up of immigrant union and labor organizers and allies who have been active on both labor and community issues for many years. In addition, the IWC is connected to what may be described as the student and anti-globalization activists. There are several reasons for this. The center has been fortunate to have student placements from law, social work, and related fields from several Montreal universities and colleges. Many of these students have been involved in student organizing, and this has helped to connect students to the issues raised by the IWC. In addition, university students have found the IWC to be an opportunity to combine radical politics and local work. At the same time, the IWC's connection with these groups has pushed its own positions on broader social issues. The IWC is a place that brings together union-community and student activists, people of different ages, ethnic, cultural, and class backgrounds to work together for social justice for immigrant workers by challenging conditions immigrants face at work and the policies of government that are supposed regulate them.

Lessons and Implications

There are several important lessons and challenges that emerge from the experiences of the IWC and other similar centers. These organizations are new forms that give voice and some power to groups of immigrant workers, who have been the most marginalized group in the labor market. These community organizations and the related organizing and advocacy cross traditional boundaries of community work. With some exceptions, labor has been the domain of the union movement. With the changes described above, however, worker centers have been founded to counter the difficulties faced by unions in the restructured labor market. It is not only linking community and labor that is an important crossover, however. Organizations like the IWC have been able to bring together younger activists, who began their engagement with the anti-globalization movement, with older activists and immigrant workers. In this way, those involved in broader social and political questions can bring their energy and analysis into local activities. On the other side, these exchanges have brought the IWC closer to wider "movement" activities such as groups working to stop deportation of those without status or failed refugee claimants. This exchange broadens both, and brings the global and local together in a concrete way; it creates an exchange between activists from different generations and from different countries and traditions. Learning is a significant consequence for all involved, and the resulting alliances have grown out of these exchanges. One result is that the IWC, as with the revival of new forms of labor organizing in the United States, takes on elements of a wider social movement and is not limited to local work (Clawson 2003). The IWC, through its many activities, has become a place for building alliances and bringing together social actors who are promoting social and economic justice.

In the history of community organizing, there has often been a division between direct service and organizing. Many community organizations are pushed to provide direct service by their funders, and as a result their organizing activities become secondary. The IWC and other centers see individual service as a key way to attract people to their organizations, and often the issues brought in contribute to building collective action and campaigns (Delgado 1996, Gordon 2005). Because individual problems are based in a workplace, they are often shared by others and form the basis for collective action. Also, for an individual to step forward to challenge their boss on an issue of working conditions is an act of courage and is inherently political. In addition, campaigns for policy change grow out of individual experiences, such as the campaign to cover domestic workers under health and safety legislation, described above. For community organizing in general, service work with individuals can be a beginning point to initiate collective action.

Another dimension to the work of the IWC is that it sees cultural events as contributing to recruitment, building connections to other groups, and as a way to promote education and a critical social analysis. The International Women's Day, March 8 event, and MayWorks were deliberate attempts to use these events to promote a critical social analysis through the eyes and experiences of immigrants. The events have been successful, as well, for bringing diverse groups of activists to the same table to participate in planning and implementing the various activities. The March 8 event has succeeded in bringing issues faced by immigrant women to the forefront of the wider women's movement. In addition, it has broadened the issues traditionally discussed during activities held on that day. MayWorks event, mentioned previously, created a place where union representatives, younger activists, and immigrant workers could meet to plan a series of events. Cultural activities were used to discuss the politics of labor. The lesson is that cultural work is a tool for recruitment, alliance building, and political education.

In this period, many community organizations have turned away from the state and have developed a strategy of local self-reliance through market-driven solutions such as local or community economic development. Others have turned to local asset mobilization as a way of creating independent services based on the energy of volunteers (DeFilippis et al. 2006). Other groups have continued in the tradition of social action and mobilization but have targeted corporations in the private sector rather than making claims on the state (see the discussion of ACORN below). Similarly, worker organizing through unions prioritizes collective agreements with these employers. Organizations like the IWC recognize that it is impossible to organize directly in the workplace because of the precarious nature of many of the jobs of immigrant workers. Therefore, the target of their campaigns has been the state, demanding improvements in conditions for everyone at the bottom end of the labor market. Policy-oriented campaigns, such as those for improvements in labor standards or extending coverage of health and safety, demand state intervention. This is shared with other immigrant labor centers. The lesson here is that the state—whether municipal, provincial/state, or national—plays a central role in shaping social and economic conditions and should not be abandoned as a target, whether through legislative efforts (Gordon 2005), renewed community development (Fisher and Shragge 2001), or corporate campaigns.

Tensions

The organizing of immigrant labor has some barriers that are difficult to overcome. Most of the workers have difficult life situations either because of the demands of jobs, often multiple, in a household while raising children, or because they do not have regular status, so it is impossible for them to be part of a public movement for improving their conditions. It is important to see the connections between work and wider migrant justice issues in order to build a movement that argues if one works, one should have full rights. As it stands, there are immigrant workers who in theory have access to rights, and those who do not, with the latter creating a pool of cheap labor. The jobs of both groups are not stable in the context of contract labor, temp agencies, just-in-time production, and so forth. Further, the combination of these kinds of jobs and the demands of family life means that it is difficult to sustain member participation in organizations. In addition, it is dangerous for people without status to participate in public in formal organizational processes. People will participate in a campaign or in an action or an event, but given the complexity of individual lives, it is challenging to expect them to enlist in a formal membership structure.

Another tension is the relationship between trade unions and worker centers. The experience of the IWC is that this relationship is complex. Sometimes unions have been important allies both for financial support and as supporters in campaigns. At other times, unions have not adequately represented members, and the members have challenged them when this happens. Further, in-house unions created by employers have created blocks to both effective representation and organizing. In addition, the types of jobs in which immigrant workers are working are difficult for unions to organize. Moreover, with recent changes linked to the global recession, more and more workers will be "difficult" to organize into traditional unions. New approaches will be needed to find ways to represent and organize a working class whose jobs are fragmented by precarious work, part-time, and service-sector employment.

The last tension faced by community-based labor organizing is the limits of working at the local level. Most worker centers attract members on the basis of specific issues in the local market, and solidarity is derived from shared workplace, neighborhood, or ethic group (Fine 2006). Most of the forces faced by labor that block economic justice are much wider than local, however. The challenge is to build a wider movement, bringing centers together to form alliances with the trade unions and other movements, at the regional and national levels, that can raise policy issues beyond specific employers. State intervention to protect workers against the forces of a largely unregulated marketplace is the goal of this organizing. There have been some attempts to do this; for example, Living-Wage campaigns and IWC have brought coalitions together for specific campaigns. But given the power of global capital, broader-based cohesion is a necessary precondition to more successful challenges. If the long-term goal is to build a class-based movement to fight for workplace justice, then a combination of unionization and community-based strategies are necessary, with much greater emphasis on common purpose.

ACORN—Building a Grassroots and National Organization

ACORN, now known as the Association of Community Organizations for Reform Now, began in 1970 in Little Rock as the Arkansas Community Organizations for Reform Now, a single community-based effort. It has expanded during its forty years into a national, even international, organization. In 2008 ACORN claimed more than 400,000 member families in more than 1,200 neighborhood chapters in 110 cities in 40 states across the United States (Delgado 1986; Johnson 1999; ACORN Web site, www.acorn.org) Whereas the lifespan of such Alinsky-style community-based organizations was once said to be about six years, ACORN, along with efforts such as the Industrial Areas Foundation and other large networks of community-based organizing, have not only survived but developed significant organizations and organizing models. On first glance, this seems a curious development in an era of neoliberalism, an era that undermines progressive social change, not to mention social movement organizations such as ACORN. On the other hand, it is this very neoliberalism, with its devolution of state responsibility to the local level, its devolution of responsibility from the public sector to the "voluntary" and nonprofit sector, its destabilization of social networks, and its decimation of inner-city neighborhoods, which has created the opportunity and demand for community-based responses. That is the essential irony of this book, that at the very moment that it takes more than a village to address the vast restructuring taking place globally, people are forced back into community work to respond to their desperate conditions. They are told, not inaccurately, that community is the site of more opportunities, more free space for social change efforts to develop and maneuver.

In this paradoxical situation, some organizations have done impressive work under very difficult conditions. This is especially true of the national and regional networks of community organizing. Examples are the Industrial Areas Foundation (IAF), with its broad organizing in the Southwest and selected cities such as Baltimore, New York, and Chicago, as well as other large networks of community organizing such as PICO (People Improving Communities through Organizing), DART (Direct Action and Research Training Center), CTWO (Center for Third World Organizing), the Gamaliel Foundation, and others. On one level, the networks, including ACORN, seem cut from one cloth—progressive, neo-Alinsky community organizing—and, accordingly, share a great deal in common (Fisher 1994). For example, the community-organizing approach of all of them is grounded in a conflict, not consensus, model. ACORN is certainly not alone in continuing to pursue a conflict model, though it does seem the most noted for it and the most vigilant about it. In addition, these networks all look beyond the local, either to statewide, regional, or national initiatives. Aside from these and other shared aspects, the overall strategy, cultures, leadership, and degree of success in these network organizations differ in significant ways. For example, IAF, PICO, and Gamaliel use a congregation-based model of community organizing (CBCO) whereas ACORN uses a door-to-door, union-oriented, and membership mobilization model. The CBCOs offer a religious-oriented "value driven" model of organizing as distinct from ACORN's "secular model" (Hart 2001; Swarts 2008). Part of the differences between ACORN's organizing model and that of the other large networks relates to their different pasts.

ACORN, as we have said, has its roots in Alinsky-style organizing. It too focuses on the community as the locus and on poor, disenfranchised citizens as the agents of social change. It also shares with the early IAF a 1930s union model of organizing. ACORN's model is geared to building a strong organization of dues-paying members working together with gifted and committed community organizers. But ACORN, with roots also in the student movement and welfare rights organizing of the 1960s, has always seen itself more as a social movement organization, as part of a broader social movement. ACORN comes directly out of Wade Rathke's experience in national welfare rights organizing, which organized welfare recipients, primarily African American women, to challenge the limits and contradictions of the expanding welfare state of the late 1960s. Combining this experience with an analysis of the virtues as well as limits of the New Left and welfare rights organizing, ACORN developed a "majoritarian strategy" to target low- and moderate-income Americans, not just welfare recipients, in order to build a broader-based organization and contribute to a more effective mass movement.

The animus for ACORN was the same as that which undergirded an insurgent consciousness, oppositional tactics, and participatory politics throughout the world in the 1960s and 1970s. But the now highly complex organization has an eclectic style; its roots are in Alinsky-style organizing but it pursues a model from that of the heirs to Alinsky organizing. Its civil rights and youth movement culture capture mainstream pragmatism but also the rebellious activist aspects of the 1960s movement. Its union model bridges critical divides: between old and new social movements as well as community and labor organizing. Its "extra-parliamentary" grassroots politics, unlike most Alinsky organizing, intentionally links with an electoral strategy and campaigns. Also critical, it sees itself as part of a broader social movement for economic justice, whereas other community organizing efforts intentionally distance their organizations from contemporary social movements or activist causes. All of these and more have enabled ACORN not only to survive and persevere for nearly forty years but also to offer a distinctive organizing model.

Perhaps equally significant for our purposes, ACORN caught a second wind between 2002 and 2008, which enabled the organization to expand dramatically in terms of both the number of constituents and local chapters, as well as the projects and issues it addressed. For example, as recently as 2002, ACORN claimed chapters in 40 cities; in 2008 this was up to 110 cities. ACORN has always been about increasing organizational size and scale—expanding operations to include ACORN housing service, support for Working Family political parties in New York and Connecticut, massive voter registration efforts, ownership of two radio stations, operation of two public schools, and so on—but between 2002 and 2008 its expansion far exceeded prior periods of growth.

In a nutshell, ACORN's basic strategy combines a focus on neighborhood-based, door-to-door organizing in essentially low-income communities of African American and Latino residents, with an emphasis on direct-action tactics. The goal is to force targets, increasingly private sector ones but also public bodies, to address issues that concern the membership and win victories that build the organization and further broaden objectives of social, economic, and political justice. There is a deep pragmatic streak in the organization, similar to that of the IAF and the labor union movement. ACORN emphasizes that community work is heavily linked to the work of organizers and the task of organization building. For ACORN, it is about mobilizing both people and money. Mobilizing people and marshaling resources are essential to social struggle. But the work is not fundamentally about values, ideals, or relationships, which are the focus of more process-oriented and cultural-minded efforts such as the CBCOs. ACORN's culture is a counterculture, one of opposition and direct action to build power and win victories. Their counterculture is evident in the activism that characterizes the organization, observable in both staff and members, and is also evident in their "culture of scarcity" that influences everything in the organization, from salary of organizing staff to the appearance of most local offices. The money goes to hire organizers, win victories for neighborhood members, and focus on building the organization and furthering the cause of economic justice. It is evident in the organization's implicit and explicit critique of mainstream dominant institutions, structures, and power arrangements. And it is obvious in its effort to offer an oppositional alternative to ruling groups and the status quo.

Moreover, and especially critical to understanding the organization's import for this study, unlike most other community organizing efforts, including other national and regional networks, ACORN's model meshes dues-paying members in local chapters within a powerful national organization with strong national leadership and professional staff. Whereas the IAF's network in Texas has scored important statewide and even regional victories, ACORN has been much more effective in orchestrating successful national campaigns. Campaigns emanate from both the local and national levels, depending on the issue. For example, campaigns against predatory home mortgage loans bubbled up from the locals, whereas the campaign around refund anticipation loans came more from the national. ACORN's recent dramatic growth and public visibility around economic justice issues such as living wage, predatory financial practices, labor organizing, voter registration, electoral campaigns, and Hurricane Katrina's destruction of New Orleans derive from its hybrid structure, which enables it to coordinate campaigns and mobilize local resources on a national as well as local basis (Fisher 2009; Atlas 2005; Atlas and Dreier 2003). Until recently, ACORN had an organizational infrastructure that could engage at both the local and national levels, in communities in more than 110 cities as well as at worksites through their labor union initiatives, around local issues as well as national ones, including electoral campaigns. Unlike the dominant forms of moderated community practices discussed in chapters 3 and 4, ACORN is a conflict-oriented organization. They engage in protest to win victories. They also provide services through vehicles such as ACORN Housing in order to meet member needs and raise funds. They helped register more than one million voters in the 2008 presidential campaign, thereby playing a major, if indirect, role in the election of Barack Obama. They understand and act on the concept that it takes more than community-based initiatives to effect change. It also takes opposition to the status quo. By 2009, ACORN had become an important and powerful national effort, the largest community organization of disproportionately low-income members.

ACORN's perspective and practice transcend boundaries that limit other community efforts. The focus is always on building the organization, building greater power, mobilizing more people and funding. Their work is not constricted by dualisms that constrain other community organizing efforts such as local or national scale, service delivery or social action, grassroots or electoral activism, community or labor organizing, and interest group or social movement organization. This makes ACORN central to our argument about the limits of community-based initiatives and what is needed to address them. It also ties to a critical debate in the literature about social-movement organizations that are rooted at the local level but connected, in strategy and structure, to the national. For example, Palmer (1980) and Goodwyn (1978) argue that in the agrarian movement of the late nineteenth century, despite extraordinary success with local organizing, the limits of the strategy of democratic localism caused farmers to seek and implement a national solution: reform the state in order to meet local needs. Local efforts needed national scale and impact. Relatedly, as mentioned briefly before, Skocpol (2003) argues that purely national organizations, especially highly professional-run advocacy efforts based in Washington, D.C., such as Common Cause, have contributed to the deterioration of contemporary civic life at the local level. National organizations without democratic grassroots are terribly limited. She argues that what is needed are membership organizations that have active and vibrant local chapters with local participation, and a national structure that interacts with the locals and has synergistic power beyond the total impact of the local efforts.

There are obvious challenges and limits to ACORN's ability to balance a powerful national organization with democratic decision making, that is, to include opportunities for voice, participation, and decision making from the bottom up as well as the top down. This has been most evident in a financial scandal related to one million dollars embezzled more than a decade ago by Dale Rathke, ACORN's chief operating officer, which resulted in 2009 in the ousting and ostracizing of Dale Rathke's brother Wade Rathke, the founder and chief organizer. In addition to the scandal, not to mention funding cuts related to the economic crisis, ACORN was the target of a broad attack, first by the Republican Party during and especially since the election and then more recent attacks by right-wing and even mainstream media regarding voter registration and other irregularities. These public allegations and negative press reports resulted in a congressional effort to prevent ACORN from receiving any public funds, such as those for housing or census taking services. All of these developments hurt the organization. Its annual budget dropped from $35 million to $25 million, which means that

ACORN was forced to cut back on its size and activities. But it also resulted in pushing the organization to become more transparent in terms of fiscal matters and develop more formal structures and processes for democratic decision making. Nevertheless, these events aside, ACORN's combination of a local and national organizational infrastructure—its engagement of members at the local level in campaigns centered on "actions" against local and national targets, and its fee-based membership, which finances a small share of ACORN's work but remains a significant part of the organization's democratic culture (most of the funding now comes from foundation support, victories won with corporate targets, and service work)—all of these provide a countermodel of organizing that addresses the limits of the local community and combines the power of organizing at both local and national scales. The ACORN model challenges the myopia of most community efforts, the failure to go beyond the local in both their practice and their analysis, that undermines most contemporary, as well as historical, community organizations.

An example of a national/local campaign is in order. During 2004, ACORN conducted a national campaign funded by the Marguerite Casey Foundation against the financial service practices of H&R Block, the largest commercial tax preparation corporation in the nation. The campaign, building on ACORN's prior work around the democratic control of finance and capital, targeted Block's use and promotion of high-interest Refund Anticipation Loans (RALs) to recipients of the Earned Income Tax Credit. One goal of the campaign was to stop the financial industry from ripping off poor people; the most vulnerable and therefore targeted tax payers were people who were eligible for the Earned Income Tax Credit program and who were most likely to be in need of instant cash. ACORN's primary tactic was to hold highly visible protests—ACORN calls them "actions"—at H&R Block offices located in the same poor communities of people of color in which ACORN organizes. This mobilized members, built the organization, and gave a Fortune 500 company, one especially vulnerable during tax season, the bad press and public visibility corporations detest. Another goal was to win resources for ACORN, which would help strengthen the national organization and enable it to reward locals with additional funding after the successful campaign.

ACORN held national days of action during tax season, from January through mid-April, at which the local chapters turned out members to protest at Block offices against predatory practices. The first nationwide action occurred on January 13, 2004. On that day national ACORN organized "Don't Be a Blockhead" actions at forty-three different Block offices across the nation in neighborhoods where ACORN had local chapters (Christie 2004). They sought to engage their membership, get visibility in their local communities, and get H&R Block's attention as well as that of the media. They were successful on all fronts. For example, ACORN recorded that the first actions were covered by at least sixty-four media outlets. In a second nationally coordinated action, on January 31, ACORN members protested at fifty-five H&R Block offices, demanding that corporate officials from H&R Block meet with representatives of ACORN to negotiate an end to predatory RAL practices. Atlas and Dreier (2003) argue that "ACORN's most impressive attribute" is its membership structure, which enables it "to work simultaneously at the neighborhood, local, state and federal levels, so that its chapter members are always 'in motion' on a variety of issues, and so that its local organizations can link up with their counterparts around the country to change national policy on key issues that can't be solved at the neighborhood or municipal level." Furthermore, the national organization enhances organizational capacity beyond the local chapters. They got Block to the bargaining table within a month of their first national day of action, won resources from Block to fund ACORN's community work as well as a repeal of some fees associated with RALs, galvanized their membership around the local actions, and showed their ability to stage enough demonstrations nationwide to force a Fortune 500 company to negotiate.

For our purposes, what is so valuable in this modest campaign and the ACORN model of community activism is the demonstration of a contemporary organizing effort that blends democratic localism with national organization and leadership, in order to begin to have the clout and power necessary to challenge global corporations. Under neoliberalism, the forces of capital concentrate while the forces of production disperse. Corporations get bigger and bigger, centralizing their power and control, in order to eliminate competition and control markets. At the same time, the nature of production becomes increasingly decentralized and localized, with operations throughout the world, often weakly tethered to place. The forces of resistance mirror this deconcentration and fragmentation, except that they are increasingly grounded to local place and community. ACORN is unusual in its ability to blend the advantages of community organizing with the power and discipline of a national, mass-based organization that can lead, unite, and reward locals to join national campaigns.

Moreover, unlike most current community-based efforts, ACORN acts as though it has a broader perspective that seeks, as Koehler and Wissen put it in a discussion of urban social movements, to "fight the destructive influences which neoliberal globalization exerts on everyday life" and politicize these contradictions through organized "urban social conflict" (2003, 949). ACORN understands that the broad reach of multinational corporations under contemporary economic globalization requires at least a national network to hold actions, as they did against H&R Block, in more than fifty cities. They understand that in the past generation, but especially under the regime of George W. Bush, it was good strategy to target large corporations, not public agencies or officials, given the shift in power and resources under contemporary policies away from the public sector in general and urban areas and city officials in particular (Weir et al. 2005). They intentionally built an oppositional organization which, while it uses a broad variety of strategies and tactics, is fundamentally known for and successful with its direct action protests against targets that epitomize the social injustice inherent in neoliberal versions of contemporary political economy.

Tensions

With all its recent success and its opportunity to serve as an organizing model for efforts to build beyond the local and still sustain an oppositional politics, ACORN has its problems. Most obvious in 2009 is the problem of ACORN's success, which has angered opponents and brought down their wrath on the organization. Moreover, there is the tension between ACORN's expanding organizational size and scope and developing a transparent and democratic organizational structure. ACORN has always privileged its members at the local level, but not at the national one. As the organization expanded dramatically, especially since 2002, it is easy to conclude that prior antiquated fiscal and decision-making mechanisms needed to be updated. A sense of trust and mutual respect between staff and members permitted a talented national staff to run the national organization on a relatively informal basis. Once, however, problems of embezzlement and unilateral decision making surfaced, it became clear that the national infrastructure was being run too much like a family business and had outlived its value. This dissonance in organizational structure might be the result of many factors, including acquired informal traditions that developed with having to survive for forty years on meager resources. The forty-year-old "culture of scarcity," which has served the organization well, may also have resulted in management decisions that seemed right at the moment but were not in the long-term interest of the organization. Nevertheless, there are inherent tensions in complex organizational structures which combine a national organization and grassroots locals and members. Such tensions need to be addressed in organizational infrastructures that strike a better balance between transparency, accountability, and democratic decision making on the one hand, and efficiency, effectiveness, and innovation, on the other (Delgado 2009; Fisher 2009).

Second, if the organization is able to survive current attacks and restore its prior strength, ACORN could be more visionary, more explicit in its analysis of contemporary problems and solutions. ACORN is a product of the nonideological, highly pragmatic organizing model associated with Saul Alinsky, which instructs that at the worst vision and analysis are part of the problem, and are at the least something potentially divisive for which organizers do not have time. But one of the lessons of the Right has been to show the power of an ideological critique that serves as a galvanizing vision of contemporary society and conditions. One of the lessons of the recent past might be the limitations of ACORN's overly pragmatic side. It has served the organization well for decades, but it is not without drawbacks. For example, ACORN took an initial leadership role on issues of predatory lending of home mortgages, but when the financial disaster struck ACORN was relatively silent, due to various signed Memoranda of Understanding, which included no-protest pledges against predatory lenders and banks. Some would also argue that this is true of ACORN's support of a large-scale Ratner housing development plan in Brooklyn. A radical vision and analysis might have led the organization in a different direction in both cases. Perhaps not. It may be presumptuous for us to second guess the complex strategic decisions of an organization that has been as successful as ACORN and to which we are outsiders. Nevertheless, ACORN does not do as good a job as some other organizations in developing a more explicit analysis and critique that could galvanize membership and offer a broader, radical vision around which not only to mobilize and expand the organization but also unite the membership. They could share with people, members especially, an analysis of political economy and wealth redistribution in a more intentional manner. Better yet, they could develop a visioning process, which could help ACORN as it moves forward with a more open organizational structure. This process could include staff and members in developing a platform of analysis and goals, one that might provide direction from the bottom up on organizational priorities and initiatives, especially at the national level (Delgado 2009; Fisher 2009). Of course, such an analysis would probably bring even greater wrath from the Right. But we should keep in mind that the Right was very effective in its use of a mobilizing economic and social analysis, and so have other groups on the Left.

Third, to its credit, ACORN sees itself as a social movement organization and has roots in the social movements of the 1960s and beyond. ACORN is not hostile, as are some community organizations, to contemporary activists and movements. Still, if ACORN can regain its size, scope, and general prominence of the organization circa 2008, a greater focus on movement building might enable ACORN to play a significant role in a larger movement for economic justice. From the start, ACORN, like most community organizations, focused on its own development. It did not have resources to look much beyond its own borders. In recent years, it has sought to work with others in coalitions and even built efforts, such as the Living Wage Resource Center, which helps advance not only ACORN's living wage movement but also other social justice groups without direct affiliation with ACORN (Luce 2009). Given ACORN's size and prominence, perhaps there is an opportunity to engage in social movement building, which would include developing more bridges with allies less powerful than ACORN. That would be a major boon to any potential economic and social justice movement in the next decade, and could serve as a model of how community organizations can contribute beyond the local to a national, even global, movement-building effort.

IN THIS CHAPTER, we have presented examples of practices and organizations that work for social and economic justice. All of the organizations have been in existence for at least nine years and one for forty, and have been able to work locally but with a wider vision than most community organizations due to their analyses, emphasis on power, and inclusion of conflict. We have not written about these and similar organizations to celebrate them or to deny their tensions and limitations, but to highlight their work and their successes. There is a continuing legacy of conflict-based organizing for social and economic justice, despite the general direction of community-based work that we have presented throughout this book. In the next chapter, we will draw out some lessons and possibilities for the emergence of a radical practice, both from these organizational examples and from the overall critique in this book, which have increased relevance for the current period.

CHAPTER 6

Radicalizing Community

WE WRITE THE CONCLUSION for this book in the midst of a crisis of global capitalism and of the neoconservative and neoliberal strategies that have dominated the world stage for the past thirty years. We are in an historical moment in which grassroots-led social change has become a possibility again. Even when the right-wing ideologies and related policies seemed impenetrable, critics and activists underscored the contradictions inherent in the hegemonic context. Thankfully and predictably, neither hegemony nor context is permanent. The global economic crisis that began in 2008 has become the backdrop for what seems to be a shift away from unquestioned market primacy and state devolution. Unbridled capitalism has exposed itself for the self-indulgent and disastrous force it can be. The question now becomes what forms of political and economic relations will be created in the wake of this crisis. And this question is not being asked by just academics; massive mobilizations about the crisis and its impacts have challenged politics as usual in Greece, Iceland, France, China, and elsewhere. As the crisis has deepened in North America and the United Kingdom, it creates possibilities amid much hardship.

We are not, however, naïve about the prospects of change. Crisis can result, as with the origins of neoliberalism in the 1970s, in simply new forms of a reasserted class power. And crises can, and certainly do, bring about surges in reactionary and xenophobic (usually anti-immigrant) politics and social movements. But neither are we pessimistic about contemporary prospects. The lessons of this book are timelier than we ever expected. If, as we argue, context plays a significant role in theory and practice, at both the community level and beyond, then the potential change in context calls forth opportunities as well as challenges for contemporary organizing. The opportunity exists for the development of new theories and practices in and about community efforts. The perspectives that presume the superiority of the market have been demonstrated to be bankrupt intellectually and morally. Making the case for forms of community effort that recognize the limitations and failures of neoliberal policies has become easier in the contemporary context.

And yet, even if the neoliberalism of the post-1980s world is newly vulnerable and more open to contestation, community-based efforts continue to be embedded in a form of global capitalism in which the primary arbiter of social relations, processes, and outcomes is the market. It is certainly not a given that neoliberalism will be replaced. Nor is it a given that we will see different forms of capitalism, let alone a non-capitalist alternative political economy, emerge from the crisis. Therefore the central premise of this book remains unaltered. Communities are vitally important, but inherently limited, arenas for social change and social change organizations. The limited capacity of community remains, as does its centrality. Accordingly, the debate over the place of community in social change should continue to locate both the possibilities and limits of practice at its core. Community organizations can be a part of a wider force of social and political opposition and can make claims to redress social inequality and injustice. In order to do so, however, those organizations which aspire to greatest impact have to raise their consciousness, situate themselves in the broader social struggles, and understand the underpinning ideologies and analysis, as well as the stakes involved and the contemporary opportunities of the present moment.

Below, we advance a series of six propositions that capture the central lessons of this book. We present these as a way to advance theory and practice, and to push debates about the potential role of communities and community organizing in the struggle for progressive social change. We do not see the propositions as utopian. We do not claim to be providing a definitive guide to contemporary community organizing, one appropriate for all types of community organizations in all types of settings. We are not convinced such a guide can be done well, and therefore we have not set out to do so here. Rather we propose steps that have been, and can be, developed and for which there are historical precedents and current examples of each.

UNDERSTAND THE IMPORTANCE
OF COMMUNITY

Our first proposition is a fairly simple one: in order for people working in communities to realize the potential within communities, they must first properly understand that potential—and its limits. As we have already stated, we find ourselves in an ambiguous position. We are advocates for and participants in community-based organizing and development efforts, but also theorists who are keenly aware of both the political limits to community in the contemporary political economy and the problems of power relations and oppression within communities—which make community a dubious goal in and of itself. And yet, we remain hopeful about community. This is for several reasons.

First, we understand that communities and local organizations are not inherently Left or Right, progressive or reactionary. The political meanings and trajectories of community organizations are not written in the first instance, but emerge from their analyses, issues, struggles, strategies, and tactics. In ways similar to how E. P. Thompson conceptualized class as "making itself," community is created through the practices of individuals, organizations, and institutions (Lustiger-Thaler 1994). This is not, by any means, to reject the important limitations placed on communities by their structural context or the language and invocation of community *for itself*. Rather we would argue that the space is there for people concerned with social change to claim and make, if they are willing, able, and moved to do so.

Second, our perspective is not limited to the experiences of the last couple of decades. The history of grassroots organizing and social movements, upon whose shoulders current efforts stand—or should stand—provides a collective memory of efforts that successfully challenged oppression and injustice and expanded political, social, and economic democracy.

Third, there are organizations currently out there doing work in communities that are oriented toward radical change. These are organizations that are continuing in the long tradition of using community-based organizing to try to effect social change that gets at the structural roots of contemporary problems. Our arguments are not being made in a vacuum of ivory-tower critique, but with the recognition that organizations are applying and have already applied many of the same principles and ideas to practice in their communities.

These brief examples from the past and present underscore the fact that despite internal and external challenges to community, such work remains integral to social change. Without rehashing the arguments laid out in chapter 1, we argue that the community is a central realm in the organization of the larger political economy. It is where we live, and build many—if not most—of our most significant social relationships. And it is also where labor is produced and reproduced, and where political meanings and understandings of the world take root. These are not, by any means, small components of life. Although much of the book is critical of how community is used and promoted, concepts such as community organizing and community building have importance. Building local organizations based on a sense of solidarity and belonging is an essential step in the creation of a broad social movement that has strong local roots. Local work in community organizations or trade unions that looks beyond the traditional boundaries of these organizations creates a base from which larger movements and campaigns can grow. Without the local work, the wider efforts cannot be sustained and will ultimately be without a base of either members or place.

But the analyses and understandings that currently inform most community efforts are problematic. In short, they are both too ambitious and too modest. They are too ambitious because they turn inward, into local efforts that inherently assume community problems are rooted in the characteristics of the community (and the people and organizations that constitute the community). That leads to community organizations promising too much, and thereby setting themselves up to fail, and disappoint funders and others who wonder why community-based efforts "don't work." But they are also, and conversely, too modest, in that they implicitly downplay the potential role community-based efforts can play in changing the larger political economy. In so doing, they lose sight of the fact that while communities may not be able to control the local-level manifestations of larger social problems, they can be a central part of changing the larger-scale social problems in the first place.

ORGANIZE BEYOND COMMUNITY

Our second proposition, which comes logically out of the first, is that community-based efforts need to understand their work as transcending the community. We see the political potential from community emerging when there is an emphasis on working "within a place," rather than "about a place." The focus of too much of the theory and practice in the contemporary world has been on community as solely "about a place." It is limited by boundaries, usually geographic but sometimes based on identity or specific interest. Local activities are thereby limited to local processes, and there is little interest in going beyond these boundaries.

In contrast to this position, we suggest that an understanding of community should be "within a place." Local work is the starting point, but it is not the ultimate goal. The community as a geographic place serves as a point of entry, but the effective community organization understands that the issues go beyond the local. While all the organizations in chapter 5 focus on local/community-based social change, they also understand that social and economic problems cannot be addressed in any substantial way solely through local work. Therefore community-based efforts must address and confront issues and problems within a community *and* create linkages beyond the local. If there are not these kinds of connections, community organizations will not be able to engage in anything beyond working to improve, in a limited way, local conditions.

Integrated into community practice must be an analysis of the context of a community organization's work. And fundamental to this analysis is an understanding of the limits of local work and the need to build an analysis that connects local work with wider social, economic, and political forces. For example, the Immigrant Workers Center understands migration as linked to all of these forces, globally. This helps the staff understand the multiple dimensions of issues as well as the importance of connecting with other organizations locally and internationally on issues related to migrant justice. ACORN has been able to examine how large corporations such as H&R Block have an impact on local communities and, equally important, ACORN has a national structure that can mobilize local power and challenge economic exploitation within and beyond the local community. ACORN's recent plan to join other efforts in blocking foreclosures and coordinating a national response to foreclosure evictions demonstrates the potential of radical organizing at the local level and beyond. These efforts began at the local level by other groups, such as City Life/Vida Urbana in Boston. ACORN, with its national organization and its presence in

110 cities, proposes to extend this critique of and opposition to exploitative corporate practices beyond the local community and give it more national visibility and power. At the same time, all of our organizational examples in chapter 5 were chosen, in part, because they recognize the importance of local work as essential to the process of building power.

Community organizations need to understand their work in a larger context in a threefold manner. First, given that the conditions in communities are the products of larger-scale social forces and processes, there are real and significant limitations to what can be achieved solely through a focus on internal community-scale issues. The scale, in short, is insufficient to solve the problems because the problems themselves exist due to processes that operate at larger scales. Second, in a politically hostile or reactionary context, internally focused social reform can seem like revolutionary work. But unless organizations are outward-looking, insofar as their efforts have a focus that includes and goes beyond the local, they are often just providing modest relief that legitimizes the larger system. That is, by staying within the community, the larger system remains unchallenged. The cliché of "think globally, act locally" is an extremely disempowering one because it discourages action beyond the local. Third, and emerging directly from the first two, is the problem that focusing community-based work solely on the level of the community enables—encourages, even—a blaming of the victim of larger-scale problems. That is, if community-focused work is predicated on the ability to solve problems locally, then the inability to solve those problems locally (which is inevitable, since those problems are not themselves rooted in any individual community) becomes a very useful way for critics to blame poor and marginalized communities for their own poverty and marginalization. Thus not only are the larger institutions of the private and public sectors let off the hook, but the communities themselves become the object of blame for failures evident within those communities.

EMPHASIZE CONFLICT AND POWER

Our third proposition is that if community organizations must remain focused on processes and structures that occur beyond their community, so too must they maintain a full range of strategies and tactics from which to draw upon in their work. If their goal is make things better in their community, then a proper understanding of the causes of the conditions in their community must include a recognition that social change is needed to ultimately make things better. And for social change to happen, conflict over power must be a key orienting direction of community organizing. The organizations we discussed in chapter 5 understand that conflict is central to their practice. This does not mean that all or even most of their activities are confrontational, but rather that conflict is part of an analysis, an overarching strategy, and a tactic to obtain desired results. With the struggle over power relations at their core, conflict is expressed in several ways.

First, in practice, conflict defines who is the opposition. It defines who benefits from the current set of power relations, and thereby is in a position to deliver the changes demanded. It also means understanding what is necessary to mobilize against those who are in positions of power. The specific tactics can vary from street-level actions to lobbying officials, but at the core there is a we/they dynamic in place, at least on the specific issues being contested.

Second, conflict is expressed through the analysis of social issues. For example, organizations must understand that power relations and structurally rooted interests are central, and problems emerge because of unequal power relations. Therefore, political education and analysis is a key part of their activities. Organizations need to be asking questions of who benefits and why, when issues are confronted. Organizing is a means of challenging structural power, whether it is based on class, gender, race, or sexuality. We recognize that stating things so starkly and nakedly is decidedly unfashionable, and that much of contemporary academic and community work masks analyses of power, runs away from conflict, and turns to partnerships in unequal power relations in the name of pragmatism. The idea of power relations being transformed and made more equitable through organizing disappears in both how these groups act and how they analyze power. But this, we would argue, is a fundamental reason why the gap between those who are in positions of power and those who are not has grown so dramatically in the last thirty years.

Third, conflict can be built into organizational practice not only through direct conflictual relations with those in positions of power but also through the creation of alternative practices that challenge dominant ones. Examples are the wide array of popularly or democratically run organizations that embody the creation of social and economic alternatives, such as cooperatives, or alternative services such as feminist-oriented health services and domestic-violence shelters. These can be understood as entering into conflict with dominant practices by developing institutions with alternative values and practices such as participatory democratic control. We see these as connecting the alternative to the oppositional (see Raymond Williams in DeFilippis 2004, 149). The challenge for oppositional organizations is to sustain this stance over time, that is, to keep their vision over the long term. Many organizations have a conflict perspective in their origins, just as many originate as part of a social movement, but this dimension is lost over time—particularly in a political economic context that is fundamentally hostile. In a recent study of the birth of the neighborhood movement in the 1970s, for example, Suleiman Osman (2008) argues that by 1975 the decline of dissent and conflict in these efforts led to their becoming instruments of conservative politics. Understanding community work as contested activity over power is a fundamental building block to creating social change.

The significance for contemporary practice is clear. Conflict against enemy targets that further economic, political, and social injustice is not something to be discouraged or feared. Proponents of communitarian ideas and practices argue that, in the face of the current economic crisis, now is the time for all to come together, to build connections in defense of our common community and common interests. They would propose, as does President Obama, who articulates many communitarian sentiments, that we need to rebuild the economy together and that partisan political attacks will only undermine progress. But a conflict perspective underscores that the causes of our crisis rest in those who were all too willing to exploit others, and from those too quick to disregard such exploitation, and that these groups remain more or less steadfast in support of highly individualistic ideas and elite interests. It underscores that the divisions and oppressions of class, race, and gender that existed before the crisis still exist. It emphasizes that community efforts must struggle against the ideas and practices of neoliberalism as well as the corporate elites, right-wing organizations, and free-market supporters who foisted their agenda and interests on the world. The enemies of the past have not retreated. The anti-canon that they represent will keep surfacing and setting back the trajectory and speed of progressive gains if it is not targeted as a primary cause of our problems, and if it is not defeated.

Organizers and community organizations should be angry over what Piven and Cloward (1979) referred to as the "new class war" of the past thirty years. Community efforts should target the corporate elites and right-wing efforts that with great audacity will undoubtedly seek to benefit and regain power from the crisis they created. Ernesto Cortes, lead organizer for the IAF in the American Southwest, likes to note that people should be angry about injustice, and by anger he refers to the Norse origins of the word, *angr*, which means "social grief." That is, anger is not individual anger or rage but collective anger over what has been done to society, anger over a social problem or injustice. Community efforts in our current context need to keep this conflict perspective, need to understand the legitimacy and importance of social anger, need to keep putting pressure on progressive regimes to not be afraid of challenging opponents. Of course, building new relationships around current challenges should not be discounted. Hegemony is not permanent, and neither are people's interests or politics. But dealings with prior enemies must come from a position of power and opposition to antidemocratic forces, not a desire for partners and a seat at their table.

UNITE COMMUNITY AND SOCIAL MOVEMENT EFFORTS

Our fourth proposition is that although community organizing efforts and social movements are almost always treated as different species, both in the literature and by practitioners, we think a critical element in moving toward a new theory and practice of local work is recognizing their common origins and elements, as well as seeing them as parts of the same overall social struggle. Social movements almost always start out as local efforts but, if the conditions and issues are right, they metamorphose into movements that are far greater than the sum of their parts. Similarly, local efforts often start out as parts of or offspring of social movements, but a change in conditions or problems in the movement usually encourages more local effort. The two clearly take on different forms and appearances, and play different roles in the struggle for social change. But we see them as highly interconnected, and offer this proposition to emphasize that for the purposes of developing new theories and strategies of community organizing, the two need each other. Accordingly, we propose that outward-looking community efforts should consider movement-building practices as well as building connections with existing, broader social movements. And social movements, if they seek greater and more long-term success, must understand the need for an active base in local communities in order to contest power effectively and to bring demands for social justice forward with the possibility of victories. Our study and observation of social change underscores how critical community and movement efforts are to each other.

This is not to suggest that the relationships between social movements and local community organizations are not complex and filled with tensions. There is a built-in strain between much contemporary community-organizing and movement-building practice, which we do not want to downplay. It is not just a case of local efforts being open to social movement efforts. In their daily work the two—community organizing and social movement activity—can seem quite different, depending, of course, on the community organizing effort and the social movement. For example, social-movement practices focus on the larger cause and building connections with other allies. They are usually multiheaded, informally organized efforts, not single organizations with formal structures. They are inherently unstable and episodic, with beginnings, peaks, and declines; to some commentators they seem more like a wave than a mountain, let alone a political organization (Zemsky and Mann 2008). On the other hand, community efforts are almost exclusively about building their organization, delivering a needed service, or, in the case of community economic development, completing a project. They focus on building a base, identifying issues and potential leaders, and teaching democratic process, whereas social movements focus on reaching out to other organizations to advance a cause or attract large numbers of individuals to engage in different forms of activities that tend to focus on a particular issue or set of related issues. Some of the leaders of large community-organizing networks in the United States, such as the IAF, think that the only good work occurs day to day at the local level. They mistrust the work and ideals of movement "activists," who they see as disconnected from real communities and mass-based, on-the-ground organizing. They fear, not without some basis, the dissipation of scarce resources on movement causes that do not show results or do not build their organization—or, worse yet, could even divide their membership.

But there has always been a dialectical relationship between social movements and community organizations. History shows us that local organizing gives birth to, galvanizes, and sustains social movements, such as the labor, civil rights, women's, or gay movements. There is not a logical progression for grassroots work to evolve into larger efforts; usually they just remain local. That is a major point of this book. But when connected to a social movement, that dynamic can change. Historically, social movements begin in local social-movement organizations such as an organizing committee, but truly burst onto the scene on a larger scale. These larger-scale interventions fuel local efforts, providing more power, sparking and giving confidence to an oppositional imagination, legitimizing claims and grassroots work, and sustaining and galvanizing community efforts. Relatedly, local/community efforts often start out as social movements, whether the "backyard revolution" of the 1970s that followed on the heels of the antiwar and student movements (Boyte 1980; Fisher 1994), or the origins of local feminist consciousness-raising groups as a product of both the New Left and civil rights movements (Evans 1979). Sometimes social movements begin at a larger level and work their way down. For example, the peace and disarmament movement in the 1980s put itself on the political landscape by organizing huge national and international demonstrations. Following them and supporting subsequent demonstrations, work on the local level included the promotion of nuclear-free zones and other campaigns that brought local organizations to the wider movement.

Problems ensue when community and movement efforts ignore each other. The "anti-corporate globalization movement" emerged in the 1990s with many groups and smaller movements coming into the streets. It was filled with potential. The year 2000 was even dubbed "the year of global protest" (Bello 2001). The movement was undercut by the repression associated with September 11, 2001, along with the shift of some of the organizations toward antiwar efforts. Nevertheless, the failure of the movement to be a current force, despite the widespread crisis of global capitalism—a crisis that the movement's critique of global capitalism largely predicted—results in part from the movement's failure to work extensively with community organizations and plant local roots (Axel-Lute 2000; DeFilippis 2001b; Fisher and Shragge 2001). On the other hand, in terms of the threat of ignoring each other, contemporary community organizing networks that do not include social movement building in their work can often be found in turf battles with comparable movements with whom they share a great deal in common and with whom an alliance would advance movement building. Or they can be found disregarding social movement activists for their lack of "real" community organizing.

Clearly context matters. In Left/Liberal contexts, movements and local organizing overlap, each influencing the other. Community organizing efforts find a second wind with the emergence of a broad, progressive social movement, as Alinsky's community organizing, more or less dormant in the 1950s, did in the 1960s and 1970s as a result of the civil rights and black power movements (Horwitt 1989). In Right/Conservative eras, such as the period since 1980, the overall New Right movement, with its economic and social and cultural bases, brought forth organizations such as the Christian Coalition, just as local and national efforts strengthened the right-wing movement. The very community development and community organizing efforts in North America which are the focus of this book exhibited clear overlaps between their local work and the wider urban social movements of the 1970s (Newman and Lake 2006). For example, one of the common links between the development of local organizing and the new social movements of the 1970s was the presence of New Left movement activists, who decided to work in neighborhoods as a strategy for social change (Hamel 1986, 1991; Shragge 2003). Finally, there is one critical tension to which we would like to call attention. It is an intellectual barrier that participants may not espouse as theory but that serves as a common explanation or supposition about the relationship between social movements and local organizing that gets in the way of understanding and improving relationships and connections between the two. This is the opposition by social-movement activists to organization building, and their preference for using spontaneous rebellion, large-scale popular education, and mobilization as their basic tactics. Some have contributed to this position by arguing that historically organization building by movements demobilizes and destroys the movement, channeling activism and the initial animus into organization building and, worse, organizational maintenance (Piven and Cloward 1979; Gittell 1980). This happens, but more because of the politics and weaknesses of the social movements, or the power of their adversaries, than to some predetermined "iron law of oligarchy" (Michels 1915). Obviously activists, organizers, and other participants need to better understand and act on what divides, as well as unites, community organizations and social movements.

CRITICAL ANALYSIS AND POLITICAL EDUCATION ARE IMPORTANT

Our fifth proposition stems from the fact that the dominant traditions of community organizing and their related organizations tend to focus their work on winning short-term gains or finding limited ways to ameliorate social conditions. We propose that for community organizations to be part of a wider, larger-scale, and longer-term movement for social change, social analysis as well as its dissemination through political education are critical. Both contribute to understanding that the specific gains made and the struggles organizations undertake are part of something larger, but so is the broader political economy that structures organizational choices. Within the neoliberal context, there has been a tendency for community organizations to back away from making demands not only on corporations that engineer neoliberalism but also on the state. Economic globalization has profited the few at the expense of our communities, especially poor and minority communities. At the same time, community efforts have become an active ingredient of state policy, and neoliberal policies reduce the role of the state in certain spheres. Thus the analysis of the relationship between community, corporations and private capital, and the state becomes of critical importance. The implication of contemporary theory and practice is that community organizations "deresponsibilize" both the state and the market. In so doing, the importance of state intervention to either regulate the market or provide programs to improve social and economic conditions is lost from view. One of the consequences has been to reduce demands on the state for improvements and greater regulation of the market from community organizations.

Clearly, one of the barriers to long-term change, in addition to the basic power relations inherent in the system, is the pragmatic and adaptive strategy of community work, which, without naming a radical politics, undermines a longer-term and more fundamental social change. Shragge (2003) argues that community work has underlying intentions or political goals. The dominant perspectives, regardless of whether they are action, development, or service, aim at social integration. They seek to bring people and organizations closer to the mainstream, whether at the individual level as workers or consumers, or at the organizational level. Fisher (1994) talks about ideologies that shape community practice which cover the political spectrum—reactionary, conservative, liberal, and radical—as a way to name the underlying beliefs of different organizing efforts. Much of his book is based on a debate between liberals who work "to promote social changes that do not challenge the existing class and economic system" (xxiii) and radicals who do. He concludes his book by calling for organizing to create democratically a more intentional ideological practice, one that can help galvanize organizations and build a social movement.

But what kind of analysis is most appropriate and best suited for contemporary conditions? Community organizing needs to name its politics and name the problem. And community organizations, when working on and often achieving specific and short-term gains for particular people, too often do not convey a broader and longer-term perspective on organizing. They fail to adequately ask and answer basic questions such as: What is the organization's vision? What are its politics? Who and what do they see as the fundamental problem, and what, more or less, is the overall solution?

Given the current political-economic context, it is important for organizations to build an analysis of political economy and how it relates to the structures of economic inequality and inequities, growing poverty and unemployment, middle- and working-class downward mobility, and related issues. Properly understood, we would argue that the causes of these problems are rooted in the exploitative dimensions of contemporary capitalism, and the state enables, produces, and reproduces the political-economic system. Even our focus on neoliberalism runs the risk of obscuring the fact that what makes neoliberalism so damaging to poor and politically marginal people is that it is a nakedly ruthless and unregulated form of capitalism—a so-called free market stripped of the supports to individuals and communities that had been built up over generations as a result of earlier manifestations of the destruction of the free market. As the economies of countries like Canada, the United States, and the United Kingdom deteriorate, the issues of income, work, and poverty have reemerged as the key questions of our time.

Historically, analyzing problems and structures and proposing alternatives has been the forte of the Left, although this is less so for community organizations, many of which still think they must be "nonideological." It is well past time to break free of the limitations imposed on community organizations by the goals of being nonideological and nonpolitical, and for them to take their place in the great tradition of examining the world as it is, and using that analysis to imagine and help create a better world.

This raises the question of agency, that is, who will be the agent of change, the basis of the movement. The main sources of mobilization around demands for economic and social justice have been class-based, often through unions and wider social movements based on race and gender. As we have discussed, there is a complex, but potentially mutually reinforcing relationship between local work and wider movements. Local work through community organizations, particularly those that have a tradition of organizing, is an important place for education, leadership, and mobilization of these and related questions. In the current contexts, both unions and social movements are relatively weak. Organizations such as ACORN, immigrant worker centers, some of the unions that are trying to expand their membership, and community organizations working on issues such as the environment, feminism, and gay rights—that is, those which are willing to engage in explicitly political practices—are the basis for new alliances that have a local base, a commitment to action and education, and an analysis of the wider political economy. These are the ingredients that can contribute to building a program and a force to push governments to implement a change in direction. At the core is local work in a context of a wider political and social agenda.

Context is ever changing; the analysis of political economy is not absolute. Organizing locally will be shaped by broader changes, which create new opportunities and constraints. If the global economy falls into deeper recession, opportunities may be there for local organizations both to build from this type of analysis and to work toward a program of action on issues of economic justice. Choosing issues that touch the everyday lives of people is a critical antidote to short-term utilitarianism. These issues should be formulated in understandable and winnable demands that raise issues about the economic context—including the roles of class, capital, and the state—and include an analysis of the possibilities for broad-based alliance building.

Building power for the long term requires informed and critical leaders and members/participants within the organization and community. Learning and education within community organizations are often ignored, or education is limited to specific skills. Political education is the basis for unmasking the central issues of power and inequality in the system and building a longer-term vision and political culture. There are many levels. The first is the learning that people gain in engaging in action. This is often experiential, growing from their everyday lives. Critical reflection contributes to greater awareness of the interconnection between the specific issues in which an organization is engaged and the wider political economy (Church et al. 2008). One of the limits of organizations like ACORN that are linked to the Alinsky tradition is their belief that they always have to have an issue that is on the front burner. The consequence is that the educational dimensions, the ongoing activities that build oppositional communities, and that contribute to a long-term vision, can become lost. A balance between organizing, mobilizing, and education can lift the necessity of always looking for the next issue and help build critical, analytic leadership. This in turn can radicalize the program of organizations, as the base itself gains confidence in its ability to build a critical consciousness. Combining ongoing education and naming the politics within community as well as national organizing and beyond contribute to the possibility of making the local a place of critical opposition that can mobilize within a broader national organization and movement for social and economic justice.

MAKE HISTORY

Our sixth and final proposition is that history is made by ordinary people in multiple ways and at multiple scales—that is, both by the powerful, who make most of the decisions, and those who choose to make history by challenging their received world (Flacks 1988). This book is about what we see as the dominant means and the primary locus of contemporary history making, the local geographic or cultural community. The local community was not always the primary locus and agent for change, but it certainly has been since the 1960s.

The history of community efforts is more than "just history," something to be recognized, maybe even referenced, but dead nevertheless. It is something more than a history removed from contemporary needs and opportunities. History serves the present and future in many critical ways, including providing a collective memory of prior struggles, strategies, victories, and defeats. It offers an instant comparative perspective with the present, filled with lessons for those with interest and time. One of the critical lessons from the past emphasized in *Contesting Community* is the powerful role played by the broader political-economic context. These structural factors heavily influence the opportunities and limits, the potential success and constrained barriers that shape contemporary community practices. On the one hand, there is no escaping these forces of history, and the sooner community efforts learn their importance the quicker they understand what is to be done to affect them. On the other hand, historical context is not a closed, overdetermined system, with community organizations playing out a narrow role of maintaining the system and making it livable.

After asserting the importance of human agency in the struggle for social justice, it is essential to keep in mind how difficult the struggle has been and how quickly opportunities are closed by those in power. Cloward and Piven (1999) assert that throughout the twentieth century, for example, there were only two five-year periods, 1933–1938 and 1963–1968, when significant gains were won. The rest of the time, progressive forces were either back on their heels, treading water, or planting seeds. This analysis does not highlight gains made by other history makers, including movement activists, trade union members, and left political formations, who struggled in all those other ninety years in the past century around so many other causes. But the gains during the ten years were definitely transformative ones, where the national political economy and especially the national state were forced to expand the social welfare system, engage in redistributionist politics, and support the broad struggles for human rights and inclusion. The authors were clearly drawing a historical lesson, more than detailing history making. And the lesson remains worth repeating.

People make history when they challenge the existing power and when the times are right. But those right times are few and far between, and they do not last very long. Community organizing has a critical role to play in the United States, United Kingdom, and Canada, and this current economic crisis offers a window of opportunity that students and makers of history should recognize and make the most of. We see the current moment as filled with potential, but only if people act. On the other hand, whether major or minor gains are made in the present, the potential shift underway that began with the economic crisis and the presidential election in the United States should play itself out for the near future, either reversing neoliberal policies of the past thirty years or reforming its gross excesses. Still, the future of democracy and the egalitarian project depends on left opposition. Mary Ellen Lease, in a similar historical moment, working with American agrarian populists, is said to have challenged her fellow history makers to "raise less corn and more hell." It was an idea and strategy in the finest traditions of democratic dissent. It would do us all well to heed the varied lessons of the past, understand history better, and seek to become the history makers feared by those who have controlled the forces of history for more than a generation.

BIBLIOGRAPHY

ACORN. 2004. ACORN Actions. Unpublished reports from local chapters on H&R Block campaign actions in January, 2004.

ACORN. 2006. Annual report, 2005.

Agnew, John. 1987. *Place and Politics: The Geographical Mediation of State and Society.* Boston: Allen and Unwin.

Amin, Ash. 2005. "Local Community on Trial." *Economy and Society* 34(4): 612–633.

Anderson, Bridget. 2000. *Doing the Dirty Work? The Global Politics of Domestic Labour.* London: Zed Books.

Atlas, John. 2005. "Out of the Past: What Anti-poverty Groups Can Learn from the American Legion." *Tikkun* 20(4): 41–45.

Atlas, John, and Peter Dreier. 2003. "Enraging the Right." *Shelterforce Online* 129. http://www.nhi.org/online/issues/129/ACORN.html.

Axel-Lute, Miriam. 2000. "Back to the Streets: Why Community Developers Should Join the Fight against Corporate Globalization." *Shelterforce,* May/June, 14–19.

Bardone, Cheryl. 1996. "Asset Management: Chicago Communities Find Hidden Strengths." *Neighborhood Works,* January/February.

Baybeck, Brady, and Scott McClurg. 2005. "What Do They Know and How Do They Know It?: An Examination of Citizen Awareness of Context." *American Politics Research* 33(4): 492–520.

Beck, Nancy, and Lindley Higgins. 2001. *Building Neighborhoods of Choice: A Workbook on Marketing Neighborhoods and Affordable Ownership Housing.* New York: Local Initiatives Support Corporation.

Bello, Walden. 2001. "2000: The Year of Global Protest." *International Socialism,* Spring, 71–77.

Bendick, Marc, and Mary Lou Egan. 1991. *Business Development in the Inner-City: Enterprise with Community Links.* New York: Community Development Research Center, New School for Social Research.

Benjamin, Walter. 1969. "Theses on the Philosophy of History." In Walter Benjamin, *Illuminations.* New York: Schocken.

Berger, Peter L., and Richard John Neuhaus. 1996 [1977]. *To Empower People.* 2nd ed. Washington, D.C.: American Enterprise Press.

Berger, Renee, and Carol Steinbach. 1992. *A Place in the Marketplace: Making Capitalism Work in Poor Communities.* Washington, D.C.: National Congress for Community Economic Development.

Berry, Margaret. 1999. "Service and Cause: Both Sides of the Coin." In Jack Rothman, ed., *Reflections on Community Organization: Enduring Themes and Critical Issues*, 106–122. Itasca, Ill.: F. E. Peacock.

Bevington, Douglas, and Chris Dixon. 2005. "Movement Relevant Theory: Rethinking Social Movement Scholarship and Activism." *Social Movement Studies* 4(3): 185–208.

Bockmeyer, Janice. 2003. "Devolution and the Transformation of Community Housing Activism." *Social Science Journal* 40(2): 175–188.

Boyte, Harry. 1980. *The Backyard Revolution: Understanding the New Citizen Movement*. Philadelphia: Temple University Press.

Bradley, Ann. 1992. "Christian Activists Score Gains in San Diego County." *Education Week*, November 18, 12.

Bradley, Bill. 1998. "America's Challenge: Revitalizing Our National Community." In E. J. Dionne, ed., *Community Works: The Revival of Civil Society in America*, 107–116. Washington, D.C.: Brookings Institution Press.

Breines, Wini. 1982. *Community and Organization in the New Left, 1962–1968: The Great Refusal*. New Brunswick: Rutgers University Press.

Brenner, Neil. 2004. *New State Spaces: Urban Governance and the Rescaling of Statehood*. New York: Oxford University Press.

Brenner, Neil, and Nik Theodore, eds. 2002. *Spaces of Neoliberalism: Urban Restructuring in North America and Europe*. Oxford: Blackwell.

Briggs, Xavier de Souza. 2008. *Democracy as Problem Solving*. Cambridge: MIT Press.

Brilliant, Eleanor L. 1990. *The United Way: Dilemmas of Organized Charity*. New York: Columbia University Press.

Brodie, Janine. 2002. "Citizenship and Solidarity: Reflections on the Canadian Way." *Citizenship Studies* 6(4): 377–394.

———. 2007. "Reforming Social Justice in Neoliberal Times." *Studies in Social Justice* 1(2): 93–107.

Brown, J. Larry, and Larry W. Beeferman. 2001. "From New Deal to New Opportunity." *American Prospect*, February 12.

Burghardt, Steve. 2009. Personal communication with Robert Fisher. April 4.

Byrne, David. 1999. *Social Exclusion*. Buckingham: Open University Press.

Calhoun, Craig. 1982. *The Question of Class Struggle: Social Foundations of Popular Radicalism during the Industrial Revolution*. Chicago: University of Chicago Press.

Capraro, James. 2004. "Community Organizing + Community Development = Community Transformation." *Journal of Urban Affairs* 26(2): 151–161.

Carr, James. 1999. "Community, Capital and Markets: A New Paradigm for Community Reinvestment." *Neighborworks Journal*, Summer, 20–23.

Carson, Clayborne. 1981. *In Struggle: SNCC and the Black Awakening of the 1960s*. Cambridge: Harvard University Press.

Chambers, Clarke A. 1963. *Seedtime of Reform: American Social Service and Social Action, 1918–1933*. Minneapolis: University of Minnesota Press.

———. 1992. "'Uphill All the Way': Reflections on the Course and Study of Welfare History." *Social Service Review* 66: 492–504.

Chambers, Edward T., and Michael A. Cowan, eds. 2005. *Roots for Radicals: Organizing for Power, Action, and Justice*. New York: Continuum, 2003.

Christie, Rebecca. 2004. "Consumer Activists to Protest H&R Block Tax Refund Loans." *Dow Jones Business News*, January 12. Available at: http://wsj.com.

Church, Kathryn, Jean-Marc Fontan, Roxana Ng, and Eric Shragge. 2008. "While No One Is Watching: Learning in Social Action among People Who Are Excluded from the Labour Market." In Kathryn Church, Nina Bascia, and Eric Shragge, eds., *Learning through Community: Exploring Participatory Practices*, 97–116. New York: Springer.

Ciezadlo, Annia. 2003. "Invisible Men." *City Limits*, May.

Cloward, Richard, and Frances Fox Piven. 1999. "Disruptive Dissensus: People and Power in the Industrial Age." In Jack Rothman, ed., *Reflections on Community Organization*, 165–193. Itasca, Ill.: F. E. Peacock.

Cnaan, Ram A. 2006. *The Other Philadelphia Story: How Local Congregations Support Quality of Life in Urban America*. Philadelphia: University of Pennsylvania Press.

Community Development Partnership Network. 2003. *Re-Shaping the Business of Community Development*. Denver: Community Development Partnership Network.

Davis, Mike. 1990. *City of Quartz: Excavating the Future in Los Angeles*. New York: Vintage Books.

DeFilippis, James. 2001a. "The Myth of Social Capital in Community Development." *Housing Policy Debate*, 12(4): 781–806.

———. 2001b. "Our Resistance Must Be as Local as Capitalism: Place, Scale, and the Anti-Globalization Protest Movement." *City: Analysis of Urban Trends, Culture, Theory, Policy, Action* 5(3): 363–373.

———. 2004. *Unmaking Goliath*. New York: Routledge.

———. 2006. "Erasing the Community in Order to Save It? Reconstructing Community and Property in Community Development." In Harris Beider, ed., *Housing, Neighbourhood Renewal, and Community Engagement*, 271–289. London: Blackwell.

DeFilippis, James, Robert Fisher, and Eric Shragge. 2006. "Neither Romance nor Regulation: Reevaluating Community." *International Journal of Urban and Regional Research* 30(3): 673–689.

Delgado, Gary. 1986. *Organizing the Movement: The Roots and Growth of ACORN*. Philadelphia: Temple University Press.

———. 1996. "How the Empress Gets Her Clothes: Asian Immigrant Women Fight Fashion Designer Jessica McClintock." In John Anner, ed., *Beyond Identity Politics: Emerging Social Justice Movements in Communities of Color*, 81–94. Cambridge, Mass.: South End Press.

———. 2009. "Does ACORN's Work Contribute to Movement Building?" In Robert Fisher, ed., *The People Shall Rule: ACORN, Community Organizing and the Struggle for Economic Justice*, 251–274. Nashville: Vanderbilt University Press.

Delgado, Melvin. 2000. *Social Work Practice in Nontraditional Urban Settings*. New York: Oxford University Press.

Diani, Mario. 1992. "The Concept of Social Movement." *Sociological Review* 40(1): 1–25.

DiIulio, John. 2007. *Godly Republic: A Centrist Blueprint for America's Faith-Based Future*. Berkeley: University of California Press.

Dionne, E. J., ed. 1998. *Community Works: The Revival of Civil Society in America.* Washington, D.C.: Brookings Institution Press.

Dixon, John, Rhys Dogan, and Alan Sanderson. 2005. "Community and Communitarianism: A Philosophical Inquiry." *Community Development Journal* 40 (1): 4–16.

Domestic Workers United. 2006. *Home Is Where the Work Is: Inside New York's Domestic Work Industry.* New York: Domestic Workers United.

Dreier, Peter. 2009. "A New Wave of Community Organizers for the Obama Era." Talking points memo. April 10. http://tpmcafe.talkingpointsmemo. com/talk/blogs/peter_dreier/2009/04/a-new-wave-of-community-organi .php#more.

DTLR (Department of Transport, Local Government and the Regions). 2002. *Neighbourhood Regeneration: Lessons and Evaluation Evidence from Ten Single Regeneration Budget Case Studies.* London: DTLR.

Eichler, Michael. 1998. "Organizing's Past, Present and Future: Look to the Future, Learn from the Past" *Shelterforce Online* 101 (September, October): n.p.

———. 2007. *Consensus Organizing: Building Communities of Mutual Self-Interest.* Thousand Oaks, Calif.: Sage.

Eisinger, Peter. 1998. "City Politics in an Era of Federal Devolution." *Urban Affairs Review* 33(3): 308–325.

Elshtain, Jean Bethke. 1998. "Not a Cure All: Civil Society Creates Citizens, It Does Not Solve Problems." In E. J. Dionne, ed., *Community Works: The Revival of Civil Society in America.* Washington, D.C.: Brookings Institution Press.

Esping-Anderson, Gøsta. 1990. *The Three Worlds of Welfare Capitalism.* Princeton: Princeton University Press.

Etzioni, Amitai. 1995. *The Spirit of Community: Rights Responsibilities and the Communitarian Agenda.* Hammersmith: Fontana Press.

Evans, Sara M. 1979. *Personal Politics: The Roots of Women's Liberation in the Civil Rights Movement and the New Left.* New York: Knopf.

Fabricant, Michael B., and Robert Fisher. 2002. *Settlement Houses under Siege.* New York: Columbia University Press.

Fetner, Tina. 2008. *How the Religious Right Shaped Lesbian and Gay Activism.* Minneapolis: University of Minnesota Press.

Field, John. 2003. *Social Capital.* London: Routledge.

Fine, Janice. 2006. *Worker Centers: Organizing Communities at the Edge of the Dream.* Ithaca: ILR Press, Cornell University Press.

Fisher, Robert. 1994. *Let the People Decide: Neighborhood Organizing in America.* 2nd ed. New York: Twayne.

———. 2009. *"The People Shall Rule": ACORN, Community Organizing, and the Struggle for Economic Justice.* Nashville: Vanderbilt University Press.

Fisher, Robert, and Michael Fabricant. 2002. "From Henry Street to Contracted Services: Financing the Settlement House." *Journal of Sociology and Social Welfare* 29(3): 3–27.

Fisher, Robert, and Howard Karger. 1997. *Social Work and Community in a Private World: Getting out in Public.* New York: Longman.

Fisher, Robert, and Joseph M. Kling. 1987. "Two Approaches to the Role of Ideology in Community Organizing." *Radical America* 21(1): 31–45.

Fisher, Robert, and Eric Shragge. 2000. "Challenging Community Organizing: Facing the 21st Century." *Journal of Community Practice* 8(3): 1–20.

———. 2001. "Bridging the Divide between Social Movements and Community Organizing." *Canadian Dimension* 35(2) (March/April): 40–42.

———. 2005. "History, Context, and Emerging Issues for Community Practice." In Marie Weil, ed., *The Handbook of Community Practice*, 34–58. Thousand Oaks, Calif.: Sage.

———. 2007. "Contextualizing Community Organizing: Lessons from the Past, Tensions in the Present, Opportunities for the Future." In Marion Orr, ed., *Transforming the City: Community Organizing and the Challenge of Political Change*, 193–217. Lawrence: University Press of Kansas.

Fisher, Robert, and Sally Tamarkin. 2009. "What ACORN and the New Right Can Teach Us about Current Trends in Community Organizing." *Social Policy* 39(1): 48–50.

Fisher, William. 1993. "The Christian Influence on Public Policy." In William Fisher, Ralph Reed, and Richard Wienhold, eds. *Christian Coalition Leadership Manual*, 5.1–5.58. Chesapeake, Va.: Christian Coalition, Political Research Associates Archive.

Fishman, Robert. 1987. *Bourgeois Utopias: The Rise and Fall of Suburbia*. New York: Basic Books.

Flacks, R. 2006. "Knowledge for What? Thoughts on the State of Social Movement Studies." In Jeff Goodwin and James M. Jasper, eds., *Rethinking Social Movements: Structure, Meaning and Emotion*, 135–153. Lanham, Md.: Rowan and Littlefield.

Flacks, Richard. 1988. *Making History: The American Left in the American Mind*. New York: Columbia University Press.

Flint, John. 2002. "Return of the Governors: Citizenship and the New Governance of Neighbourhood Disorder in the U.K." *Citizenship Studies* 6(3): 245–264.

Fogelson, Robert M. 2005. *Bourgeois Nightmares: Suburbia, 1870–1930*. New Haven: Yale University Press.

Ford Foundation. 2006. http://www.fordfound.org/program/asset.

Frazer, Elizabeth. 1999. *The Problems of Communitarian Politics*. Oxford: Oxford University Press.

Fremeaux, Isabelle. 2005. "New Labour's Appropriation of the Concept of Community: A Critique." *Community Development Journal* 40(3): 265–274.

Friedman, Milton. 2002 [1962]. *Capitalism and Freedom*. 40th anniversary edition. Chicago: University of Chicago Press.

Frost, Jennifer. 2001. *An Interracial Movement of the Poor: Community Organizing and the New Left in the 1960s*. New York: New York University Press.

Fung, Archon, and Eric Olin Wright. 2003. *Deepening Democracy: Institutional Innovations in Empowered Participatory Democracy*. London: Verso.

Garb, Margaret. 2005. *City of American Dreams: A History of Home Ownership and Housing Reform in Chicago, 1871–1919*. Chicago: University of Chicago Press.

Geddes, Michael 1999. "Partnership and Local Development in the European Union." In Graham Haughton, ed., *Community Economic Development: Regions, Cities and Public Policy*, 47–64. London: Stationery Office.

Getter, Keith, and Leonardo Vazquez. 2007. "Out Front and in Sync: What Kind of Leadership Does the Community Development Field Demand in the 21st Century?" *Shelterforce*, Winter.

Gibelman, Margaret. 1995. "Purchasing Social Services." In R. Edwards, ed., *Encyclopedia of Social Work*, 1998–2007. Silver Springs, Md.: NASW.

Giddens, Anthony. 1998. *The Third Way: The Renewal of Social Democracy.* Cambridge: Polity Press.

————. 2000. *The Third Way and Its Critics.* Cambridge: Polity Press.

Gilmore, Ruth Wilson. 2007. "In the Shadow of the Shadow State." In Incite! Women of Color against Violence, ed., *The Revolution Will Not Be Funded: Beyond the Non-Profit Industrial Complex.* Boston: South End Press.

Gittell, Marilyn. 1980. *Limits to Citizen Participation: The Decline of Community Organizations.* Beverly Hills, Calif.: Sage.

Gittell, Marilyn, and Avis Vidal. 1998. *Community Organizing: Building Social Capital as a Development Strategy.* Thousand Oaks, Calif.: Sage.

Goetz, Edward. 1995. "Potential Effects of Federal Policy Devolution on Local Housing Expenditures." *Publius* 25 (Summer): 99–116.

Goodwyn, Lawrence. 1978. *Democratic Promise: The Populist Moment in America.* New York: Oxford University Press.

Gordon, Jennifer. 2005. *Suburban Sweatshops: The Fight for Immigrant Rights.* Cambridge: Belknap Press, Harvard University Press.

Gotham, Kevin Fox. 2000. "Urban Space, Restrictive Covenants and the Origins of Racial Residential Segregation in a U.S. City, 1900–50." *International Journal of Urban and Regional Research* 24(3): 616–633.

Gough, Jamie, Aram Eisenschitz, and Andrew McCulloch. 2006. *Spaces of Social Exclusion*, London: Routledge.

Greenberg, David. 2004. "Ways of Contending: Community Organizing and Development in Neighborhood Context." PhD dissertation, Massachusetts Institute of Technology.

Greider, William. 2009. *Come Home, America.* New York: Rodale.

Grogan, Paul S., and Tony Proscio. 2000. *Comeback Cities.* Boulder: Westview.

Gunn, Christopher. 2004. *Third-Sector Development: Making up for the Market.* Ithaca: Cornell University Press.

Hackworth, Jason. 2007. *The Neoliberal City.* Ithaca: Cornell University Press.

Hamel, Pierre 1986. *Les mouvements urbains à Montreal dans la conjoncture des années 80: Perspectives théoriques et defis politiques.* Montreal: Université du Québec à Montréal.

————. 1991. *Action collective et démocratie locale: Les mouvements urbains montréalais.* Montreal: Presses de l'Université de Montréal.

Hardisty, Jean V. 1999. *Mobilizing Resentment.* Boston: Beacon.

Harrell, David Edwin, Jr. 1987. *Pat Robertson: A Personal, Religious, Political Portrait.* San Francisco: Harper and Row.

Harrison, Bennett, and Marcus Weiss. 1998. *Workforce Development Networks: Community-Based Organizations and Regional Alliances.* Thousand Oaks, Calif.: Sage.

Hart, Stephen. 2001. *Cultural Dilemmas of Progressive Politics: Styles of Engagement among Grassroots Activists.* Chicago: University of Chicago Press.

Harvey, David. 1989. "From Managerialism to Entrepreneurialism: The Transformation in Urban Governance in Late Capitalism." *Geografiska Annaler B* 71: 3–17.

———. 2005. *A Brief History of Neoliberalism*. New York: Oxford University Press.

Haughton, Graham, ed. 1999. *Community Economic Development*, 47–64. London: Regions Cities and Public Policy, Stationery Office.

Hayden, Dolores. 2002. *Redesigning the American Dream: Gender, Housing and Family Life*. New York: W. W. Norton.

Hayes, Christopher. 2009. "Notes on Change." *The Nation*, May 1. http://www.thenation.com/doc/20090511/hayes.

Health Nexus (Ontario Prevention Clearing House). http://www.healthnexus.ca/index_eng.php.

Herrick, John M. 1970. "A Holy Discontent: The History of the New York City Social Settlements in the Inter-war Era, 1919–1941." PhD dissertation, University of Minnesota.

Hess, David. 1999. "Community Organizing, Building and Developing: Their Relationship to Comprehensive Community Initiatives." Paper presented on COMM-ORG: The On-Line Conference on Community Organizing and Development. http://comm-org.wisc.edu/papers.htm.

Himmelfarb, Gertrude. 1998. "Second Thoughts on Civil Society." In E. J. Dionne, ed., *Community Works: The Revival of Civil Society in America*, 117–122. Washington, D.C.: Brookings Institution Press.

Hines, Colin. 2000. *Localisation: A Global Manifesto*. London: Earthscan.

Hinson, Sandra. 2008. "Eviction Resistance, Then and Now." Grassroots Policy Project. http://www.grassrootspolicy.org/node/87.

Hirota, Janice, Prudence Brown, William Mollard, and Hannah Richman. 1997. *Pathways to Change: Settlement Houses and the Strengthening of Community*. Chicago: Chapin Hall Center for Children.

Hodgson, Lesley, 2004. "Manufactured Civil Society: Counting the Costs." *Critical Social Policy* 24(2): 139–164.

Hoggart, Keith. 1999. "Where Has Social Housing Gone? Politics, Housing Need and Social Housing Construction in England." *Space and Polity* 3(1): 35–65.

Homan, Mark S. 1999. *Promoting Community Change: Making It Happen in the Real World*. 2nd ed. Pacific Grove, Calif.: Brooks Cole.

Horton, John 1968. "Order and Conflict Theories of Social Problems." In Frank Lindenfeld, ed., *Radical Perspectives on Social Problems*, 34–51. London: Macmillan.

Horwitt, Sanford D. 1989. *Let Them Call Me Rebel: Saul Alinsky, His Life and Legacy*. New York: Knopf.

Husock, Howard. 1990. "Fighting Poverty the Old-Fashioned Way," *Wilson Quarterly* 15 (Spring): 79–91.

———. 2001. "Don't Let CDCs Fool You." *City Journal*. Summer.

IFAS. 1995. "Freedom Writer." March. www.publiceye.org.

Imrie, Rob, and Mike Raco, eds. 2003. *Urban Renaissance?: New Labour, Community and Urban Policy*. Bristol: Policy Press.

Independent Sector, The. 2009. *Facts and Figures about Charitable Organizations*. Washington, D.C.: The Independent Sector.

Jessop, Bob. 2002. "Liberalism, Neoliberalism and Urban Governance: A State-Theoretical Perspective." In Neil Brenner and Nik Theodore, eds., *Spaces of Neoliberalism: Urban Restructuring in North America and Europe*, 105–125. Oxford: Blackwell.

Johnson, Kemba. 1999. "ACORN branches out." *City Limits* (February): 2–4.

Jordan, Grant. 2007. "Policy without Learning: Double Devolution and Abuse of the Deliberative Idea." *Public Policy and Administration* 22(1): 48–73.

Joseph, Miranda. 2002. *Against the Romance of Community*. Minneapolis: University of Minnesota Press.

Kaplan, Thomas. 2000. "Wisconsin Works." In Sarah F. Liebschutz, ed., *Managing Welfare Reform in Five States: The Challenge of Devolution*, 103–121. Albany: Rockefeller Institute Press.

Kasinitz, Philip, and Jan Rosenberg. 1996. "Missing the Connection: Social Isolation and Employment on the Brooklyn Waterfront." *Social Problems* 43(2): 180–196.

Kay, Alan. 2006. "Social Capital, the Social Economy, and Community Development." *Community Development Journal* 41(2): 160–173.

Kearns, Alan. 2003. "Social Capital, Regeneration, and Urban Policy." In Rob Imrie and Mike Raco, eds., *Urban Renaissance? New Labour, Community and Urban Policy*, 37–60. Bristol: Policy Press.

Kendall, Jeremy, and Steven Almond. 1999. "United Kingdom." In Lester M. Salamon, et al., eds. *Global Civil Society: Dimensions of the Non-Profit Sector*. Baltimore: Johns Hopkins Center for Civil Society Studies.

Kleinman, Mark. 1990. "The Future Provision of Social Housing in Britain." In Willem van Vliet and Jan van Weesep, eds. *Government and Housing: Developments in Seven Countries*. Newbury Park, Calif.: Sage.

Kling, Joseph M., and Prudence S. Posner, eds. 1990. *Dilemmas of Activism*. Philadelphia: Temple University Press.

Koehler, Bettina., and Markus Wissen. 2003. "Glocalizing Protest: Urban Conflicts and Urban Social Movements." *International Journal of Urban and Regional Research* 27(4) (December): 942–951.

Kogut, Alvin. 1972. "The Settlements and Ethnicity, 1890–1914." *Social Work* 17: 99–108.

Lake, Robert, and Kathe Newman. 2002. "Differential Citizenship in the Shadow State." *GeoJournal* 58: 109–120.

Lassiter, Matthew D. 2006. *The Silent Majority: Suburban Politics in the Sunbelt South*. Princeton: Princeton University Press.

Lawless, Paul. 2006. "Area Based Urban Interventions: Rationale and Outcomes: The New Deal for Communities Programme in England." *Urban Studies* 43(11): 1991–2011.

Lawson, Dan. 2003. *The Next Upsurge: Labor and New Social Movements*. Ithaca: ILR Press, Cornell University Press.

Levitas, Ruth. 2005. *The Inclusive Society? Social Exclusion and New Labour*. 2nd ed. New York: Palgrave Macmillan.

Leviten-Reid, Eric. 2004. "Reflections on Vibrant Communities." Caledon Institute, March. Loewen, James W. 2005. *Sundown Towns: A Hidden Dimension of American Racism*. New York: New Press.

Lind, Michael. 1996. *Up from Conservatism: Why the Right Is Wrong for America.* New York: Free Press.

Logan, John, and Harvey Molotch. 1987. *Urban Fortunes: The Political Economy of Place.* Berkeley: University of California Press.

Louie, Miriam Ching Yoon. 2001. *Sweatshop Warriors: Immigrant Women Workers Take on the Global Factory.* Cambridge, Mass.: South End Press.

Lubove, Roy. 1975. *The Professional Altruist.* New York: Atheneum.

Luce, Stephanie. 2009. "Living Wage Campaigns." In Robert Fisher, ed., *The People Shall Rule*, 131–152. Knoxville: Vanderbilt University Press.

Lundblad, Karen. 1995. "Jane Addams and Social Reform: A Role Model for the 1990s." *Social Work* 40(5): 661–669.

Lustiger-Thaler, Henri. 1994. "Community and Social Practices: The Contingency of Everyday Life." In Vered Amit-Talai and Henri Lustiger-Thaler, eds., *Urban Lives; Fragmentation and Resistance*, 20–44. Toronto: McClelland and Stewart.

Lynd, Staughton, and Andrej Grubacic. 2008. *Wobblies & Zapatistas: Conversations on Anarchism, Marxism and Radical History.* Oakland, Calif.: PM Press.

MacLeavy, Julie. 2009. "(Re)Analysing Community Empowerment: Rationalities and Technologies of Government in Bristol's New Deal for Communities." *Urban Studies* 46(4): 849–865.

Macmillan, Rob, and Alan Townsend. 2006. "A 'New Institutional Fix'? The 'Community Turn' and the Changing Role of the Voluntary Sector." In Christine Milligan and David Conradson, eds., *Landscapes of Voluntarism*, 15–32. Bristol: Policy Press.

Marley, David John. 2007. *Pat Robertson: An American Life.* Lanham, Md.: Rowman & Littlefield.

Martinelli, Frank. 2004. *How Community-Based Organizations Can Start Charter Schools.* New York: Local Initiatives Support Corporation.

Marwell, Nicole. 2007. *Bargaining for Brooklyn: Community Organizations in the Entrepreneurial City.* Chicago: University of Chicago Press.

Marx, Karl, and Friedrich Engels. 1967 [1848]. *The Communist Manifesto.* New York: Penguin Books.

Massey, Doreen. 1995. *Spatial Divisions of Labor: Social Structures and the Geography of Production.* 2nd ed. New York: Routledge.

Mathew, Biju. 2005. *Taxi! Cabs and Capitalism in New York City.* New York: New Press.

Mayer, Margit. 2003. "The Onward Sweep of Social Capital: Causes and Consequences from Understanding Cities, Communities and Urban Movements." *International Journal of Urban and Regional Research* 27(1): 110–132.

———. 2006. "Manuel Castells' The City and the Grassroots." *International Journal of Urban and Regional Research* 30(1) (March): 202–206.

McGrath, Siobhan, and James DeFilippis. 2009. "Social Reproduction as Unregulated Work." *Work, Employment, and Society* 23(1): 66–83.

McKee, Kim. 2008. "Community Ownership of Social Housing in Glasgow: Building More Sustainable, Cohesive Communities?" *People, Place and Policy Online* 2(2): 101–111.

McKnight, John. 1995. *The Careless Society: Community and Its Counterfeits.* New York: Basic Books.

McKnight, John L., and Jody P. Kretzmann. 1999. "Mapping Community Capacity." In Meredith Minkler, ed., *Community Organizing and Community Building for Health*, 157–172. New Brunswick: Rutgers University Press.

McLaurin, Charles. n.d. "To Overcome Fear." Frame 55–56, Reel 40, SNCC Papers. Retrieved March 15, 2008, from http://www.firstofthemonth .org/nation/nation_hogan_politics.html.

Michels, Robert. 1915. *Political Parties: A Sociological Study of the Oligarchical Tendencies of Modern Democracy*. Updated edition. Free Press/Macmillan, 1962.

Midgley, James. 1986. *Community Participation, Social Development, and the State*. London: Methuen.

Miller, Mike. 1992. "Saul Alinsky and the Democratic Spirit." *Christianity and Crisis* 52 (May 25), copy sent to author, no page numbers.

Ministry of Communities and Local Government. 2008. *Communities in Control: Real People, Real Power*. Presented to the Parliament by the Secretary of State for Communities and Local Government. London.

Mollenkopf, John. 1981. "Community and Accumulation." In Michael Dear and Allen Scott, eds., *Urbanization and Urban Planning in Capitalist Society*, 319–338. London: Methuen.

Montgomery, Mark, Richard Stren, Barney Cohen, and Holly Reed. 2003. *Cities Transformed: Demographic Change and Its Implications in the Developing World*. Washington, D.C.: National Academies Press.

Morel, Sylvie. 2002 *The Insertion Model or the Workfare Model? The Transformation of Social Assistance within Quebec and Canada*. Ottawa: Status of Women Canada, Government of Canada.

Morris, Aldon. 1986. *The Origins of the Civil Rights Movements*. New York: Free Press.

Morrison, John, Joy Howard, Casey Johnson, Francisco Navarro, Beth Plachrtka, and Tony Bell. 1998. "Strengthening Neighborhoods by Developing Community Networks." In Patricia Ewalt, Edith Freeman, and Dennis Poole, eds., *Community Building–Renewal, Well-Being, and Shared Responsibility*, 107–116. Washington, D.C.: NASW Press.

Mullins, David. 2006. "Competing Institutional Logics? Local Accountability and Scale and Efficiency in an Expanding Non-Profit Housing Sector." *Public Policy and Administration* 21(3): 6–24.

Naison, Mark. 2004. *Communists in Harlem during the Depression*. Champaign: University of Illinois Press.

National Congress for Community Economic Development. 2006. *Reaching New Heights: Trends and Achievements of Community-Based Development Organizations*. Washington, D.C.: National Congress for Community Economic Development.

National Council of Voluntary Organisations. 2007. *The UK Civil Society Almanac 2007*. London: National Council of Voluntary Organisations.

National Low Income Housing Coalition. 2004. *Changing Priorities: The Federal Budget and Housing Assistance: 1976–2005*. Washington, D.C.: National Low Income Housing Coalition.

Needleman, Ruth. 1998. "Building Relationships for the Long Haul: Unions and Community-Based Groups Working Together to Organize Low-Wage

Workers." In Kate Bronfenbrenner et al., eds., *Organizing to Win: New Research on Union Strategies*, 71–86. Ithaca: ILR Press, Cornell University Press.

Nelson, Steve, James R. Barrett, and Rob Ruck. 1981. *Steve Nelson: American Radical*. Pittsburgh: University of Pittsburgh Press.

Ness, Immanuel. 1998. "Organizing Immigrant Communities: UNITE's Workers' Center Strategy." In Kate Bronfenbrenner et al. eds., *Organizing to Win: New Research on Union Strategies*, 87–101. Ithaca: ILR Press, Cornell University Press.

———. 2005. *Immigrants, Unions, and the New U.S. Labor Market*. Philadelphia: Temple University Press.

Newman, Kathe, and Robert Lake. 2006. "Democracy, Bureaucracy, and Difference in US Community Development Politics since 1968." *Progress in Human Geography* 30(1): 44–61.

Nicholls, Alex, ed. 2006. *Social Entrepreneurship: New Models of Sustainable Social Change*. New York: Oxford University Press

Nicholls, Walter, and Justin Beaumont. 2004. "The Urbanization of Justice Movements? Possibilities and Constraints for the City as a Space of Contentious Struggle." *Space and Polity* 8(2): 119–135.

Nowak, Jeremy. 1998. "Expanding the Scope of Community Development." *Shelterforce* 97 (January/February).

O'Connor, Alice. 2008. "Swimming against the Tide: A Brief History of Federal Policy in Poor Communities." In James DeFilippis and Susan Saegert, eds., *The Community Development Reader*, 9–27. New York: Routledge.

Osborne, David. 1990. *Laboratories of Democracy*. Boston: Harvard Business School Press.

Osborne, David, and Ted Gaebler. 1992. *Reinventing Government: How the Entrepreneurial Spirit Is Transforming the Public Sector*. Reading, Mass.: Addison-Wesley.

Osman, Suleiman. 2008. "The Decade of the Neighborhood." In Bruce J. Schulman and Julan E. Zelizer, eds., *Rightward Bound: Making America Conservative in the 1970s*, 106–127. Cambridge: Harvard University Press.

Palmer, Bruce. 1980. *"Man over Money": The Southern Populist Critique of American Capitalism*. Chapel Hill: University of North Carolina Press.

Payne, Bruce. 1966. "SNCC: An Overview Two Years Later." In Mitchell Cohen and Dennis Hale, eds., *The New Student Left: An Anthology*. Boston: Beacon.

Peck, Jamie. 2001. *Workfare States*. New York: Guilford Press.

Peck, Jamie, and Adam Tickell. 2002. "Neoliberalizing Space." In Neil Brenner and Nik Theodore, eds. *Spaces of Neoliberalism: Urban Restructuring in North America and Europe*, 33–57. Oxford: Blackwell.

Pendras, Mark. 2002. "From Local Consciousness to Global Change: Asserting Power at the Local Scale." *International Journal of Urban and Regional Research* 26: 823–833.

Pickvance, Chris. 2003. "From Urban Social Movements to Urban Movements: A Review and Introduction to a Symposium on Urban Movements." *International Journal of Urban and Regional Research* 27(1): 102–109.

Pierce, Neal R., and Carol F. Steinbach. 1987. *Corrective Capitalism: The Rise of America's Community Development Corporations*. New York: Ford Foundation.

Piven, Frances Fox, and Richard Cloward. 1979. *Poor People's Movements: Why They Succeed, How They Fail.* New York: Vintage.

Plotkin, Wendy. 2001. "Hemmed in: The Struggle against Racial Restrictive Covenants and Deed Restrictions in Post-WWII Chicago." *Journal of the Illinois State Historical Society* 94 (1): 39–69.

———. 2005. "Restrictive Covenants." In Richard S. Levy, ed., *Antisemitism: A Historical Encyclopedia of Prejudice and Persecution.* Santa Barbara, Calif.: ABC-Clio.

Porter, Michael. 1997. "New Strategies for Inner-City Economic Development." *Economic Development Quarterly* 11(1): 11–27.

Powell, Fred, and Martin Geoghegan. 2004. *The Politics of Community Development.* Dublin: A. & A. Farmar.

Primary Source Media. n.d. *Archives of the Settlement Movement: National Federation of Settlements and Successors, 1899–1958.* http://www.galegroup.com/servlet/ItemDetailServlet?region=9&imprint=745&titleCode=PSM300&type=4&id=V613.

Primus, Richard A. 1998. "Canon, Anti-canon, and Judicial Dissent." *Duke Law Journal* 48(2): 243–303.

Putnam, Robert. 1996. "The Strange Disappearance of Civic America." *American Prospect* 24 (Winter): 22–38.

———. 2000. *Bowling Alone: The Collapse and Revival of American Community.* New York: Simon and Schuster.

Quandt, Jean B. 1970. *From the Small Town to the Great Community: The Social Thought of Progressive Intellectuals.* New Brunswick: Rutgers University Press.

Rangan, Kasturi, Herman Leonard, and Susan McDonald. 2008. *The Future of Social Enterprise.* Harvard Business School Working Paper. Cambridge: Harvard Business School.

Ranney, David. 2003. *Global Decisions: Local Collisions.* Philadelphia: Temple University Press.

Reed, Ralph. 1994. *Politically Incorrect: The Emerging Faith Factor in American Politics.* Dallas: Word Publishing.

———. 1996. *Active Faith: How Christians Are Changing the Soul of American Politics.* New York: Free Press.

Repo, Marjaleena. 1977. "The Fallacy of 'Community Control.'" In John Cowley et al., eds., *Community or Class Struggle?* London: Stage 1.

Restaurant Opportunities Center New York. http://www.rocny.org.

Rizk, Christie. 2007. "Battle over Fifth Ave Housing." *Brooklyn Paper*, April 14.

Rothman, Jack. 1968. "Three Models of Community Organization Practice." In Fred M. Cox et al., eds. *Strategies of Community Organization.* Itasca, Ill.: F. E. Peacock.

Rubin, Herb. 1994. "There Aren't Going to Be Any Bakeries Here if There Is No Money to Afford Jellyrolls: The Organic Theory of Community Development." *Social Problems* 41(3): 401–424.

Rubin, Julia Sass, and Gregory Stankiewicz. n.d. "A Funny Thing Happened on the Way to New Markets: Implementing and Managing the New Markets Initiative." Manuscript, Bloustein School of Planning and Public Policy, Rutgers University.

Saegert, Susan, J. Phillip Thompson, and Mark R. Warren, eds. 2001. *Social Capital and Poor Communities*. New York: Russell Sage.

Samuelson, Robert. 2009. "Our Depression Obsession." *Newsweek*, April 27, 40.

Schambra, William. 1998. "All Community Is Local: The Key to America's Civic Renewal." In E. J. Dionne, ed., *Community Works: The Revival of Civil Society in America*, 44–49. Washington, D.C.: Brookings Institution Press.

Schwartz, Alex. 2006. *Housing Policy in the United States: An Introduction*. New York: Routledge.

Schwartz, Meyer. 1965. "Community Organization." In H. L. Lurie, ed., *Encyclopedia of Social Work*, 177–190. 19th ed. New York: NASW Press.

Seedco Policy Center. 2007. *The Limits of Social Enterprise*. New York: Seedco Policy Center.

Seligman, Amanda. 2005. *Block by Block: Neighborhoods and Public Policy on Chicago's West Side*. Chicago: University of Chicago Press.

Sen, Rinku. 2003. *Stir It Up: Lessons in Community Organizing and Advocacy*. San Francisco: John Wiley.

Sennett, Richard. 1998. *The Corrosion of Character: The Personal Consequences of Work in the New Capitalism*. New York: W. W. Norton.

———. 2007. *The Culture of the New Capitalism*. New Haven: Yale University Press.

Shapiro, Edward S. 1978. "Robert A. Woods and the Settlement House Impulse." *Social Service Review* 52: 215–226.

Shragge, Eric. 1990. "Community Based Practice: Political Alternatives or New State Forms?" In Linda Davies and Eric Shragge, eds., *Bureaucracy and Community*, 137–173. Montreal: Black Rose Books.

———, ed. 1997. *Workfare: An Ideology for a New Underclass*. Toronto: Garamond.

———. 2003. *Activism and Social Change Lessons for Local and Community Organizing*, Guelph: Broadview.

Shragge, Eric, and Michael Toye. 2006. *Community Economic Development: Building for Social Change*. Sydney, N.S.: Cape Breton University Press.

Shuman, Michael. 2000. *Going Local: Creating Self-Reliant Communities in a Global Age*. New York: Routledge.

Shuman, Michael H., and Merrian Fuller. 2005. "The Revolution Will Not Be Grant Funded." *Shelterforce Online* 143 (September/October), no page numbers.

Skocpol, Theda. 2003. *Diminished Democracy: From Membership to Management in American Civic Life*. Norman: University of Oklahoma Press.

Skocpol, Theda, Marshall Ganz, and Ziad Munson. 2000. "A Nation of Organizers: The Institutional Origins of Civic Voluntarism in the United States." *American Political Science Review* 94(3): 527–546.

Smith, Adam. 1998 [1776]. *The Wealth of Nations*. Oxford: Oxford University Press.

Smith, Steven R., and Michael Lipsky. 1993. *Nonprofits for Hire: The Welfare State in the Age of Contracting*. Cambridge: Harvard University Press.

Social Enterprise Coalition. 2009. *What Is Social Enterprise?* London: Social Enterprise Coalition.

Statistics Canada. 2008. "Satellite Account of Non-profit Institutions and Volunteering." *The Daily*, December 3. Ottawa: Statistics Canada.

Stoecker, Randy. 1997. "The Community Development Corporation Model of Urban Redevelopment: A Critique and an Alternative." *Journal of Urban Affairs* 19: 1–23.

———. 2001. "Community Development and Community Organizing: Apples and Oranges? Chicken and Egg?" Manuscript.

———. 2003. "Understanding the Development-Organizing Dialectic." *Journal of Urban Affairs* 25(4): 493–512.

Stone, Leroy, and Hasheem Nouroz. 2007. "Labour Inputs to Non-profit Organizations." *Statistics Canada, Perspectives*, June, 5–12.

Sugrue, Thomas. 1996. *The Origins of the Urban Crisis: Race and Inequality in Postwar Detroit*. Princeton: Princeton University Press.

Susser, Ida, ed. 2001. *The Castells Reader on Cities and Social Theory*. New York: Blackwell.

Swanstrom, Todd. 1999. "The Nonprofitization of United States Housing Policy: Dilemmas of Community Development." *Community Development Journal* 34: 28–37.

Swartz, Heidi J. 2008. *Organizing Urban America: Secular and Faith-based Progressive Movements*. Minneapolis: University of Minnesota Press.

Szakos, Kristin Layng, and Joe Szakos. 2007. *We Make Change: Community Organizers Talk about What They Do—and Why*. Nashville: Vanderbilt University Press.

Tait, Vanessa. 2005. *Poor Workers' Unions: Rebuilding Labor from Below*. Cambridge, Mass.: South End Press.

Tamarack Institute. "About Vibrant Communities." http://tamarackcommunity.ca/g2s1.html.

Tilly, Charles. 1974. "Do Communities Act?" In Marcia Pelly, ed., *The Community: Approaches and Applications*. New York: Free Press.

Tönnies, Ferdinand. 1957 [1887]. Charles Loomis, trans. and ed., *Community and Society (Gemeinschaft und Gesellschaft)*. East Lansing: Michigan State University Press.

Torjman, Sherri. 2007. *Shared Space: The Communities Agenda*. Ottawa: Renouf Publishing.

Toye, Michael, and Nicole Chaland. 2007. "CED in Canada: A Review of Definitions and Profile of Practice." In Eric Shragge and Michael Toye, eds, *Community Economic Development: Building for Social Change*, 21–41. Sydney, N.S.: Cape Breton University Press.

Traynor, Bill. 2008. "Community Building: Limitations and Promise." In James DeFilippis and Susan Saegert, eds., *The Community Development Reader*, 214–224. New York: Routledge.

Trolander, Judith Ann. 1975. *Settlement Houses and the Great Depression*. Detroit: Wayne State University Press.

Trudeau, Daniel. 2008. "Towards a Relational View of the Shadow State." *Political Geography* 27: 669–690.

———. n.d. "Junior Partner of Empowered Community? The Role of Nonprofit Social Service Providers amidst State Restructuring." Manuscript.

Wagner, David. 1993. *Checkerboard Square: Culture and Resistance in a Homeless Community*. Boulder: Westview.

———. 2000. *What's Love Got to Do with It?: A Critical Look at American Charity*. New York: New Press.

Wainwright, Hilary. 2003. *Reclaim the State: Experiments in Popular Democracy*. London: Verso.

Waldinger, Roger, et al. 1998. "Helots No More: A Case Study of the Justice for Janitors Campaign in Los Angeles." In Kate Bronfenbrenner et al., eds., *Organizing to Win: New Research on Union Strategies*, 102–120. Ithaca: ILR Press, Cornell University Press.

Walkowitz, Daniel. 1999. *Working with Class: Social Workers and the Politics of Middle-class Identity*. Chapel Hill: University of North Carolina Press.

Wall, James. M. 1993. "Organizing the Precincts: Strategies of the Religious Right—Editorial." In *Christian Century*, April 21.

Walsh, Dee, and Robert Zdenek. 2007. "Balancing Act: Old Definitions May Be Obsolete as CDCs Weigh Whether to Grow and How to Build Their Impact in Today's Social and Economic Environment." *Shelterforce*, Winter.

Walzer, Michael. 1998. "The Idea of Civil Society: A Path to Social Reconstruction." In E. J. Dionne, ed., *Community Works: The Revival of Civil Society in America*, 123–143. Washington, D.C.: Brookings Institution Press.

Warren, Mark R. 2001. *Dry Bones Rattling: Community Building to Revitalize American Democracy*. Princeton: Princeton University Press.

Watson, Justin. 1997. *The Christian Coalition: Dreams of Restoration, Demands for Recognition*. New York: St. Martin's Press.

Weir, Margaret, et al. 2005. "The Calculus of Coalitions: Cities, Suburbs and the Metropolitan Agenda." *Urban Affairs Review* 40(6): 730–760.

Weissbourd, Robert, and Riccardo Bodini. 2005. *Market-Based Community Economic Development*. Washington, D.C.: Brookings Institution Metropolitan Policy Program.

Williams, Raymond. 1988 [1976]. *Keywords: A Vocabulary of Culture and Society*. London: Fontana.

Williamson, Thad, David Imbroscio, and Gar Alperovitz. 2002. *Making a Place for Community: Local Democracy in Global Era*. New York: Routledge.

Wilson, William Julius. 1987. *The Truly Disadvantaged: The Inner City, the Underclass, and Public Policy*. Chicago: University of Chicago Press.

Winkelman, Lee. 1998. "Organizing Renaissance." *Shelterforce* 101 (September/October).

Wirth, Louis. 1938. "Urbanism as a Way of Life." *American Journal of Sociology* 44(1): 1–24.

Wolch, Jennifer. 1990. *The Shadow State*. New York: Foundation Center.

———. 1999. "Decentering the Nonprofit Sector." *Voluntas* 10: 25–36.

Zemsky, Beth, and David Mann. 2008. "Building Organizations in a Movement Moment." *Social Policy* 38(3) (Spring/Summer): 9–17.

Index

About the Authors

James DeFilippis is an associate professor in the Bloustein School of Planning and Public Policy at Rutgers University. He has written extensively on issues of community development, affordable housing, and the political economy of urban economic development. He is the author of *Unmaking Goliath*, which was named "Best Book in Urban Politics, 2004" by the American Political Science Association, and is the co-editor of *The Community Development Reader* (2007).

Robert Fisher has been teaching and researching, and engaged with, community organizing since the early 1970s. He has authored or edited six other books and many articles on the past and present of community activism. His latest book is an edited collection, *The People Shall Rule: ACORN, Community Organizing, and the Struggle for Economic Justice* (2009). He is a professor at the University of Connecticut, School of Social Work.

Eric Shragge teaches in the School of Community and Public Affairs at Concordia University, Montreal. He has edited and written books in the fields of community organizing and social policy, including *Activism and Social Change* (Broadview Press, 2003) and *Fight Back: Workplace Justice for Immigrants* (Fernwood, 2009), co-authored with Aziz Choudry, Jill Hanley, Steve Jordan, and Martha Stiegman.

CPSIA information can be obtained at www.ICGtesting.com
Printed in the USA
BVOW010603140312

285043BV00001B/23/P